MARRIAGE STUDIES V

SOURCES IN MATRIMONIAL LAW

Gerald T. Jorgensen
Editor

Canon Law Society of America
Catholic University of America
Washington, DC 20064

Reformatted and edited in 2022 for second printing

2022 ISBN: 978-1-932208-62-7
Original 2004 10-digit ISBN: 1-932208-04-6 (978-1-932208-04-7)
SAN: 237-6296

Printed in the United States of America

Canon Law Society of America
415 Michigan Ave., NE, Suite 101
Washington, DC 20017

Table of Contents

ACKNOWLEDGMENTS

The Marriage Research Committee members, on the completion of this project, wish to thank all previous committee members who devoted their time and energy to this project throughout its development and who laid the groundwork for this final product. We also thank the many canonists who contributed to this project and who have been faithful to the project over the years. Each canonist associated with a specific resource section is identified and brief biographies of the canonists appear at the end of this text. The committee members indicated below edited each resource section and made the final decisions regarding content, style, and language. Moreover, the Committee gratefully acknowledges the secretarial work of Alice R. Dahl and Nora D. Smith of the Tribunal staff of the Diocese of Dallas.

Finally, the Committee is appreciative of the persistence and assistance of Rev. Msgr. Robert P. Deeley and Rev. Arthur J. Espelage, OFM, in bringing this project to fruition. The Committee especially acknowledges the editorial expertise and advice of Rev. Patrick J. Cogan, SA.

Gerald T. Jorgensen, Chairperson
John P. Donovan
Ronald W. Gainer
Margaret Gillett

December 30, 2003

ACRONYMS AND ABBREVIATIONS

AAS	*Acta Apostolicae Sedis*
ap. exhort.	apostolic exhortation
CCEO	*Codex canonum Ecclesiarum orientalium* (1990)
CLSA	Canon Law Society of America
Comm	*Communicationes*
Dec	Apostolicum Rotae Romanae Tribunal, *Decisiones seu sententiae selectae*, 73 (1981) +
EIC	*Ephemerides iuris canonici*
FC	*Familiaris consortio*
GS	*Gaudium et spes*
IC	*Ius canonicum*
IDE	*Il Diritto ecclesiastico*
IE	*Ius Ecclesiae*
Jur	*The Jurist*
LG	*Lumen gentium*
LS	Wrenn, Lawrence G. *Law Sections*, Washington, D.C.,
MDGBI	CLSA (1994)
ME	*Matrimonial Decisions of Great Britain and Ireland*
Per	*Monitor Ecclesiasticus*
REDC	*Periodica*
RRDec	*Revista Española de Derecho Canónico*
	Apostolicum Rotae Romanae Rotae, Decisiones seu
SC	*sententiae selectae,* 73 (1981) +
	Studia canonica

INTRODUCTION

Since its beginnings the Canon Law Society of America has been concerned with the ongoing development of canonical jurisprudence. John Paul II, in his first allocution to the Rota after the 1983 code became effective, noted the role of jurisprudence in the interpretation and application of the law.

> The interpretative power, however, is to be placed, above all, in the formation of jurisprudence, that is, of that ensemble of concordant decisions, which – without having the absoluteness of the ancient "the authority of cases always decided in the same way" (*auctoritas rerum perpetuo similiter indicatarum*, Dig. I. 3. *De legibus*, 1, 38. *Nam Imperator*), nevertheless plays a notable role in filling possible lacunae in the law (see c. 19).
>
> 7. The value of the Rota's jurisprudence in the Church has always been noteworthy, given the knowledge and experience of the judges and the authority they enjoy as papal judges. Canon 19 of the new code expressly confirms this.
>
> In the new code, especially in the matter of marriage consent, not a few explanations of natural law from the Rota's jurisprudence have been codified. There still remain canons of great importance in matrimonial law, however, which have been necessarily formulated in a generic way and which await further determination, to which especially the expert jurisprudence of the Rota could make a valuable contribution. (*AAS* 76 [1984] 643-649; and William H. Woestman *Papal Allocutions to the Roman Rota 1939-2002* [Ottawa:St. Paul University, 2002] 184-185, hereafter English trans. from Woestman, *Papal Allocutions*)

Over the years, the Society has not lost a focus on ecclesiastical law and jurisprudence concerning marriage. In 1978, the Society constituted the Marriage Research Committee as an on-going committee of the Society. Then in 1987, the Marriage Research Committee commissioned Augustine Mendonça to continue his research and to compile an annotated index of rotal decisions since 1971, ultimately agreeing to publish the fruit of his research. Thus, in 1992, the Society, through the work of the Marriage Research Committee, published *Rotal Anthology: An Annotated Index of Rotal Decisions from 1971 to 1988*, as compiled by Augustine Mendonça.

It was not long until the Marriage Research Committee again was charged with a major research and potential publication endeavor. At the

1994 Atlanta annual convention and meeting of the Society, a resolution was passed directing the Canon Law Society of America to publish a collection of selected marriage nullity decisions issued by various tribunals throughout the United States. All those speaking in favor of the resolution spoke to the need of the Society to promote a better understanding of jurisprudence within the context of marriage nullity cases. The Board of Governors assigned the implementation of the "Atlanta Resolution" to the Marriage Research Committee. This project has been a major focus of the Committee's work since that time.

As a result of such efforts, *Jurisprudence: A Collection of U.S. Tribunal Decisions* became available in summer 2002. The book is a collection of thirty-two actual court decisions from church tribunals across the United States. In each entry, one can read a judicial decision in its traditional format. The volume divides into matrimonial and non-matrimonial cases. The first and larger section provides examples of marriage cases tried on a variety of different grounds. In this section, the reader will find the theological principles and law by which the Catholic Church upholds the validity of marriage as well as how in a particular case that presumption can be overturned in the face of the facts offered.

However, no matter how instructive it is to read an actual law section, an advocate, defender of the bond or judge still must address the peculiarities of a case before him or her. A previously composed text, even though it may contain the principles of the relevant law, remains remote from specific cases. Thus, the development of the current volume in the CLSA series known as *Marriage Studies* is another distinct effort to contribute to the evolution of jurisprudence, as well as to facilitate the construction of a relevant law section, which every case requires.

The volume before you, *Marriage Studies V: Sources in Matrimonial Law*, contains a collection of resources for the composition of law sections on eighteen different grounds used in the adjudication of marriage nullity cases. The content of each section concerning a particular ground follows the same sequence: 1) citations of pertinent canons; 2) Papal and/or conciliar teachings on marriage, with special emphasis on the aspects of marriage subsumed within the specific ground, and on papal allocutions to the Rota addressing the ground or issues within the ground; 3) passages from rotal jurisprudence; 4) types of proofs required for the specific ground; and 5) a final subsection entitled *Related Issues*, which provides lengthier references or presents specialized matters relative to the specific ground.

This volume is meant to be user friendly and to be truly a resource for canonists actively involved in tribunal ministry. The bound volume also comes with a CD of the complete text. To access the contents of the CD it is possible either to read them directly from the CD or to copy them to a hard drive and into a special folder, for example, MarrLawRes. As indicated above, each grounds specific section follows the same sequence so that the user can refer to the relevant subsection as he or she develops the *Law Section* for the decision being written.

The sequence of subsections for each section corresponds to the traditional format of the *Law Section* in a formal nullity decision. Thus, each section begins by providing the most common canons potentially pertinent to the specific ground under consideration. It is unlikely that any user would ever use all the canons listed for any one law section on that ground; however, the intent is to provide all the canons that might be necessary in writing a law section to address the peculiarities of the specific case before the user. The English translation of the canons referenced may be found in the latest CLSA translation of the 1983 code.

Next, a traditional law section most often addresses key theological principles and church teaching from which the law derived. Thus, the next subsection of each section of the volume provides citations from church documents, rotal allocutions, and canonical doctrine applicable to the specific ground. Again, the user would not use all the references provided but only those pieces that assist the user in developing an understanding of the law at issue, and in interpreting the law in view of the specific facts of the case before the user.

Then, in concluding, a traditional law section incorporates pertinent rotal jurisprudence concerning the ground. This present collection of rotal jurisprudence not only aids or guides interpretation by the local judge but also frequently clarifies what needs to be proven. Once again, the user would not necessarily use all the jurisprudence provided but would select the jurisprudence that would seem most appropriate for the peculiarities of the case before him or her. In the final subsection of each section in this volume are often references to additional materials for improved understanding as well as some peculiar nuances of this specific ground in general or in the face of a certain fact scenario.

The user does have to provide the connecting and transition phrases as well as critical analysis and logic necessary for a readable, intelligible, and applicable *Law Section*. However, the all-important "raw materials" are readily available and easily used. Moreover, the user needs to note that the English translation of the original texts not in English either is cited in the source documents or is the contributor's translation. The committee did not take formal efforts to exclude all danger of inaccuracy in or misinterpretation of the translations.

Finally, as stated in numerous ways and times by John Paul II throughout his pontificate, the Church supports, defends, and fosters the dignity, sanctity, and indissolubility of marriage. The Church fulfills this task in many ways but in a special way through the ministry of its judicial power. The intent of this volume, Volume V, of *Marriage Studies* is the support and facilitation of these goals by assisting the personnel of marriage tribunals as each duly constituted court administers justice, with equity, and seeks to protect the dignity, sanctity and indissolubility of marriage.

Chapter I

Sources For Canon 1095, 1°

INCAPACITY BECAUSE LACK SUFFICIENT USE OF REASON

Carlotta Bartone, SHJC, JCL and Melissa Truman Schools, JCL
with John P. Donovan, JCL and Gerald T. Jorgensen, PhD, JCL

I. Pertinent Canons

A. See canon 1095, 1°.

B. See the following allied canons: 1095, 3°; 1055, §1; 1056; 1057, §2; 1680; 1579, §1; 1579; §2.

II. Conciliar and/or Papal Teachings

A. Pius XII, 1942 allocution to the Rota (*AAS* 34 [1942] 338-343):

> The conscientious observance of these norms [jurisprudential principles as enunciated in rotal jurisprudence or canonical doctrine/science] is a matter of duty for the judge; but on the other hand in their application he must remember that they are not ends in themselves, but means to an end, that is, to attain and guarantee a moral certainty with an objective foundation as to the reality of fact. It should not come about that, what the will of the legislator intended as a help and security for discovering the truth, become instead an obstacle to its discovery. If ever the observance of formal rules of law results in injustice or is contrary to equity, there is always a right of recourse to the legislator. (English trans. from Woestman, *Papal Allocutions*, 20.)

B. John Paul II, 1981 ap. exhort., *Familiaris consortio* (*FC*):

> Consequently, sexuality, by means of which a man and woman give themselves to one another through the acts which are proper and exclusive to spouses, is by no means something purely biological, but concerns the innermost being of the

human person as such. It is realized in a truly human way only if it is an integral part of the love by which a man and a woman commit themselves totally to one another until death. The total physical self-giving would be a lie if it were not the sign and fruit of a total personal self-giving, in which the whole person, including the temporal dimension, is present; if the person were to withhold something or reserve the possibility of deciding otherwise in the future, by this very fact he or she would not be giving totally. (A. Flannery, ed. *Vatican Council II: More Postconciliar Documents*. [Grand Rapids: Wm. B. Eerdmans Publishing Co., 1982] 822; hereafter Flannery, *Vatican Council II*.)

C. John Paul II, 1984 allocution to the Rota (*AAS* 76 [1984] 643-649):

The concern to safeguard the dignity and indissolubility of marriage by checking abuses and irresponsibility, which, unfortunately must often be sadly noted in this matter, cannot prescind from the real and undeniable progress of the biological, psychological, psychiatric, and social sciences. Otherwise, one would contradict the very value to be protected namely, a truly existing marriage, not one which has only the appearance of such, since it is null from the outset. (English trans. from Woestman, *Papal Allocutions,* 185.)

D. John Paul II, 1987 allocution to the Rota (*AAS* 79 [1987] 1453-1459):

7. For the canonist, the principle must remain that only *incapacity* and not *difficulty* in giving consent and in realizing a true community of life and love invalidates a marriage. Moreover, a breakdown of a marriage union is never in itself proof of such incapacity on the part of the contracting parties. They may have neglected or used badly the means, both natural and supernatural, at their disposal; or they may have failed to accept the inevitable limitations and burdens of married life, either because of blocks of an unconscious nature or because of slight pathological disturbances which leave substantially intact human freedom; or finally because of failures of a moral order. The hypothesis of real incapacity is to be considered only when an anomaly of a serious nature is present, which, however, it may be defined, must substantially

vitiate the capacity of the individual to understand and/or to will. (English trans. from Woestman, *Papal Allocutions*, 194.)

E. John Paul II, 1997 allocution to the Rota (*AAS* 89 [1997] 486-489):

Marriage certainly has an *essential nature*, described in canon 1055, which pervades the entire teaching concerning marriage, as can be seen in the concepts of 'essential property,' 'essential element,' 'essential rights and obligations,' etc. This essential reality is a possibility open in principle to every man and woman; indeed, it represents a true vocation for the great majority of the human race. (English trans. from Woestman, *Papal Allocutions*, 243.)

F. John Paul II, 1999 allocution to the Rota (*AAS* 91 [1999] 622-627):

This consent is nothing other than the conscious, responsible assumption of a commitment through a juridical act by which, in reciprocal self-giving, the spouses promise total and definitive love to each other. They are free to celebrate marriage after having chosen each other with equal freedom, but as soon as they perform this act they establish a personal state in which love becomes something that is owed, entailing effects of a juridical nature as well. (English trans. from Woestman, *Papal Allocutions*, 251.)

III. Rotal Jurisprudence

A. *Coram* Grazioli of 1 July 1933 (James H. Provost, "Cases: Sources for Canon 1095, 1°, Part One," *Jur* 54 [1994] 279-292.) was a case of *dementia praecox* in the Respondent, Anna. Two points of note were addressed in the law section. First, it is stressed that a person must at least have the use of reason of a seven year old (citing *CIC* 1917 c. 88, 3°) and, further, that knowledge sufficient to be not-ignorant of the substance of marriage is presumed after puberty (n. 2). A discretion or maturity of judgment proportionate to the contract is required. (n. 3). Second, "[t]he court also noted that if antecedent and consequent amentia are proven, then concomitant amentia is rightly deduced (n. 4)" (James H. Provost, "Cases: Sources for Canon 1095, 1°, Part Two," *Jur* 54 [1994] 630). The facts of the case clearly proved the dementia praecox of the Respondent.

B. *Coram* Wynen of 13 April 1943 treats in its law section a further consideration of what is required for "sufficient use of reason," that is, a consciousness that a human act is being placed and that the object of consent is at least marginally understood and freely undertaken. The Petitioner, Andrew, had suffered head injuries in a fall that had, in fact, at one point, deprived him of the use of his reason. Careful examination of facts and medical records, however, determined that the Petitioner had recovered sufficient use of reason by the time he contracted marriage two years after his accident. This case is cited also as a source for canon 1095, 2° and may have come to an affirmative decision for nullity, had the ground existed, but lack of sufficient use of reason was not proven (Provost, "Sources, Part One," *Jur* 54 [1994] 293-303).

C. *Coram* Felici of 22 May 1956 (Ibid. 54:323-333) considers the mental state of Respondent, Vanda, who suffered from some weakness of mind, want of education and from loose morals, but nevertheless is not proven to lack "sufficient use of reason" to contract marriage.

1. The law section discusses "phrenesthesia, … also oegophrenia" (mental retardation) in its varying degrees, of which one degree is "imbecility." It is asserted that "imbeciles can be educated and instructed" and the question is raised in the form of whether "phrenesthetics have the necessary discretion," not sufficient use of reason (n. 3).

2. A distinction is made between the phrenesthesia of the case in question (which is "only ... some diminution of discretionary faculty") and "an intimate disturbance of the mind, such as, for example, in paranoia, schizophrenia, or depressive melancholy" (n. 4). Felici concurs with the decision *coram* Canestri of 16 July 1943 cautioning against holding the qualifications for marriage so high as to exclude simple people from marrying.

D. *Coram* Felici of 3 December 1957 (Provost, "Sources, Part Two," *Jur* 54 [1994] 658-669.) discusses the development of the intellect, affected by "somatic dispositions," and lists contributing factors of adolescence, noetic elements, endotypical elements and societal elements (n. 2). The argument makes an interesting point, stating that the Petitioner, André, was of a chronological age sufficient to allow him to contract marriage, but his inherited syphilis had caused a degeneration of his mental faculties such that the court ruled that by the time of the marriage, he had not yet reached the necessary psychological age to contract validly (n. 13). The court found that the presumption of discretion for marriage at puberty was overturned by the facts of the case, citing "natural law" and the "prescriptions of positive law." The decision also makes a distinction between amentia and mental illness sufficient to vitiate consent: "Thus, when the marriage was contracted, even though André cannot yet be said to be *amens*, he was in such a mental state that he could not validly undertake matrimonial obligations" (n. 12).

E. Though *coram* Sabattani of 24 February 1961 (Provost, "Sources, Part Two," *Jur* 54 [1994] 670-691) addresses most of its law section to what would more fittingly apply to canon 1095, 2°, there are some worthy contributions to the jurisprudence for canon 1095, 1°. Provost lists these as follows:

    1. It [the sentence] cautions against using penal law standards that determine imputability (*CIC* 1917 c. 2201) in evaluating capacity to consent (n. 3);
    2. It provides strong and convincing arguments to reject the concept of semi-amentia as well as the so-called lucid intervals (n. 6);
    3. It recognizes that mental debility can progress to insanity, and may indeed have that effect well before it is otherwise recognized (n. 9);
    4. It corrects the basis for evaluating whether intoxication produced a lack of use of reason sufficient to invalidate consent (n. 11);
    5. It provides very useful principles to guide judges in cases involving chronic alcoholism (nn. 12-13). (Provost, "Sources, Part Two," *Jur* 54 [1994] 633)

F. *Coram* Mattioli of 4 April 1966 (Provost, "Sources, Part Two," *Jur* 54 [1994] 706-722) was a rather contentious and confusing case, with the two parties "counter-suing" so to speak: the man maintaining the woman's exclusion of children; the woman alleging the man's amentia. It seems that through the first two instances and into the third (by which time the man had accepted the allegations of amentia), there was much dubious evidence introduced as well.
    1. In the law section, however, the sentence still offers some valuable points and holds that amentia is not the illness of the

mind itself, but rather the condition resulting from the illness or injury or whatever cause (n. 2). This allows for a broader interpretation of what causes amentia and therefore, lack of sufficient use of reason vitiating consent. A second point was made that the existence of some mental illness alone is not enough to invalidate consent for marriage. It must be demonstrated that "the patient's mind was so disordered that he must no longer be considered to be the master of his own actions" (n. 2).

2. This decision is similar to the case decided *coram* Felici of 22 May 1956 which affirmed that weakness of mind is not identical to lack of use of reason.

G. *Coram* Serrano of 7 November 1980, "finds for the affirmative due to the Respondent lacking the capacity to intend freely because of mental retardation. Serrano utilizes jurisprudence and a lengthy treaty on personality to demonstrate the women's incapacity to assume the essential obligations of marriage, but more importantly to highlight the necessity to have the capacity to exercise discretion towards consent." (Augustine Mendonça, *Rotal Anthology: An Annotated Index of Rotal Decisions from 1971 to 1988*, [Washington, CLSA: 1992] 54, hereafter Mendonça, *Rotal Anthology*.)

H. *Coram* Egan of 2 April 1981 examines thoroughly the incapacitating nature of epilepsy. Not all who suffer from seizures are incapable of consent. However, each case is worthy of being addressed on its own merits and concrete circumstances. The history of epileptic convulsive and twilight states may give rise to psychopathy that could diminish the capacity to give free consent. If a person exchanged consent at the time of a seizure, that itself could be invalidating. (Mendonça, *Rotal Anthology*, 57.) See also *coram* Colagiovanni of 18 October 1986, who applied these same criteria and concluded in the negative stating that the evidence of epilepsy being incapacitating was not proven, it must be in a serious stage that would impede one's judgment. (Ibid. 80)

I. *Coram* Giannecchini of 13 May 1983 states that the person suffering from schizophrenia disassociates, thus, can be incapable of rendering consent. It should be noted that remission, if possible, is not a cure and therefore the person's mental health prior to, at the time of and immediately after consent would need to be examined as medication can allow someone to appear in remission as well. (Mendonça, *Rotal Anthology*, 64.) *Coram* Fiore of 20 October 1984 adds that schizophrenia creates a contradiction between the action and consent. (Mendonça, *Rotal Anthology*, 74)

J. *Coram* Colagiovanni of 8 May 1984 concludes that drug dependence or addiction is incapacitating towards consent (Mendonça, *Rotal Anthology,* 71). Mendonça summarizes five highlights of the sentence that are effects of addiction:

1. Persistence of disturbed condition even during abstinence;
2. Serious disturbance in practical judgment with break in reality contact;
3. Serious blockage in one's capacity to establish interpersonal relationships with others;
4. Internal disturbance in the presence of external normality;
5. Long periods of treatment, with serious relapses in the process of regaining physical and mental health.

"A person suffering from drug-dependence is radically incompetent to elicit the act of consent and to establish the intimate communion of life" (Mendonça, *Rotal Anthology,* 71).

K. *Coram* Di Felice of 14 May 1984 stresses the importance of internal freedom. Individuals who are subject to psychotic episodes can be impeded from such freedom, which is not to say all people who marry must have perfect mental health. It is the court's responsibility to evaluate the medical and judicial differences between incapacity and lack of judgment (Mendonça, *Rotal Anthology,* 71).

L. *Coram* Ragni of 26 November 1985 argues that alcoholism can cause the incapacity of a person to exchange consent due to a lack of sufficient reasoning; and an incapacity of comprehending and fulfilling the obligations of marriage. He relies on jurisprudence and reemphasizes the physical and mental elements of alcohol and its power to render the Respondent at hand to be without the critical faculty for there to have been valid consent (Mendonça, *Rotal Anthology*, 77).

IV. Types of Proofs Required

A. In addition to the testimony of the Petitioner and his witnesses, every effort should be made to procure the testimony of the Respondent, who is usually the party whose lack of reason is alleged.

B. It is clear that, particularly when the cause of the lack of sufficient reason is a habitual disorder, the services of an expert are required. When the cause is of a transitory nature, the use of an expert is at the discretion of the judge.

C. Originally, included under this heading were those defects and illnesses listed under the common heading of *amentia.* Edward Hudson points out, however, "[…] there is the greatest variety with respect to the definition and diagnosis of these illnesses, and there are likewise […] different degrees and gravity in the same illness" [J. Edward Hudson, *Documentation II on Marriage Nullity Cases* (compiled for private distribution only and published by Faculty of Canon Law, Saint Paul University, Ottawa 1979) 171].

V. Related Issues

A. Since the publication of the *Diagnostic and Statistical Manual of Mental Disorders* and its general acceptance in the English-speaking world as the standard for diagnoses of all types of psychological disorders and illnesses, the term *amentia* has fallen out of use. As Ladislas Örsy, S.J., notes in *Marriage in Canon Law* (Wilmington, DE: Michael Glazier, 1986), though empirical psychology and medical psychiatry are newcomers in the field of sciences, they have developed by leaps and bounds and even canon law has felt their impact. Örsy says, "[…] Canon 1095 in the New Code […] has opened the door to the findings of contemporary psychology and psychiatry" (Örsy, *Marriage in Canon Law*, 129).

B. James Provost writes in "Canon 1095: Past, Present and Future," *Jur* 54 [1994] 81-112:

1. "Given its antecedents in jurisprudence, it could be assumed that this number [c. 1095, 1°] is but a restatement of jurisprudence on *amentia.* If so, it would be reserved to the most serious psychic disturbances. But if the canon is something new [to 1983], and not merely a restatement of the law on *amentia,* it requires, at least at the time consent is to be exchanged, that a person would have to lack the use of reason

that is necessary and sufficient to know what marriage is (c. 1096)" (Provost "Canon 1095," *Jur* 54 [1994] 93).

2. "Tribunal personnel must attend to the two dimensions of this number: the degree of lack of the use of reason in the person who attempts marital consent, and the relationship of that lack of use of reason to the object of marital consent itself." (Provost "Canon 1095," *Jur* 54 [1994] 93).

C. Augustine Mendonça states in "Consensual Incapacity for Marriage" (*Jur* 54 [1994] 477-559):

> "Among the three species of consensual incapacity expressed in this Canon (1095) the first one, that is, 'lack of sufficient use of reason', seems to have had its role in canonical history. In my opinion, this *caput* offers no scope of further development both in theory and application in light of the very nature of the *caput* of 'lack of discretion of judgment'" (Mendonça, "Consensual Incapacity for Marriage," *Jur* 54 [1994] 558).

To deprive a person of *sufficient* use of reason to contract marriage, a mental impairment must be relatively severe and pervasive in its affect. The cause can be habitual disorder, such as a psychosis or severe mental retardation, or a transient disturbance, such as drug or alcohol intoxication or a serious psychic trauma. In other words, a person may be judged to lack sufficient use of reason whether his condition is temporary or permanent so long as the condition was present at the time of consent and was serious.

D. *The Canon Law, Letter & Spirit* (The Canon Law Society of Great Britain and Ireland in association with the Canadian Canon Law Society, [Collegeville: Liturgical Press, 1995] 610.) states that "it is not the *content of the intellect* that is in question here [...] but the *fundamental ability to know*. If this is lacking entirely or seriously inadequate, a person simply cannot consent."

E. Examples of deprivation of use of reason.

1. An example of a temporary deprivation of use of reason would be drunkenness. Other conditions that qualify as depriving a person of his intellectual function have been cited: the effect of drugs, epileptic

twilight, delirious fever, somnambulism, or some psychic trauma such as hypnosis or shock.

2. An example of a permanent condition rendering a person incapable of exercising sufficient use of reason would be a psychosis. Other conditions that qualify have been cited: severe mental retardation, the effects of brain damage, schizophrenia, untreated bi-polar disorder.

F. *The Invalid Marriage* (Lawrence G. Wrenn *The Invalid Marriage* [Washington: Canon Law Society of America, 1998], 21) notes that canon 1095, 1° is not referring to a simple use of reason or suggesting that once one has attained the use of reason and can place a human act he or she is capable of marriage. Rather, in order to be capable of marriage one must have arrived at a degree of reasoning ability sufficient to understand the Church's teaching on marriage.

G. John Beal, quoting Mendonça, notes that "when a disruption of the 'psychological process involved in forming the human act [...] seriously impeded the rational function of the mind and deprived a person of any meaningful deliberation concerning personal capacity for marital commitment and the choice of the object of consent', he or she may be judged to lack sufficient use of reason." ("Matrimonial Consent," in John Beal, James A. Coriden, Thomas J. Green, eds. *New Commentary on the Code of Canon Law* [Mahwah, NJ: Paulist Press, 2000] 1298.)

Chapter II

Sources For Canon 1095, 2°

INCAPACITY BECAUSE GRAVE DEFECT OF DISCRETION

Michael J. Cariglio, JCL with Gerald T. Jorgensen, PhD, JCL

I. Pertinent Canons

A. See canon 1095, 2°.

B. See the following allied cannons: 1055, §1; 1056; 1057, §1; 1057, §2; 1579, §1; 1579, §2; 1680.

II. Conciliar and/or Papal Teachings

A. John Paul II, 1987 allocution to the Rota:

> For the canonist, the principal must remain clear that only *incapacity* and not *difficulty* in giving consent and in realizing a true community of life and love invalidates a marriage. Moreover, the breakdown of such marriage union is never in itself proof of such incapacity on the part of the contracting parties. They may have neglected or used badly the means, both natural and supernatural, at their disposal. Alternatively, they may have failed to accept the inevitable limitations and burdens of married life, either because of blocks of an unconscious nature or because of slight pathological disturbances which leave substantially intact human freedom, or finally because of failures of moral order. The hypothesis of real incapacity is to be considered only when an anomaly of a serious nature is present, which, however it may be defined, must substantially vitiate the capacity to understand and/or to consent.
>
> The judge therefore cannot and ought not expect from the expert a judgment on the nullity of marriage, and still less must he feel bound by any such judgment which the expert may in the event express. It is for the judge and for him alone to pronounce judgment on nullity of marriage. The task of the expert is only

> that of providing the elements of information which have to do with his specific competence, that is, the nature and extent of the psychic and psychiatric realities on grounds of which the nullity of the marriage has been alleged. In fact, the code, in cc. 1578-1579, explicitly demands from the judge that he evaluate the reports of experts. In this evaluation it is important that he should not allow himself to be misled, either by superficial judgments or by the expressions that are apparently neutral but which in reality contain unacceptable anthropological presuppositions. (English trans. From Woestman, *Papal Allocutions*, 194-195.)

B. John Paul II, 1997 allocution to the Rota:

> *Marriage* certainly has an *essential nature*, described in canon 1055, which pervades the entire teaching concerning marriage, as can be seen in the concepts of 'essential property', 'essential element', 'essential rights and obligations of marriage', etc. This essential right is a possibility open in principle to every man and woman; indeed, it represents a true vocation for the great majority of the human race. Consequently, in assessing the capacity or the act of the consent necessary for the celebration of a valid marriage, one cannot demand what it is not possible to require of the majority of people. It is not a question of a pragmatic or convenient minimalism, but of a *realistic view of the human person*, as a being always growing called to make responsible choices with his/her inborn abilities, continuously enriching them by his own efforts and the help of grace.
>
> From this perspective, the *favor matrimonii* and the resulting presumption of the validity of marriage [cf. c. 1060] can be seen not only as the application of a general principle of law, but as consequences perfectly in keeping with the specific reality of matrimony. However, there remains the difficult task, as you well know, of determining, including with the help of human sciences, that minimum without which one can speak of the capacity or sufficient consent for a true marriage. (English trans. from Woestman, *Papal Allocutions*, 243.)

C. See Chapter III on "Sources for Canon 1095, 3°" for related teachings.

III. Rotal Jurisprudence

A. In *coram* Colagiovanni, 28 May 1994, (*ME* 123 [1998] 273-294):

> To say that *discretion* is the capacity to want the marriage properly so called, is not enough, because one must mean that particular marriage wanted by God and restored by Jesus who enriched it with the indissoluble, exclusive and sacramental characters (see Canons 1055 & 1056) … The jurisprudence of the Rota stemmed from the positive consideration of the *discretion of judgment*. In the famous decision *coram* Felici of December 3, 1957, reported together with the one *coram* Sabattani of February 24, 1961, we read: 'The only criterion of a sufficient consent is the discretion of judgment proportionate to the marriage. The cognitive faculty is not enough, as it consists merely in the perception of truth, but a discriminating power is required which is the capacity to deliberate and decide, and to combine deliberations into one, so that a new judgment may logically be deduced'. The 'harmonious order' is required not just between intellect and will, but also within the individual faculties there must exist that harmonious and structural interrelationship that may give rise to the decisive fiat of the final decision which is precisely the marriage consent. (*Lack of discretion of judgment and incapacity to assume essential obligations of marriage.* Canonical jurisprudence and interpretation in *Forum*: A Review of the Maltese Ecclesiastical Tribunal, I [1991].) [English original]

B. In *coram* Burke, 24 November 1994:

> 2. Incapacity implies an absolute condition. To speak of degrees of incapacity ('grave', 'less grave', 'partial' incapacity, etc.), is incorrect (although at times it is carelessly done). Consensual incapacity must always be *total*. There is no such thing in canon law as partial incapacity for marital consent.
>
> Certainly one can speak of a reduced psychic capacity, just as one can of a physical capacity. For the purposes of c. 1095, however, a reduced psychic capacity of itself does no more than increase the possible difficulty which a person may experience in coming to a decision or in carrying it out.

Difficulty and incapacity are not to be confused, according to the principle well established and often repeated in rotal jurisprudence. Reduced capacity is not invalidating, unless the impairment or reduction in psychic powers is so grave that the subject is thereby made truly incapable. In other words, the question of gravity regards the *cause* of the alleged incapacity; this cause must indeed be grave, sufficiently grave as to produce the effect of true incapacity. In practice an affirmative decision in a case of alleged consensual incapacity seems unjustified unless one can trace the incapacity to a grave root or cause (perhaps constitutional or inherited, perhaps circumstantial) which strikes at the person's estimative or elective faculties regarding to the choice of marriage. [...]

4. Canon 1095 is concerned with the adequacy of the act of consent. Consent is not valid unless it: a) is the result of due understanding (proportionate to the seriousness of the commitment being undertaken) of the essential rights and obligations involved in this marital commitment; and b) proceeds from a free will capable of actually observing these essential rights and duties. Number 2 of the canon considers the case where consent is rendered invalid by a grave defect in discretion of judgment, i.e., a gravely defective exercise of the critical-estimative faculty. The essential rights/obligations of marriage (considered in themselves) constitute the object of this defective judgment – which is juridically examined solely in respect of the moment of consent, with no necessary reference to the future. As a result there is no difficulty in accepting that a lack of discretion of judgment, sufficient to invalidate consent, may later vanish or be overcome. Hence it is clear that the duration of the incapacitating condition does not matter in no. 2. There is nothing inconsistent in allowing that a grave defect of discretion can be produced by a transient cause and may have a transient duration, being mitigated or cease completely with the passage of time. It is sufficient that it be present and operative at the moment of consent. [...]

9. So we see a clear contrast between nos. 2 and 3 of c. 1095. When it is a question of evaluating a person's discretionary powers, as exercised in one particular moment, one may indeed judge that circumstances were then present which impeded due exercise of discretion and so invalidated consent;

nor is the force of this judgment weakened by the fact that these circumstances may disappear later – even shortly afterwards – and so the person becomes quite capable of marital consent. [...] (*Forum* 10 [1999] 168-173.)

C. In *coram* Turnaturi, 22 April 1998:

7. [...] The matrimonial or conjugal covenant established by God, and raised by Christ to the dignity of a sacrament (canon 1055, §2), arises only out of a human act, by – which the spouses mutually give and accept one another in order to constitute marriage (canon 1055, §1). Thus given the gravity or particularity of establishing the consenting acts of the parties, the spouses 'require a psychological capacity for proffering consent, which, given the intimate connection between the cognitional, affective and voluntative spheres in the same person, three species of capacity are needed, namely: a) intellective capacity; b) discretionary capacity; c) assumptive capacity' (*coram* Stankiewicz, 21 July 1994, unpublished, n. 4). With this in mind the case above needs to be treated only as a second and third instance case from the aforementioned canon 1095, namely defect of discretionary judgment.

8. Although canon 1057, §2 needs to be kept in mind, namely that matrimonial consent is said to consist in an act of the will, capacity to consent occurs when it exists in the whole person whether with regard to the cognitive or with regard to the voluntative function, so that no disturbance in the affections (marital) exists of psychological or psychiatric nature. As it is said in a sentence *coram* Stankiewicz, 16th December 1994, 'although the concept of grave defect of discretionary judgment in the stricter sense according to the terms of the words (of the canon) suggests substantial dysfunctions of intellectual activity by way of a disturbance (*perturbatio*) or of an inadequate maturity, by reason of age (cc. 891 and 989), according to the accepted jurisprudence it may just as equally refer also to dysfunctions of voluntative activity due to factors in the psychological make-up of the person of a cognitional and/or voluntative nature.

Indeed a grave defect of discretionary judgment may arise from a disorder of the cognitional faculty in its ability to evaluate out of which one's understanding or evaluation of the substantial normative value of the mutual give-and-take of the couple in their communion of life is blocked especially with regard to the essential rights and obligations of marriage. It may, however, also arise from the faculty of choice which would impede the freedom of judgment in choosing a person as party with whom to realize the mutual self-giving that is the cause of marriage, and in appropriating in a specific way the essential rights and duties of marriage.' (See *coram* Anton Stankiewicz, 24th February 1994, in *Rotae Romanae Decisiones* (*RRDec.*) 86 [1994] 108-109, nn. 6-7 or *ME* 124 [1999] 293-333.)

D. The following rotal decisions are taken from Augustine Mendonça, *Rotal Anthology*.

1. 11/25/76 *coram* Parisella, *Dec.* 68 (1987) 460-467; *EIC* 33 (1977) 335-338; Aff., Rome, Italy (Depressive neurosis; Immature personality)

   The diagnosis given by experts consulted in this case described the Petitioner as an indecisive and anxiety ridden person with depressive neurosis. Parisella briefly explains how psychoneurosis can affect the act of consent. He distinguishes a twofold knowledge in discretion of judgment, one critical and the other estimative. Estimative knowledge consists in weighing the essential obligations of marriage. This estimative knowledge can be disturbed by mental illness including psychoneurosis. The judge must be convinced that the psychic disturbance has actually affected the will of the contractant at the time of marriage. The assistance of experts could be most helpful in such cases (Mendonça, *Rotal Anthology*, 29).

2. 01/25/77 *coram* Palazzini, *EIC* 34 (1978) 145-149; Aff., Paris, France (Affective immaturity)

   This published portion of the sentence contains only the *in iure* section. Palazzini defines 'voluntarium' as 'a voluntary and free human act' and explains its different aspects. The aspects of a ‘voluntary’ and ‘free’ human act are of their nature joined together. A deliberate choice is the very will which determines the practical judgment concerning its acts and the very act of election after proportionate deliberation. This requires discretion of judgment and critical knowledge of the object and of the acts. ‘Voluntarium’ required to place the act of consent can be impeded either by immaturity of character or judgment, or by affective immaturity which directly affects the will. Palazzini explains further the notion of ‘affective immaturity’ and its effect on personality and will (Mendonça, *Rotal Anthology*, 29).

3. 01/11/78 *coram* Palazzini, *Dec.* 70 (1988) 1-12; Aff., Venice, Italy (Affective disorder; Depressive personality)

   This marriage case was initially presented on grounds of ‘exclusion of the right to sexual acts’, but it received a negative decision. The Petitioner requested the Rota to judge this case also on grounds of lack of discretion of judgment, and more specifically: defect of free and deliberate consent. The second instance court gave an affirmative decision on the newly introduced caput and a negative decision on exclusion of the right to sexual acts. The third instance court *coram* Palazzini dealt with the case on ‘lack of discretion’ grounds. Palazzini focuses his analysis of the act of matrimonial consent on the aspect of internal freedom. He says that there are certain disorders of personality which disturb the unity within the personality in such a way that the person affected by it is not free to make a deliberate choice. It is only when affective immaturity renders a person incapable of eliciting a free act, it constitutes a defect sufficient to declare the marriage null. Neurosis, here depressive syndrome, can cause such a defect and render consent invalid. The Petitioner was diagnosed by experts as suffering from depressive neurosis, and therefore, the court concluded that he could not weigh things critically. He rushed into marriage because he felt that he had found the ideal woman (in this case 17 years his senior) (Mendonça, *Rotal Anthology*, 34).

4. 11/25/78 *coram* Pompedda, *Dec.* 70 (1988) 508-515; Aff., Turin, Italy (Borderline personality)

[...] From the description of the disorder the Respondent was probably suffering from a borderline personality disorder. Pompedda says that such a disorder can nullify the act of consent. According to Pompedda, lack of discretion or maturity of judgment is verified when: a) there is a lack of sufficient intellectual knowledge of the object of consent; b) there is a lack of sufficient estimative or critical knowledge of the contract; c) there is a lack of sufficient internal freedom for self-determination with regard to the choice of marriage (Mendonça, *Rotal Anthology*, 39).

5. 10/12/79 *coram* Pinto, *Dec.* 71 (1988) 440-452; *IDE* 91-II (1980) 19-29; *ME* 105 (1980) 165-176; Aff., Nancy, France (Anxiety neurosis)

   In this sentence Pinto presents an excellent analysis of the notion of discretion of judgment and of neurosis. Pinto's conclusion with regard to the effects of neurosis on matrimonial consent is that, if serious, it affects the free deliberation of the will in making the choice. In this case, the Respondent was diagnosed as suffering from serious neurotic anxiety (Mendonça, *Rotal Anthology*, 46).

6. 10/11/82 *coram* Ragni, *Dec.* 74 (1987) 452-468; *ME* 108 (1983) 254-268; Aff., Venice, Italy (Psychoneurosis; Use/abuse of prescription drugs)

   This is an important sentence dealing with the effects of personality disorder and use (abuse) of prescription drugs (Surmontil, Valium, Nesal, Librium, etc.) on matrimonial consent. The juridic element of consent focused in this case is the internal freedom to determine oneself to contract marriage. The Respondent in this case was diagnosed by experts as suffering from psychoneurosis and was in the habit of using prescription drugs to alleviate her anxiety and phobic symptoms. As a matter of fact she had used the drugs prior to nuptials and continued to use them after the marriage. This sentence is very informative on the psychological and juridic aspects of the case (Mendonça, *Rotal Anthology*, 60).

7. 07/05/83 *coram* Agustoni, *Dec.* 75 (1988) 379-389; Aff., Santiago de Chile, Chile (Affective immaturity; Obsessive-compulsive personality)

   The Petitioner in this case was diagnosed as suffering from serious affective immaturity and obsessive-compulsive personality. Agustoni states that such a disorder can impede a person's capacity for free deliberation. An anomaly does not have to be an illness or disease. Even a serious personality disorder, which is not an illness, as such can disturb mental faculties in such a way that a free choice is rendered impossible (Mendonça, *Rotal Anthology*, 65).

8. 05/14/84 *coram* Pompedda, *Dec.* 76 (1989) 272-278; Aff., Venice, Italy (Affective immaturity)

   [...] Pompedda insists that proportionate maturity is necessary to elicit the act of consent. Discretion of judgment consists of three essential elements, namely sufficient knowledge of the object; sufficient evaluation of the value of the object; and sufficient freedom of choice. Sufficient psychological maturity is the basis of a mature decision. Therefore, if a person is psychologically immature, he/she may not be capable of eliciting a mature decision. The Petitioner in this case was diagnosed as suffering from a 'neurotic-dysthymic' and 'psychosexual' disorder (Mendonça, *Rotal Anthology*, 71).

9. 12/14/84 *coram* Pinto, *ME* 113 (1988) 445-454; *IDE* 97-II (1986) 62-71; Aff.; Medellin, Colombia (Affective immaturity)

   [...] In this sentence, Pinto presents some useful points for consideration by ecclesiastical tribunals. He says that 'affective immaturity' must be understood in a 'juridic' and not 'psychiatric' sense. Ecclesiastical legislator uses a mixed method, that is, psychological and psychiatric, in determining the elements of consent. The psychological method provides insights into the process involved in forming the acts of consent while the psychiatric method enlightens the judge on the pathological condition of the process. From a juridic point of view lack of discretion of judgment proportionate to the obligations of marriage can be caused by affective immaturity.

Therefore, the correct way of determining grounds in such a case would be 'Whether there is sufficient evidence in favor of nullity of marriage due to lack of discretion mentioned in canon 1095, §2, because of affective immaturity on the part of X.' Pinto then elaborates on the threefold elements of discretion of judgment, namely knowledge, critical faculty and freedom. Pinto also gives a brief description of antisocial personality disorder as an expression of affective immaturity. The rotal court ruled affirmatively only on the basis of condition (Mendonça, *Rotal Anthology*, 75-76).

10. 02/16/85 *coram* Di Felice, *ME* 111 (1986) 253-266; Aff., Santiago de Chile, Chile (Psychic immaturity)

This sentence confirms the affirmative rotal decision of July 5, 1983, rendered *coram* Agustoni. Di Felice affirms that among sources giving rise to lack of discretion of judgment is affective or psychic immaturity which weakens the will in such a way that a person affected by it cannot elicit a free decision. The juridic emphasis is on the element of 'free choice'. Persons who are suffering from 'immature psychological development' are prone to obsessive ideas or to ideas suggested by others. Lacking sufficient critical ability due to retarded psychological evolution, persons affected by it are easily led by suggestions from others and thus lack internal freedom. In this case the Petitioner (woman) was diagnosed as an immature person who was easily led in making decisions (Mendonça, *Rotal Anthology*, 76).

11. 05/30/86 *coram* Bruno, *ME* 112 (1987) 449-463; Aff., Rockville Centre, U.S.A. (Psychic immaturity)

The first instance decision by the Rockville Centre tribunal was negative on grounds of lack of discretion of judgment. The appeal court of New York overturned that decision. In this sentence Bruno states that canon 1095 implies three essential species of capacity on the part of those who intend to contract marriage: the capacity to know, to weigh, and to hand over and assume the object of consent. If one of these capacities is missing, matrimonial consent is invalid. The Respondent (woman) was described by experts and witnesses as 'immature' and incompetent to judge the weight of matrimonial duties, and consequently to fulfill them in marriage. This sentence is important for a study on 'psychic immaturity' and its effects on consent (Mendonça, *Rotal Anthology*, 79).

12. 12/16/88 *coram* Bruno, *ME* 114 (1989) 298-308; Aff., Malta, Malta (Affective immaturity)

    The grounds proposed for the nullity of marriage in this case were intention against fidelity and lack of discretion of judgment. The first instance decision was affirmative only on lack of discretion of judgment. The second instance court at the Rota pronounced negatively on both grounds. In this sentence, which represents an affirmative decision, Bruno defines discretion of judgment in terms of reason and will proportionate to the obligations of marriage. He says that it is difficult to list those obligations. However, he admits that the following can be considered certain elements: a) the right to the body for the generation and education of offspring; b) the good of fidelity and sacrament; c) the good of spouses. At the very heart of conjugal consortium is the complete union of the spouses in all the aspects of their spiritual, intellectual, emotional, economic, social and physical life. Besides carnal union, interpersonal relationship is of great importance in marriage. Among interpersonal relationships love undoubtedly holds real weight, but it certainly does not pertain to the essence of marriage. Therefore, one should not doubt that a marriage celebrated without love is valid. However, if a person is radically incapable of placing an act of oblative love because of psychic disorder he/she cannot be considered to have consented validly because such a person is incapable of offering to the partner valid interpersonal relations for the purpose of promoting the moral, spiritual and social good of the spouse. A disorder of affect can disturb a person in such a way that she/he cannot elicit a mature decision concerning marriage. The psychic disorder of the Respondent was diagnosed as serious affective immaturity (Mendonça, *Rotal Anthology*, 81-82).

E. The following rotal decisions are taken from *Canon Law Abstracts* Nos. 67, 71, 75, 72, 75, 74, 76:

1. 02/23/90 *coram* Stankiewicz, *ME* 116 1-2/91, 297-313; Aff., Tribunal of the Roman Rota

Both parties were drug addicts before and after the wedding. S. distinguishes between the act of willing, the capacity of will and willingness, a state of being ready to decide. Only psychologically pathological states directly affect the will. He then explores the category of Psychoactive Substance Use Disorders (DSM-III-R). The effects of different categories of drugs are discussed in some detail, and especially the cocktail of cannabis, L.S.D. and cocaine involved in this case, with extensive references to rotal decisions on drug related cases. Occasional use of drugs does not generally indicate the presence of a mental pathology, but addiction in the proper sense does (*Canon Law Abstracts* 67:45-46).

2. 02/20/92 *coram* Davino, *ME* 117 1-2/93, 185-193; Neg., Philadelphia, U.S.A.

The case concerned a widowed man with two children, who remarried a woman twenty years his junior. After an affirmative first and second instance, the Respondent asked the Rota for a new hearing. The argument in favour of the Petitioner's lack of discretionary judgment had been based on the speed with which the marriage had been arranged and insufficient thought given to the age gap. D. sets out succinctly what is meant by 'lack of balance' and 'immaturity'. These cannot be identified with a lifelong process of maturation, or just any confusion of thought (*Canon Law Abstracts* 71:44).

3. 03/04/92 *coram* Faltin, *ME* 119 4/94, 943-506; Aff., Paris, France

In the law section F. emphasizes the importance of a capacity for the interpersonal relationship without which the communion of life, which distinguishes the marriage contract, and the exchange of rights cannot even be conceived. The case concerned the freedom of choice for a woman abandoned as a child and passed from pillar to post, who had severe obsessive-compulsive symptoms (*Canon Law Abstracts* 75:36).

4. 10/15/92 *coram* Burke, *ME* 118 4/93, 567-679; Neg., Dublin, Ireland

   B. reflects on the meaning of maturity in the context of canon 1095, 2°. As a term it is indeterminate, a matter of growth measured in terms of fullness, whereas discretionary judgment must be measured in proportion to the object of consent. Clearly the minimum age for marriage sets a standard for the level required for valid consent. The further one moves from that age, the greater the abnormality that will be required measured against the age group. If a degree of pathological immaturity is required at 16 or 18, this is even more true at 25 or 30. Again the suggestion that affective immaturity by itself leads to lack of due discretion, even when there is no sign of any defect in the intellect or will, does not seem well founded (*Canon Law Abstracts* 72:28).

5. 03/25/93 *coram* Stankewicz, *ME* 119 4/94, 449-464; Neg., Long Island, U.S.A.

   [...] Gravity is measured in terms of the incongruence with the obligations, but at the same time incapacity can be verified only when there is a serious psychological anomaly. The mere fact that a psychological expert diagnoses a personality disorder does not suffice, without an indication of its seriousness in terms not just of the symptoms, but the individual's psychological structure and its effect on the capacity to understand and evaluate (*Canon Law Abstracts* 75:36).

6. 02/10/94 *coram* Serrano Ruiz, *ME* 119 3/94, 307-319; Aff., Dublin, Ireland

   S. upholds the second instance affirmative decision. One should eschew attempts to define in an abstract way the minimum quid required for marriage. Discretionary judgment involves a number of factors: the maturity of each party must be studied as a presupposition for marriage; the level of maturity must be evaluated in the specific context of consent for marriage; the disposition of each party for a partnership of life and love must also be considered. S. draws particular attention to the relevance of situations of prolonged emotional tension, which are of greater importance for individual development than isolated events. The Petitioner had been adversely affected by the loss of his parents at an early age, and became involved in a world of drug taking, crime and prostitution. The Respondent was of low intelligence, childish, and into prostitution, marrying the Petitioner on impulse because he was concerned about them living in sin (*Canon Law Abstracts* 74:42).

7. 07/28/94 *coram* Colagiovanni, *ME* 120 3/95; 369-379; Neg., Galveston – Houston, U.S.A.

   [...] Immaturity can indeed lead to grave lack of discretionary judgment, but this must be measured not in terms of some lifelong process of maturation, but rather in proportion to the essential elements and properties of marriage. Equally a capacity for marriage presupposes not just an ability to recognize the essential obligations, but to deliver them, the attainment of a stable and lasting condition in regard to the essentials, but one still capable of development in other ways (*Canon Law Abstracts* 76:69-70).

IV. Types of Proofs Required

A. For proof, the evidence is gathered based on premarital and post-marital style of thinking and acting (adapted from Lawrence G. Wrenn, *Law Sections* [*LS*], [Washington: CLSA, 1994] 26-27).

B. As already noted, the defect in discretion must be grave. This gravity is measured in terms of the partnership that must be formed as indicated in canon 1055, §1. There must be, therefore, an adequate critical judgment to discern the nature and obligations of the partnership and also a personal ability to put the truly conjugal relationship into practice. As for proof, Fennel notes, "While some *a priori* indications may be available from the time of courtship from other relationships, much of this proof must be sought *a posteriori* in balancing the acts of consent and the lived reality, the ability to put into practice the essential obligations of consent" (*coram* Fennel, 9 July 1987, *MDGBI* 24, 1988).

C. The following is an example of proof, based upon the evidence of past premarital and post-marital style of thinking and acting. On July 7, 1995 the rotal decision *coram* R.P.D. Francesco Bruno granted an affirmative decision on the ground of grave lack of discretion in the case of a man who entered the seminary at the early age of eleven, then later ordained led a checkered career. He then left the ministry and sought laicization. He then married and later discovered that he loved all women. This type of behavior indicated that his sudden change in plans without regard for the consequence show instinctive response rather than carefully weighed decisions that characterized true discretion of judgment (*ME* 121 2/96, 198-213).

D. For proof, especially when grave lack of discretion involves a mental disorder, the role of an expert witness is imperative according to canon 1680. See "Sources for Canon 1095, 3°" for greater elaboration on this issue.

V. Related Issues

A. Donal Kelly in *The Canon Law, Letter & Spirit* notes that the concept of discretion of judgment is not so much about intellectual or cognitive ability per se as it is about "being able to use such intellectual ability in a practical way." Since the decision to marry is of great weight in that it involves lifelong consequences, the powers of judgment in a person must be adequate and reasonably mature.

B. According to the canon the invalidity of marriage occurs only when the lack of discretion is so grave that it removes the power of judgment entirely or so clouds the judgment that it renders the individual "incapable of consenting." The commentary mentions some factors which may precipitate grave lack of discretion: alcohol or the use of drugs, serious pressure to marry due to premarital pregnancy.

C. Victor J. Pospishil in his commentary on the Eastern Catholic Church Law (*Eastern Catholic Church Law, Second Revised and Augmented Edition*, [Staten Island, NY: Saint Maron Publications, 1996]) addresses the invalidity of marriage of those who are subjects of grave lack of discretion in canon 818, 2° of *CCEO*. He addresses the necessity to be able to make a sound judgment about the essential rights and obligations of marriage, to understand and comprehend the situation; all of which is something more than mere intellectual ability. "The ability of a marriage partner to foresee and plan may be unimpaired, but the translation of this intellectual foresight into daily human actions may be disturbed by compulsive neuroses, paranoid fantasies, unjustified suspicion of the surrounding, schizoid psychopathologies, chronic or continuous hysteric overreactions to daily occurrences, permanent immaturity of psychosocial development, and similar mental interferences of discretional ability of making judgments that are necessary in married life" (p. 551).

D. Therefore in grave lack of discretion cases we look for a significant flaw in evaluative cognition rather than mere or only conceptual cognition. Evaluative cognition assesses the true meaning and concerns of the Church's understanding of marriage. It grasps the appreciation of its authentic value and worth as a partnership of the whole of life.

E. James H. Provost, in his *Jurist* article "Canon 1095, 2° Seen from Its Sources," (*Jur* 56 [1996] 824-874) notes five rotal decisions which were part of the discussion of the canons at the time of drafting the schema for the 1983 *Code of Canon Law.*

> [...] there may be some advantage for those engaged in the work of local tribunals to have an appreciation for the seriousness with which the Roman Rota has approached the various cases which gave rise to canon 1095, and which were influential in drafting the canon as attested to in the discussions reported in *Communicationes* [...] Five rotal decisions were given as the sources for Canon 1095, 2° by the Pontifical Commission for the Authentic Interpretation of the Code of Canon Law. They are, in chronological order, *coram* Felici, December 3, 1957; *coram* Wynen, April 13, 1943; *coram* Felici, December 3, 1957; *coram* Sabattani, February 24, 1961; and *coram* Pinto, February 4, 1974.

F. See Wrenn, Lawrence G. "Lack of Due Discretion," *LS* (Washington: CLSA, 1994) 24-28.

Chapter III

Sources For Canon 1095, 3°

Incapacity Because of Inability to Assume the Essential Obligations of Marriage

Gerald T. Jorgensen, PhD, JCL

I. Pertinent Canons

A. See canon 1095, 3°.

B. See the following allied canons: 1057, §1; 1056; 1055, §1; 1057, §2; 1680; 1579, §1; 1579, §2.

II. Conciliar and/or Papal Teachings

A. Pius XII, 1941 allocution to the Rota:

> The Sacred Rota has recently been occupied with cases concerning psychic incapacity, based upon some pathological defect; and on these occasions the judicial sentence had to apply certain theories which are presented as very recent by modern psychiatrists and psychologists. Surely this is a matter of congratulation and a sign of painstaking and broad judicial scrutiny; for ecclesiastical jurisprudence cannot and must not ignore the genuine progress on the moral and juridical sciences; nor can it deem it permissible and proper to reject the findings merely because they are new. Is novelty inimical to science? Without taking new strides beyond the truth, which has already been acquired, how could human knowledge in the immense field of nature make any progress? (English trans. from Woestman, *Papal Allocutions*, 12-13.)

B. Pius XII, 1942 allocution to the Rota:

> The conscientious observance of these norms [jurisprudential principles as enunciated in rotal jurisprudence or canonical doctrine/science] is a matter of duty for the judge; but on the

other hand in their application he must remember that they are not ends in themselves, but means to an end, that is, to attain and guarantee a moral certainty with an objective foundation as to the reality of fact. It should not come about that what the will of the legislator intended as a help and security for discovering the truth become instead an obstacle to its discovery. If ever the observance of formal rules of law results in injustice or is contrary to equity, there is always a right of recourse to the legislator. (English trans. from Woestman, *Papal Allocutions*, 20.)

C. Pope Pius XII, 1944 allocution to the Rota:

But the jurists – who as such look to mere law and rigid justice – are wont to show an instinctive aloofness from the ideas and preoccupations of the care of souls, and champion a clear separation between the two fora, the forum of conscience and the external juridico-social forum of human society. This inclination toward a definite line of demarcation between the two is, to a certain extent, legitimate inasmuch as the Judge and his collaborators in the judiciary process do not have directly the pastoral responsibility as their proper office. But it would be a fatal error to deny that they too, in the last and definitive instance, are in the service of souls. For thus they would, in the ecclesiastical trial, exclude themselves from the end and unity of action, which belong to the Church by divine institution. They would be like members of a body, which are no longer inserted in the whole and are no longer ready to subordinate and direct their activity to the end of the whole organism. (English trans. from Woestman, *Papal Allocutions*, 30.)

D. John Paul II, 1984 allocution to the Rota:

The concern to safeguard the dignity and indissolubility of marriage by checking abuses and irresponsibility, which, unfortunately must often be sadly noted in this matter, cannot prescind from the real and undeniable progress of the biological, psychological, psychiatric, and social sciences. Otherwise one would contradict the very value to be protected namely, a truly existing marriage, not one which has only the appearance of such, since it is null from the outset. (English trans. from Woestman, *Papal Allocutions*, 185.)

E. John Paul II, 1987 allocution to the Rota:

> For the canonist, the principle must remain that only *incapacity* and not *difficulty* in giving consent and in realizing a true community of life and love invalidates a marriage. Moreover, the breakdown of a marriage union is never in itself proof of such incapacity on the part of the contracting parties. They may have neglected or used badly the means, both natural and supernatural, at their disposal; or they may have failed to accept the inevitable limitations and burdens of married life, either because of blocks of an unconscious nature or because of slight pathological disturbances which leave substantially intact human freedom; or finally because of failures of a moral order. The hypothesis of real incapacity is to be considered only when an anomaly of a serious nature is present, which, however, it may be defined, must substantially vitiate the capacity of the individual to understand and/or to will. (English trans. from Woestman, *Papal Allocutions*, 194.)

F. John Paul II, 1997 allocution to the Rota:

> [...] *Marriage* certainly has an *essential nature*, described in canon 1055, which pervades the entire teaching concerning marriage, as can be seen in the concepts of 'essential property', 'essential element', 'essential rights and obligations', etc. This essential reality is a possibility open in principle to every man and woman; indeed, it represents a true vocation for the great majority of the human race. (English trans. from Woestman, *Papal Allocutions*, 243.)

G. John Paul II, 1997 allocution to the Rota:

> [...] Relations between spouses, in fact, like those between parents and children, are constitutively *relations of justice*, and for that reason have in themselves juridical significance. Conjugal and parent-child love is not merely an instinctive inclination, nor an arbitrary and reversible choice, but *is rather a love that is due*. Therefore, putting the person at the center of the civility of love does not exclude the law, but instead demands it, leading to a rediscovery of law as an interpersonal reality and to a vision of juridical institutions that highlights their constitutive link with

persons themselves, which is so essential in the case of marriage and the family. (English trans. from Woestman, *Papal Allocutions*, 242.)

H. John Paul II, 1999 allocution to the Rota:

[...] This consent is nothing other than the conscious, responsible assumption of a commitment through a juridical act by which, in reciprocal self-giving, the spouses promise total and definitive love to each other. They are free to celebrate marriage, after having chosen each other with equal freedom, but as soon as they perform this act they establish a personal state in which love becomes something that is owed, entailing effects of a juridical nature as well. (English trans. from Woestman, *Papal Allocutions*, 251.)

I. John Paul II, 1981 ap. exhort., *FC*:

Consequently, sexuality, by means of which man and woman give themselves to one another through the acts which are proper and exclusive to spouses, is by no means something purely biological, but concerns the innermost being of the human person as such. It is realized in a truly human way only if it is an integral part of the love by which a man and a woman commit themselves totally to one another until death. The total physical self-giving would be a lie if it were not the sign and fruit of a total personal self-giving, in which the whole person, including the temporal dimension, is present; if the person were to withhold something or reserve the possibility of deciding otherwise in the future, by this very fact he or she would not be giving totally. (Flannery, *Vatican Council II*, 2:822.)

III. Rotal Jurisprudence

A. *Coram* Serrano, 22 November 1985, *RRDec.,* 77:517-518:

In order to understand the newest species of incapacity, one must keep the following in mind:

The incapacity for establishing interpersonal relationship should extend to the total person of both spouses, that is, to those aspects of one's character bonding the persons to each other. This is not only because the term '*se*' ('themselves') means it and the law has placed it within the totality of the union – 'they establish between themselves a partnership of the whole of life' (c. 1055) – but also because, with the teaching of Vatican Council II [...] *Gaudium et spes*, n. 48: 'intimate community of life and conjugal love is established by the irrevocable personal consent', – present law no longer restricts the term of conjugal consent to 'acts per se apt for the generation of offspring'.

The specific incapacity for establishing a true and apt relationship between the two persons corresponding to the meaning and significance of the words 'mutually give and accept' is also expressed in law (c. 1057). If we are not mistaken, these words imply relative suitability to be considered between two determined persons and not between anyone else, not even between one or both with someone else.

Moreover, stability and strength of constancy are essential since it is not directed only to the act, as it would in case [...] of capacity related to the act of consent in two other legal suppositions, but to the rights and duties which are of their nature perpetual and grave. [Private translation]

B. *Coram* Serrano, 12 July 1991, *ME* 117 [1992] 358-359:

Ecclesial law clearly requires a certain 'quality of gravity' (*qualitas gravitatis*) for any *defect* to affect the validity of marriage. This principle is applicable to each norm of c. 1095.

In a marriage case, it is not sufficient to prove that a certain disorder is 'beyond the norm' (*extra normam*) or 'below the norm' (*infra normam*) to invalidate marriage. These concepts do not coincide and therefore, a judge should not declare a marriage null just because it is 'peculiar' (*matrimonium singulare*) because a 'peculiar marriage' is not necessarily a 'null marriage' (*matrimonium nullum*). [English original]

C. *Coram* Bruno, 19 July 1991, *RRDec.,* 83:463-477; also published in *ME* 117 [1992] 169, 170, 173:

Certainly it is not easy to determine and list the essential rights and obligations flowing from marriage. Without doubt, however, we must consider among them, as can be deduced from cc. 1055-1056, the giving and acceptance of the right to the body ordered to the generation and education of children, and this constitutes the element toward which the conjugal covenant is specifically ordered; the good of fidelity and of the sacrament, which are the essential properties, and the good of the spouses, a proper element proposed by the new Code under the influence of Vatican Council II, and derived from ancient secular definition.

[...] The *good of the spouses*, as an end and essential element of the nuptial covenant, is the sum of all the goods which flow from the interpersonal relationship of the same spouses. If they do not suffer from any psychic anomaly of personality, (then) they together, through apt interpersonal relationship, enrich each other as individual persons and the entire conjugal life.

[...] And truly, if the man or the woman or both spouses lack the capacity for establishing an interpersonal relationship, it would be impossible for them to have a tolerable common life, and the 'good of spouses', which is the end and essential element of conjugal covenant, would be hopelessly difficult. (The text of the sentence as found in *ME* 117:169-170 is used here.)

D. *Coram* Bruno, 19 July 1991, *RRDec.,* 83:463-477; also published in *ME* 117 [1992] 171:

The incapacity of the person must exist, at least in a latent and stable form, at the time of the celebration of the marriage and it must be certain; doubtful incapacity neither impedes the celebration of the marriage nor does it allow a declaration of nullity of the marriage.

[...] After some initial hesitation, the consolidated jurisprudence of the Rota *passim* teaches that *it is not at all necessary to insist on perpetual incapacity*. (The text of the sentence as found in *ME* 117:171 is used here.)

E. *Coram* Pompedda, 11 April 1988, *RRDec.,* 80:202.

Indeed our opinion is that the question ought to be changed so that the good of the spouses – the only one treated in the new code, which no longer makes mention of the right to communion of life – ought to be understood and brought about as the right (and correlative obligation) to the communion of life: understood in its broad significance, ideally inspired toward conjugal love as the Second Vatican Council placed it, and expressed juridically by the rights and obligations associated with a unique or specific way of acting in interpersonal relationships proper to spouses, determined by what is essentially required and adequate form the nature of marriage and having juridical importance. [Private translation]

F. *Coram* Bruno, 18 December 1986, *RRDec.,* 78:759 (addressing when a disorder becomes evident only after the celebration of the marriage; in this specific case the disorder was chronic alcoholism):

If, however, a certain diagnosis of chronic alcoholism is made at the time of the wedding, but serious disturbances erupted only shortly after the marriage, it can be concluded with moral certainty in favor of invalidity of the marriage, because the contractant, in view of the progressive nature of the disease, was incapable of assuming and fulfilling conjugal duties. The incapacity was already present at the time of the wedding, although in a latent form. (Trans. by Augustine Mendonça in *ME* 125 [2000] 555.)

G. *Coram* Defilippi, *ME* 125 (2000) 478-483:

6 – To say it briefly, according to c. 1095, 3° of *C.I.C.*, there is incapacity to contract marriage if the following three elements simultaneously concur: a) *impossibility to assume;* b) *the essential obligations of marriage;* c) *because of causes of a psychic nature.*

a) In what refers to the first element, it must be recalled that the condition should be such that, because of it the person about to marry is in fact *morally incapable* of assuming the duties of marriage. Consequently we must keep in mind the appropriate distinction between 'mere difficulty' and 'moral incapacity', as timely recalled by the Supreme Pontiff in his Address to N.A.T. on 5 February 1987: 'For the canonist the principle must remain clear that only *incapacity* and not *difficulty* in giving consent and of realizing a true community of life and love invalidates a marriage' (*AAS* 79 [1987] 1457).

When the real incapacity to assume and fulfil the conjugal duties, persisting during the time of the wedding celebration, has been proven, it is no longer necessary to raise the questions of 'seriousness' or 'perpetuity' concerning that incapacity (cf. *coram* Pompedda, 15 July 1994, *RRDec.*, 86:395-396, nn. 9-11).

b) The alleged incapacity must refer to 'the essential matrimonial obligations', which are different from those other obligations that complement the conjugal covenant.

Those essential duties refer to the duties of justice between the two persons, contained within the juridical bond itself, by which a man and a woman become husband and wife (cf. J. Hervada, *Obligaciones esenciales del matrimonio: Ius Canonicum* [1991] 61).

Although it is difficult to determine and enumerate each and all the essential obligations of marriage, 'without any doubt, those obligations are to be counted that derive from the essential properties of marriage according to c. 1056, i.e., from unity and indissolubility, and, from the ends of c. 1055, §1, which are specifically rooted in marriage. Attention is to be paid also to the definition of matrimonial consent provided by c. 1057, §2, according to which the contracting parties, by an irrevocable covenant, mutually give and accept each other for the purpose of establishing a partnership of their entire life "which is ordered, of its own very nature, to the good of the spouses and to the procreation and upbringing of offspring" (c. 1055, §1)' (*coram* Funghini, 19 December 1994, *RRDec.*, 86:766, n. 2).

c) Finally, the incapacity must derive from 'a cause of a psychic nature', that is to say, as the Supreme Pontiff teaches us in the above mentioned address of 5 February 1987, 'the hypothesis of real incapacity is possible only if a serious anomaly is present' (*AAS* 79 [1987] 1456).

It must be noted that the alleged 'anomaly' or 'cause of a psychic nature', is not the ground of nullity of marriage but the 'determining cause' of the incapacity to assume an essential obligation of marriage. Therefore, both the existence of the cause of a psychic nature and the same cause's influence in the failed marriage should be investigated.

That anomaly must be a disorder 'of a psychic nature', present 'at the moment of manifesting consent, at least in a latent state or *in actu primo proximo*' (*coram* Bruno, 25 November 1988, *RRDec.*, 80:680, n. 5).

That alleged disorder, which 'will be found in the personality itself, or rooted in the character of the subject, since it must refer not so much to the act (of consent) but to the conjugal partnership' (*coram* Serrano, 27 November 1992, *RRDec.*, 84:595, n. 3), is described with different words in the decisions of N.A.T. as a 'distortion of character or mood pervading the entire personality' (*coram* Colagiovanni, 8 March 1990, *RRDec.*, 82:359, n. 10), or 'a serious disturbance or pathology of the human "psyche"' (*coram* Burke, 22 July 1991, *RRDec.*, 83:502, n. 4), or a 'deflection or deviation from normality' (*coram* Stankiewicz, 27 February 1992, *RRDec.*, 84:106, n. 6), or 'abnormal personality' (*coram* Ragni, 19 May 1992, *RRDec.*, 84:265, n. 5), etc.

7 – In those cases 'the judge is to use the services of one or more experts' (c. 1680).

The role of the expert, however, is not to issue a judgment about the nullity of marriage but 'to provide the elements of information which have to do with his specific competence, that is, the nature and extent of the psychic and psychiatric realities on grounds of which the nullity of marriage has been alleged', and to explain, therefore, 'the nature and the degree of the psychic processes in relation with matrimonial consent...' (*Allocution of John Paul II to the Rotal Auditors*, 5 February 1987, *op. cit.*, pp. 1454 and 1458).

Finally, the judge is the only one competent to issue the judgment on the nullity of marriage, and in order to reach his own juridical conclusion, he 'is to weigh carefully not only the expert's conclusions ... but also all the other circumstances of the case (c. 1579, §1)'. Furthermore, 'when he is giving the reasons for his decision, the judge must state on what grounds he accepts or rejects the conclusions of the experts' (c. 1579). (The *turnus* for this case was the following: Mario F. Pompedda, Dean, Joseph M. Serrano Ruiz, and John Baptista Defilippi, *Ponens*.)

H. *Coram* Pompedda, 31 October 1986, *RRDec.,* 78:569-588.

Augustine Mendonça in *ME* 125 (2000) 566-570 offers excellent insights into this decision and the juridical principles elucidated by Pompedda when addressing the allegation that a person is incapable of assuming the essential obligations of marriage. First, Pompedda admits that "intimate communion of life" or "intimate interpersonal relationship" is an essential aspect of marriage; but in order for one's consent to be invalid, there must be true incapacity for that relationship that is specifically conjugal in nature. Pompedda argues that mere incompatibility is not a juridical option for true incapacity for interpersonal relationship. Second, even the greatest difficulty to sustain the relationship, which emerges only after the celebration of the marriage, cannot prove the unsuitability of the parties to establish the partnership of the whole of life. Impossibility for assuming and fulfilling the specifically conjugal partnership of their entire life must be proven to have been present in the person at the time of the exchange of consent. Pompedda says that only a personality disorder or psychic disorder, which is found to be serious at the time of exchanging consent, would invalidate it. In a concrete case, in order to declare a marriage invalid, it is not sufficient to have a diagnosis only, it is also important to take into consideration the age of the person(s), the length of relationship, when the alleged disorder actually emerged, what was the quality of the conjugal life of the parties for the first several years after the wedding, etc. (*coram* Pompedda, 31 October 1986, *RRDec.*, 78:576)

I. *Coram* Burke, 2 December 1993, *RRDec.,* 85:746-751; English trans. in *SC* 29 (1995) 509-514; also in *ME* 123 (1998) 36-51 [Latin-English text]:

[...] while an inability to refrain from certain vices is clearly an incapacity, there is need to specify the object, scope, and effect of this incapacity, for it may embrace many areas of life, or few; it may relate to substantial or quite accidental aspects of these areas, etc. This is of particular importance in pleas of nullity of marriage brought under c. 1095, 3° when a person's alcoholism or drug addiction, etc., is alleged as proof or partial proof of consensual incapacity.

Not only must proof be furnished of the *existence at the time of the marriage* of the dependent condition in question, but its *gravity* has also to be established. Further, it has to be strictly shown that the fulfillment of marital duties was rendered not just more difficult by the dependence, but actually *impossible* for the person laboring under it. Above all what must be pondered and recognized is that the duty or duties whose fulfillment was made impossible by the addiction or dependence were *essential* marital duties. (*SC* 29:511)

J. *Coram* Civili, 22 November 1994, *RRDec.,* 86:570:

The causes of a psychic *nature*, therefore, need not necessarily be *pathological*; but it cannot be denied that proof of incapacity will be easier if a pathological element is added. This can easily happen, for example, in cases of grave affective immaturity, in obsessive neuroses, in congenital or acquired defects, such as alcoholism.

K. Civili's *turnus* in the decision cited immediately above also clearly disagreed with the view that the incapacity of canon 1095, 3° does not render marriage null if, within a reasonable period of time, it can be cured by ordinary and licit medical means. According to Civili, it is sufficient in the case of incapacity to assume that it be present at the very moment of eliciting consent, from which the bond arises. And in fact, more recent rotal jurisprudence is unanimous in affirming that antecedence is not necessary, nor is the perpetuity of the incapacity. Certainly, antecedence will be useful to strengthen the proof of the existence of incapacity at the time of marriage. (See *coram* Civili, ibid. 571.)

IV. Types of Proofs Required

A. Canon 1095, 3° confirms that the incapacity to assume the essential marital obligations *must* be due to "causes of a psychic nature." It appears that during the preparation of the 1983 code, various terms expressive of causes or an inability to assume were suggested (cf.

Comm 7 [1975] 44-52; 9 [1977] 369-370). Thus, the final choice of "*ob causas naturae psychicae*" was probably a compromise with differences of opinion as to its exact meaning remaining (cf. John Paul II, 1987 allocution to the Rota for interpreting or evaluating a law section). "In this area, the Commission tried to propose certain principles, that are expressions of natural law, to help jurisprudence give more explicit criteria of those things that are contained in that general principle that "consent makes the marriage" (*Congregatio Plenaria*, session 5, 24 October 1981 in *Acta et documenta Pontificiae Commissionis Codici Iuris Canonici recognoscendo,* [Vatican City. 1991] 437)." However, the phrase "causes of a psychic nature" appears sufficiently inclusive to account for any psychological or psychiatric disorder that would render a person incapable of assuming obligations essential to marriage.

B. In the judge's decision making process the following directives of the current Pontiff seem most helpful and to the point. First, "only incapacity invalidates marriage" under this canon. It is the incapacity to assume and not the psychological defect that is endowed with juridic relevance ("an anomaly of a serious nature is present, which, however, it may be defined must substantially vitiate the capacity of the individual to understand and/or to will"). The disproportionality in the act of consent is what is juridically relevant, not the anomaly per se. Second, the words "however it may be defined" suggest that psychiatric diagnosis, as such, has little significance. In assessing the disproportionality, the effect of the anomaly is what becomes the judge's focal point.

C. *Coram* Burke, 24 November 1994, *Forum* 10 (1999) 170-171, 174-178:

> 4. Canon 1095 is concerned with the adequacy of the act of consent. Consent is not valid unless it: a) is the result of due understanding (proportionate to the seriousness of the commitment being undertaken) of the essential rights and obligations involved in this marital commitment; and (b) proceeds from a free will capable of actually observing these essential rights and duties. [...]
>
> 5. The matter does not appear in quite the same light when we turn to the 'incapacity for assuming' considered in no. 3 of the canon. Consent is equally invalidated by the person's incapacity,

but in this particular case the incapacity has of necessity a projection toward the future. The person is incapable of assuming because he or she is incapable of fulfilling. Fulfillment (a future event) *will* prove impossible to him because of a fundamental inadequacy of will residing in him *right* now.

The truth and importance of this appear most clearly when one considers the requirements for proving this particular ground. Proof that a person was incapable under c. 1095, 3° seems impossible in practice, unless it can be shown beyond doubt that in subsequent conjugal life he or she did not in fact fulfill some essential obligation of marriage. So while the canon speaks of an *incapacitas assumendi* (in the moment of consent), post-matrimonial conduct has a much greater bearing on the process than in the case of a grave defect of discretion of judgment. Hence the opinion that the subsequent possible recovery from, or overcoming of, the incapacitating condition should be evaluated differently according to whether it is no. 2 or no. 3 of c. 1095 that is in question. [...]

10. Whatever the merits of the view presented here, it is important that the core of the argument be accurately grasped. What is maintained is not that perpetuity enters as an essential element of the *incapacitas assumendi*, or that perpetuity has to be proved if incapacity is to be established (in practice such proof would be well-nigh impossible). What is being suggested is that *non*-perpetuity [of the anomaly or disorder] quite undermines the claim or hypothesis of original incapacity from a probative point of view. Where non-perpetuity is a verified fact in a particular case (because the party's alleged incapacitating condition has disappeared or has been cured), this so fundamentally debilitates the proof of consensual incapacity as to render impossible the attribution of moral (or scientific) certainty to any diagnosis presented to the Court of an incapacity actually present at the moment of consent.

Therefore we have no interest in proposing a positive thesis- that perpetuity is an essential component of incapacity. Our argument is pragmatic and negative: in the face of an actual cure or recovery from a condition diagnosed as disabling, it does not seem possible to resolve with judicial certainty the question whether the condition was a true incapacity, and not a simple difficulty.

On the theoretical level of doctrine therefore, one can legitimately argue that an incapacity for assuming does not have to be marked by perpetuity. In practice however, if at the time of the canonical process an alleged incapacity has turned out to be temporary (because it has disappeared or been cured), then proper judicial reasoning seems to call for the conclusion that at the time of consent it was a transient (though perhaps serious) difficulty at most, and not a real incapacity in the canonical sense. [...]

One notes too Msgr. Giannecchini's words in a decision of October 4, 1991: 'Antecedence and perpetuity or incurability are not necessarily required; these traits *rather help the process of proof,* inasmuch as a *transient incapacity*, that is, one which is short-term and curable by licit means, *is presumed not to be grave or true*, but rather a difficulty' (vol. 83:520). The last observation seems fully in line with the considerations outlined above; if so, the whole passage could be taken as a refinement more than a contradiction of what the same Ponens wrote three years earlier in a (non-published) sentence: 'an incapacity which results from the disorder must be true, antecedent and *perpetual*' (*Medellen.*, Dec. 20, 1988, n. 3). The same practical connection between [non-]perpetuity and proof of incapacity is noted by other auditors who favor the theoretical position that perpetuity is not required: 'On the other hand, the incurability of the incapacity is not required, even though *this can provide an excellent criterion* to distinguish a true incapacity from a mere difficulty' (*c.* Civili, July 10, 1990, 82:598).

13. A sentence *c.* Stankiewicz of Nov. 14, 1985 states that 'While a perpetual incapacity for assuming the essential obligations of marriage is not formally required by ecclesiastical law (cf. can. 1095, n. 3) so as to invalidate matrimonial consent, nevertheless [perpetuity] is *rightly insisted upon in the order of proof of incapacity*, since 'unless incurability is proved, one cannot conclude to a true incapacity for permanent obligations' (J.M. Pinto: "Incapacitas assumendi matrimonii onera in Novo C.I.C.," in *Dilexit Iustitiam*, [1984] 25)' (vol. 77, p. 490; cf. dec. of the same Ponens of May 28, 1991: vol. 83, 349).

The principle quoted here from Msgr. Pinto (and repeated by him in many rotal sentences along with those noted above; e.g. Dec. 3, 1982, vol. 74, 571; d. 27 maii 1983; May 30, 1986; Feb. 6, 1987, vol. 79, 34, etc.) seems an over-statement of the matter. According to the opinion put forward here, it is not that the perpetuity or incurableness of the incapacitating condition must be established in order to give an affirmative decision under c. 1095, 3°; it is rather that the cessation or cure of the condition – diagnosed as incapacitating – must bring into question the juridic value of the diagnosis, and leave uncertainty in the judges' minds as to the basic question whether what had been diagnosed as a true incapacity was in fact a mere difficulty - that *could* have been overcome at the time of consent (using proper means), as it was in fact overcome later.

D. Depending on the disorder at issue in the specific case, the judge may have to enunciate in his or her law section a description of the disorder and in light of the specific disorder the juridic principles pertinent to the case at bar. If it is a traditional psychiatric disorder, the DSM-IV diagnostic manual as published by the American Psychiatric Association may provide the information necessary to explicate the negative effects of the disorder on the parties' conjugal partnership of the whole of life. If it is not a traditional psychiatric disorder, then the judge will have to rely on experts or recognized psychiatric or psychological textbooks to provide the necessary information. (See *coram* de Lanversin, 1 March 1989, *RRDec.,* 81:176-189 and Mendonça's discussion of the same decision in *ME* 125 [2000] 570-573.)

E. Because a declaration of a person's incapacity to assume and fulfill the essential obligations of marriage concerns one of the most basic human rights, that is, the right to marry, caution must be exercised lest that right be arbitrarily denied to a person with a psychiatric disorder. The effects of mental illness or a diagnosed mental disorder are not to be unduly generalized. (See *coram* Burke 1993 decision cited above, pp. 511-512 of the *SC* translation [cf. p. 29, letter I] and Mendonça's discussion of the Burke decision in *ME* 125 [2000] 574-577.)

F. Although the fact of the party's mental disorder may not be in doubt at the time of the marital separation and/or civil divorce, what is important is the time in the relationship that the reported facts began to occur at a serious level. Even if a mental disorder is considered chronic, it has no effect on the presentation of consent in the act of assuming the responsibilities if it emerged only as a result of the vicissitudes of married life. (See *coram* Colagiovanni, 20 January 1994, *RRDec.,* 86:26; *coram* Pompedda, 31 October 1986, *RRDec.,* 78:588.)

G. In the declaration of the Supreme Tribunal of the Apostolic Signatura, Prot. N. 2852/97 VT:

In cases based on grounds which are dealt with in canon 1095, 'unless it is obvious from the circumstances that this would be useless', the services of experts are required (cf. c. 1680 and the address of John Paul II to the Rota of the 5th February 1987: *AAS* 79 [1987] 1453-1459 and of the 25th January 1988 *AAS* 80 [1988] 922-927). Therefore in such cases the services of a psychiatrist or psychologist are mostly required to distinguish the psychic condition of the party or parties at the time of the marriage. [...] The services of experts in such cases are to be employed not only because they have been prescribed by law, but especially because such services are an instrument of proof, which, as happens in most cases, the judge cannot ignore in order to derive moral certainty 'from the acts and proofs', so as to be able to pronounce sentence in favour of the nullity of a marriage. An expert report about the psychic state of the party can seem to be 'evidently useless' in order to prove the nullity of a marriage: a.) when, even if the matter in hand is not 'expert report' in the technical sense, in the acts there exists a document or testimonial, which is so qualified, that it provides sufficient relevant proof to the judge; b) when from proven facts and circumstances, without any doubt, there appears either a lack of sufficient use of reason or a serious lack of discretion of judgement or an incapacity to assume the essential obligations of marriage. The reason is that in this case the nullity of the marriage can be declared on account of an evident lack of consent, without the need of a carefully drawn up diagnosis of the psychic cause due to which there exists that defect. However, in such cases the judge can ask the expert to explain some document or fact, which exists or is alleged in the acts. Indeed, here we are dealing with two cases which should not be considered except as exceptions from the general rule. However, if a party refuses to subject himself to an examination by an expert, it is usual for the judge to ask the expert for a 'report' (*votum*) based on the acts alone, even if such a '*votum*' is not considered in psychiatry or psychology as 'an expert report' (*peritia*) in the technical sense. Evidently in this case one can ask the same expert to explain the importance of such a '*votum*' in order to distinguish the true nature of the psychic defect. It is clear that this same '*votum*' should not be assessed in psychiatry or psychology in the same way as a '*peritia*' in the technical sense. (English translation in *Forum* 9 [1998] 51-57, esp. nn. 2, 4-6.)

Chapter IV

Sources For Canon 1096

IGNORANCE

Girard M. Sherba, JCD

I. Pertinent Canons

A. See canons 15, §1; 124, §1; 124, §2; 126; 1096, §1; and 1096, §2.

B. See the following allied cannons: 1584; 1055, §1; 1056; 1057, §1; and 1057, §2.

II. Conciliar and/or Papal Teaching

A. Vatican Council II, *Gaudium et spes* (*GS*) 47-52, *AAS* 58 [1966] 1067-1068.

We have the articulation of the Church's teaching concerning marriage and family life. Of particular significance is number 48:

> The intimate partnership of life and the love which constitutes the married state has been established by the creator and endowed by him with its own proper laws: it is rooted in the contract of its partners, that is, in their irrevocable personal consent. It is an institution confirmed by divine law and receiving its stability, even in the eyes of society also, from the human act by which the partners mutually surrender themselves to each other; for the good of the partners, of the children, and of society this sacred bond no longer depends on human decision alone [...] By its very nature the institution of marriage and married love are ordered to the procreation and education of the offspring and it is in them that it finds its crowning glory. Thus the man and woman, who 'are no longer two but one' (Mt. 19:6), help and serve each other by their marriage partnership; they become conscious of their unity and experience it more deeply from day to day. The intimate union of marriage, as a mutual giving of two persons, and the good of the children demand total fidelity from the

spouses and require an unbreak-able unity between them. (Flannery, *Vatican Council II*, 2:950.)

B. Pope Paul VI, *Humanae vitae*. See *AAS* 60 (1968) 485-487:

> [H]usband and wife, through that mutual gift of themselves [in marriage], which is specific and exclusive to them alone, seek to develop that kind of personal union in which they complement one another in order to co-operate with God in the generation and education of new lives [...]
>
> [Married] love is above all fully *human* [...] It is not, then, merely a question of natural instinct or emotional drive. It is also, and above all, an act of the free will [...]
>
> Then it is a love which is *total* – that very special form of personal friendship in which the husband and wife generously share everything [...] content to be able to enrich the other with the gift of himself.
>
> Again, married love is *faithful* and *exclusive* of all other, and this until death. Though this fidelity of husband and wife sometimes presents difficulties, no one can assert that it is impossible [...]
>
> And finally this love is *creative for life*, for it is not exhausted by the loving interchange of husband and wife, but also contrives to go beyond this to bring new life into being. 'Marriage and married love are by their character ordained to the procreation and bringing up of children. Children are the outstanding gift of marriage' [*GS* 50; *AAS* 58 (1966) 1070-1072].
>
> Married love, therefore, requires of husband and wife the full awareness of their obligations in the matter of responsible parenthood [...] Responsible parenthood, moreover, in the terms in which we use the phrase, retains a further and deeper significance of paramount importance which refers to the objective *moral* order instituted by God, – the order of which a right conscience is the true interpreter." (Flannery, *Vatican Council II*, 2.400-402.)

C. John Paul II, ap. exhort., *FC* nn. 18-20. See *AAS* 74 (1982) 100-104:

While *Humanae vitae* speaks of conjugal love rather than *consortium*, the values set forth, i.e., fully human, total, faithful and exclusive, creative for life (fruitful) and moral, are important for our understanding, because conjugal love arises within the context of the *consortium*. These same values were further reiterated by the Holy Father in his 1981 apostolic exhortation, *FC*, nn. 18-20.

The family, which is founded and given life by love, is a community of persons: of husband and wife, of parents and children, of relatives. Its first task is to live with fidelity the reality of communion in a constant effort to develop an authentic community of persons [...] The love between husband and wife . . . is given life and sustenance by an unceasing inner dynamism leading the family to ever deeper and more intense *communion*, which is the foundation and soul of the *community* of marriage and the family [...] The first communion is the one which is established and which develops between husband and wife: by virtue of the covenant of married life, the man and the woman 'are no longer two but one flesh' [Mt 19:6; cf. Gen 2:24] and they are called to grow continually in their communion through day-today fidelity to their marriage promise of total mutual self-giving [...] Such a communion is radically contradicted by polygamy: this, in fact, directly negates the plan of God which was revealed from the beginning, because it is contrary to the equal personal dignity of men and women who in matrimony give themselves with a love that is total and therefore unique and exclusive [...] Conjugal communion is characterized not only by its unity but also by its indissolubility: 'As a mutual gift of two persons, this intimate union, as well as the good of children, imposes total fidelity on the spouses and argues for an unbreakable oneness between them' (*GS* 48). (Flannery, *Vatican Council II*, 2:828-831.)

D. Pope John Paul II repeated this teaching in his 1982 allocution to the Rota. See *AAS* 74 (1982) 450-451:

The Council saw marriage as a covenant of love (see *GS*, no. 48). This covenant is 'freely and consciously chosen, whereby man and woman accept the intimate community of life and love willed by God himself' (*Familiaris consortio*, no. 11) [...] Love is essentially a gift. Speaking of the act of love the Council envisages an act of giving, which is one, decisive, irrevocable because it is a total giving which wants to be and remain mutual and fruitful [...] Marriage consent is an act of the will which signifies and involves a mutual giving which unites the spouses between themselves and at the same time binds them to the children which they may eventually have, with whom they constitute one family, one single home, a 'domestic Church' (*LG*, no. 11). (English trans. from Woestman, *Papal Allocutions*, 172.)

E. In the *Catechism of the Catholic Church* concerning the Sacrament of Matrimony, we read:

§§1661 The sacrament of Matrimony signifies the union of Christ and the Church. It gives spouses the grace to love each other with the love with which Christ has loved his Church; the grace of the sacrament thus perfects the human love of the spouses, strengthens their indissoluble unity and sanctifies them on the way to eternal life (cf. Council of Trent: *DS* 1799).

§§1664 Unity, indissolubility and openness to fertility are essential to marriage. Polygamy is incompatible with the unity of marriage; divorce separates what God has joined together; the refusal of fertility turns married life away from its 'supreme gift', the child (*GS* 50, §1).

F. Taking into consideration the Church's teaching on marriage as seen in *GS*, the teachings of Pope Paul VI and Pope John Paul II and the *Catechism of the Catholic Church*, we now have laid the foundation for how ignorance may effect matrimonial consent.

III. Rotal Jurisprudence

A. It is to be noted that between *GS* (1965) and the 1983 *Code of Canon Law*, there have been a number of referenced rotal decisions pertaining to ignorance. In only two cases, *coram* Serrano of 25 April 1975 (*RRDec.,* 67:368-375) and *coram* Pompedda of 29 October 1979, (*RRDec.,* 71:460-467) is reference made to Vatican II, the latter implicitly.

Until Serrano's decision in 1975, the basic focus of the decisions was the evaluation of the knowledge of the person(s) pertaining to the procreation of children. The evaluation considered whether the person knew that procreation was part of the nature of marriage or, more often, how much knowledge of the physical *copula* was necessary. Of course the evaluation of knowledge had to take into consideration the presumption of *CIC* 1917, c. 1082, §2 that the person is presumed to have such knowledge after having reached puberty. All of the judges, with the exception of Masala in his 30 May 1977 decision (*RRDec.,* 69:157-171), demonstrate that there is more to the knowledge of marriage than the physical joining of bodies.

B. Also of note is the fact that there appears to have been no cases adjudicated in the Rota on the ground of ignorance since the promulgation of the 1983 *Code of Canon Law.*

C. It is in the 22 March 1963 landmark decision *coram* Sabattani based on ignorance that we find listed four criteria to utilize when weighing proofs in order to establish whether ignorance is verified or not: the psycho-physical, the educational, the prenuptial and the postnuptial, (See *RRDec.,* 55:209-210) These criteria can be readily applied to the 1983 code just as they were to the 1917 code:

1. *Psycho-physical criterion*: Ignorance of sexual things is more likely present in those whose psycho-physical development is imperfect and who have, as a result, subnormal sexual drives, than in others.

2. *Educational criterion*: The location and social context in which the party was raised can provide circumstantial indications that the plea of invalidating ignorance is credible. Ignorance is more likely in those whose education was rigid and narrow, who received an outdated and constricted moral formation, and whose parents were severe. Likewise, if the party was shy of friendships and lived a solitary adolescence.

3. *Prenuptial criterion*: Ignorance is more likely in people who were pressurized to marry, or who, during the courtship, acted and spoke in childish, uncontrolled, silly and thoughtless ways.

4. *Postnuptial criterion*: The reaction of the party to the first act of sexual intercourse can be of juridical value. If this was a reaction of horror and repugnance, or if the party made it clear to

the other party that she/he did not know what was expected of her/him, or, even after being instructed by the other party, she/he could not be persuaded to have sexual intercourse, then there is a presumption that the party was truly ignorant about the giving and acceptance of the right to acts which of their nature are open to the procreation of children.

IV. Types of Proofs Required

A. Canon 1096 succinctly states that a person must at least not be ignorant that marriage is a (1) permanent, (2) *consortium*, (3) between a man and a woman, (4) ordered for the procreation of offspring (5) by means of some sexual cooperation. In other words, this canon states that the essence of marriage includes two elements: the *personalist* element (the 'permanent *consortium* between a man and a woman') and the *procreational* element ('ordered to the procreation of offspring by means of some sexual cooperation'). (See Lawrence G. Wrenn, *Decisions*, 2nd rev. ed., [Washington: CLSA, 1983] 129.) The canon further indicates that substantial ignorance regarding some portion of either element can invalidate marriage. However, a person should have more than an abstract notion of marital consent: there is to be a realization of the personal implications of that to which he or she is consenting. Thus, according to canon 1096, the spouses must know that marriage is a permanent relationship of a special nature between a man and a woman. They must also know that this relationship is ordered to the generation of children through sexual cooperation.

B. The 1983 code maintains the presumption of law found in canon 1082, §2 of the 1917 code, i.e., after puberty (twelve for girls, fourteen for boys), knowledge of marriage is presumed. Before puberty, ignorance is presumed. Since this is a presumption of law, it can yield to contrary proof (cf. c. 1584).

C. Canon 1096 and its parallel, *CCEO* canon 819, are examples of areas which determine that ignorance hinders the effectiveness of invalidating or disqualifying laws, which, generally speaking, it does not according to canon 15, §1 and its parallel, *CCEO* canon 1497, §1. Two details need to be pointed out concerning these canons: (1) they refer to both ignorance and error, but the concern is only with ignorance; and (2) generally speaking according to these canons, both ignorance and error do not hinder the effectiveness of invalidating or disqualifying laws unless expressly stated in the law.

D. Marriage is a juridic act and thus subject to the regulations delineated in the canons pertaining to juridic acts (cc. 124-128). For validity, canon 124 is followed. Thus, for a juridic act to be valid, the person must be capable (both naturally and juridically) of placing it; it must include all of its essential elements; and the formalities and requirements imposed by law for validity must be observed. Ignorance is specifically mentioned in canon 126.

E. Ignorance about the essential nature of marriage is best understood in the Thomistic sense. It is not only the privation or lack of knowledge in a person who is naturally capable of such knowledge, but also, more specifically, it is the lack of *due* knowledge, i.e., the degree of knowledge that a person within a given situation is expected to have. Thus, ignorance is distinguished from nescience, which is the total absence of knowledge. A minimal knowledge of the nature of marriage is required by the natural law itself, since one cannot intend or will to enter the marriage covenant without knowing what it is, following the adage *nil volitum nisi praecognitum* ("Nothing can be willed unless it is known before").

F. Detailed and sophisticated knowledge of the essence of marriage is not required; canon 1096 presents the minimum which is needed for a person or persons to enter into marriage by presenting the basic, yet essential, description of marriage: a (1) permanent, (2) *consortium* (partnership), (3) between a man and a woman, (4) for the procreation of offspring, (5) by means of some sexual cooperation.

V. Related Issues

A. Pope Paul VI set forth five values of conjugal love (total, fully human, exclusive, creative and moral) which, if we take them into consideration in light of the following five elements, respectively, we can see a correspondence between them. Let us describe each of these elements individually:

1. *permanent*: all that is required is that the parties know that marriage is a stable relationship; one that is not sporadic or fleeting. They must also know, as stated *coram* Serrano (25 April 1975) that the relationship is, of its nature, permanent and cannot be terminated

by the parties themselves. One does not need to intend an indissoluble union, however, failure to include such an understanding could come under canon 1099.

2. *consortium (partnership)*: the *consortium* referred to in the canon is understood not simply as the context within which procreative sexual acts take place. It is the total self-giving partnership of the spouses, which is clearly seen in the Church's teaching (*GS* 47-52; c. 1055). This requires the knowledge that some mutual cooperation, support, and companionship is required. Pompedda, in his 29 October 1979 decision, writes that the minimum knowledge required on the part of the contractants to consent validly concerns marriage as a permanent society, that is, a perpetual communion of life and a communion between two sexually distinct persons and ordered to a specific end. However, a formal understanding of indissolubility is not required in this knowledge.

3. *between a man and a woman*: the partnership established in marriage is a permanent one, it is thus exclusive, not allowing for more than the two spouses. Furthermore, since it is for the procreation of offspring, it is heterosexual; i.e., between a man and a woman. The natural law or canon law institute of marriage does not, by its very nature, allow for same sex unions.

4. *for the procreation of offspring*: it is the ordering of the marital *consortium* for the procreation of children, which differentiates it from any other relationship. Marriage is more than a partnership of friendship, service, economics, etc. Marriage is a conjugal relationship that calls for the specific element of sexuality, which, in turn, finds its fullness in procreation.

5. *by means of some sexual cooperation*: the 1983 code explicitly states that the procreation of children is by some means of sexual cooperation. While the couple need not have complete knowledge of the details of sexual copulation, they are to know specifically that it is sexual, i.e., genital, and not merely something physical in a generic kind of way. (See *coram* Ewers, 1 February 1975 in *RRDec.,* 67:27-33; *coram* Masala, 30 March 1977 in *RRDec.,* 69:157-171.)

B. Ignorance is more properly ascribed to those who have the basic capacity for knowledge but lacked the opportunity rather than the capacity to learn. Confusing and conflicting social customs and value systems can prevent a person from learning that the notions of permanent commitment and self-sacrifice are acceptable facets of life. Because of these social realities, canonical jurisprudence no longer presumes that all persons marry in the manner intended by God, as stated in *coram* Ewers, 18 May 1968. (*RRDec.,* 60:343-355)

C. Consequently, a person could go through a wedding ceremony and yet be ignorant of the fact that the subsequent marriage involves a self-sacrificing community of life ordered to the good of the spouses and the procreation and education of children. Therefore, taking all these factors into consideration, if there is ignorance, i.e., lack of due knowledge, on the part of the contractant(s) in one or more of the five elements we have described in the canon, the marriage is invalid.

Chapter V

Sources For Canon 1097, §1

Error of Person

Marianne Burkhard, OSB, JCL

I. Pertinent Canons

A. See canon 1097, §1.

B. See the following allied canons: 126; 1055, §1; 1056; 1057, §1; and 1057, §2.

II. Conciliar and/or Papal Teaching

A. Vatican Council II, *GS* 61:

> Nowadays, much more than in the past it is difficult to form a synthesis of the arts and of the different branches of knowledge while, in fact, the volume and diversity of the constituent elements of culture are on the increase, there is a decrease in the individual's capacity to perceive and harmonize them, so that the picture of 'a universal man' has almost disappeared. Still, it remains each one's duty to safeguard the notion of the human person as a totality in which predominate values of intellect, will, conscience, and brotherhood, since these values were established by the creator and wondrously restored and elevated by Christ. (Flannery, *Vatican Council II*, 1:965.)

B. Pope John Paul II, *FC* 11:

> As an incarnate spirit, that is a soul which expresses itself in a body and a body informed by an immortal spirit, man is called to love in his unified totality. (Flannery, *Vatican Council II*, 2:822.)

C. Pope John Paul II, allocution to the Rota, 29 January 1993:

> Subjecting canon law to caprice or contrived interpretations, in the name of an ambiguous and indefinite *humanitarian principle*, would mean destroying the very dignity of man, even before the norm (6). [...] In the matter of *error of fact (*error *facti)* too, especially when it is a question of 'error of person' (*error in persona*) [c. 1097, §1], one may not attribute to the terms used by the legislator a meaning alien to canonical tradition (7). (English trans. from Woestman, *Papal Allocutions*, 226.)

III. Rotal Jurisprudence

A. *Error of person* in the sense of a mistaken identity, as in the case of Jacob who wants to marry Rachel, but instead is given Leah in marriage (Gen 29: 6-31), does not occur in Western culture in our time. Jurisprudence concerning error of person thus addresses mainly the definition of error and of its juridic effects on marriage. Therefore this jurisprudence is also applicable to canon 1097, §2, and the jurisprudence quoted here comes from cases involving canon 1083, §2 *CIC* 1917, the precursor of canon 1097, §2 *CIC* 1983.

B. *Coram* Faltin, 19 May 1989 (unpubl.), excerpted in F. Rocca (ed.), "Massimario Rotale" in *Diritto Matrimoniale Canonico* [1995] 4:173-176, n. 43:

> Since an error is an erroneous perception of a thing, it must not be confused with ignorance which is the absence of due knowledge of a certain subject. In the case of an error one has a positive judgment, but an erroneous one about some object which moves the will. While on the contrary, in the case of ignorance any judgment is lacking, and thus the will cannot be moved by any object. Cf. the prescriptions about *error* and *ignorance* with regard to juridic acts in general in c. 126 which entirely reproduces c. 104 of the 'Old Code'. [...] Therefore one has to distinguish between an error, which concerns that which constitutes the substance [of the act] and an accidental error which does not concern that which constitutes the substance of the act. (Rocca, 4:173.)

C. *Coram* Funghini, 20 December 1989, *RRDec.,* 81:775-788:

To have a valid consent and a marriage that is in truth contracted it is required that the consent be placed between persons who are by law able to do so, do it with the right intention and full freedom of choice, in the legitimate form and also with a due understanding of its object. The latest condition is not verified where there is error, that is, an erroneous judgment of the matter or a false representation of it inasmuch as these do not correspond to reality. For error implies a discrepancy between comprehension and reality: 'it designates something false or a defined or particular fallacy which therefore has the appearance of a positive or probable content, but which is in fact negative' (S. Caramella, *Errore*, in *Enciclopedia Filosofica*, vol. II [1957], col. 30). In our province the practical error is of interest because consent is an act of the will and 'an act of the will presupposes an appraisal or a judgment of anything on which it has a bearing' (S. Thomas, *Summa Theol.*, III, q. 51, art.1).

An error, as 'an assent to something false' (cf. Boyer, *Cursus philosophiae*, vol. II, [1939], 229) has a juridical importance and weight inasmuch as it determines the formation and the expression of the will which in this matter is not brought to its effect because of that erroneous judgment or that false representation of reality which definitely and properly constitute an error. This differs from ignorance because an error implies a positive discrepancy between the mind and the comprehension of its object while ignorance is merely a negative discrepancy. In other words, an error is an incorrect comprehension, ignorance is in fact an absence of comprehension. (*RRDec.*, 81:776-777.)

D. *Coram* Jarawan, 10 February 1993, *RRDec.,* 85:42-46:

Error holds the first place among the defects of consent. Ontologically error is the false apprehension of a matter or an erroneous assent that is opposed to logical truth or to the conformity of the intellect with the matter. Error is well distinguished from ignorance which is merely the absence of knowledge while error, on the contrary, is a positive, but erroneous judgment about an object by which the will is moved (*RRDec.*, 85:43.)

E. *Coram* Giannecchini, 4 March 1994, *RRDec.,* 86:134-43:

> Matrimonial consent is an human act in which two persons of different sex mutually give and accept each in an irrevocable covenant in order to establish marriage. Besides wanting to obtain the specific object of the contract, a consortium of the whole of life, which is by its very nature ordered toward the good of the spouses and the generation and education of children (cc. 1055, 1057), the contractant also wants a determined and chosen person with whom he wants to contract marriage here and now. Because the matrimonial contract is for all people most personal and the person of the contractant constitutes in different ways the essential object of the consent, thus the figure of subject and object is introduced. If someone errs about this figure, the contract suffers from nullity. (*RRDec.*, 86:135.)

F. In rotal jurisprudence there has been an attempt to broaden the notion of 'person' to that of 'personality'. On the basis of a sentence *coram* Canals of 21 April 1970 (*RRDec.,* 62:370-375) a number of writers challenged the traditional concept of person claiming that the Second Vatican Council understood 'person' not as a physical identity, but a "substantial identity representing one's integral personality structure, including physical, spiritual, religious, moral, social, ethical aspects." (A. Mendonça, "Error of Fact: Doctrine and Jurisprudence on Canon 1097," in *SC* 34 (2000) 39; J. H. Provost, "Error as Ground in Marriage Cases," *CLSA Proceedings* 57 [1995] 319.)

G. In an article entitled "Error in *persona* (c. 1097, §1)" in *Per* 87 [1998] 352- 404, U. Navarrete discusses this at length and concludes that the entire canonical tradition has always understood the term 'person' in the sense of an individual human being, the subject of rights and obligations and that at no time in the history of canonical legislation the term 'person' has been understood as 'personality', a psychological term which does not have a universally defined concept (352-371). Cf. also A. Mendonça, (39f.). Pope John Paul II has responded to this discussion in his 1993 allocution to the Rota stating that the term 'person' used in the sense of 'personality' was not germane to canonical tradition.

H. There is a total rejection this broader meaning of person in *coram* Pompedda, 6 February 1992 *RRDec.,* 84:49-63:

From all the authors quoted it is very clear that the word 'person' only 'entails one meaning in canon law and in doctrine, namely that of an individual physically distinct from others'. (*RRDec.*, 84:53.)

I. *Coram* Stankiewicz, 22 July 1993, *RRDec.,* 85:590-600, likewise understands "person" to be the individual, physical person:

Yet the concept of 'person', in whom the error may fall, cannot be any other than that of 'physical person' (cf. cc. 96ff.) (n. 6, 592). [...] One cannot call into doubt the certain and constant jurisprudential principle according to which the notion of 'person', mentioned in c. 1097, §1, can only entail one meaning in canonical legislation, i.e. an 'individual physically distinct from others' (cf. *coram* Pompedda, above). [...] Indeed in canon law (cf. cc. 96-98, 100) the word person has only the meaning of 'a subject who, in the last analysis, has rights and obligations in his/her individuality and identity while prescinding entirely from the qualities or defects inherent in, or affecting, the person' [...] (U. Navarrete, "Error circa personam et error circa qualitates communes seu non identificantes personam c. 1097," *Per* 82 [1993] 663, 85:593-594.)

J. Also, in the same direction, see the decision *coram* Funghini, April 1997, *Forum* 10 (1999) 349-401:

[...] an error concerning the person impedes the formation and the existence itself of the consent rather than simply impairs it, inasmuch as the object of the consent, in its very source, are the contracting parties considered in their certain and definite individuality and identity: 'the person who is known in a determinate way to the contracting party is the substantial object of the marriage consent' (*coram* Sincero, Rome, 27 May 1911, *RRDec.,* 3:178, n. 14). The same contracting parties, insofar as they are also the exclusive subjects of the conjugal bond, are, in their individuality and identity, an inescapable cognitive premise of the willingness of the act, which cannot be formed and be effective when the preceding cognition is lacking, according to the principle 'nothing is willed without being known before'. The reason is that 'whatever hinders a cause, of its very nature hinders the effect likewise. Now consent is the cause of matrimony, as stated above. Hence whatever voids the consent, voids marriage' (St. Thomas, *Summ. Theol., Supplementum*, q.51, art.1).

[...] there must be no longer any dispute about the genuine meaning of the word 'person' in the first paragraph of can. 1097 and everyone cannot help noticing the context of the regulation laid down therein, if one keeps in mind the serious warning of the present Holy Father in the Address of January 29, 1993 to the Prelates of the Roman Rota: 'specifically when it is a question of 'error of person' one may not attribute to the terms used by the legislator a meaning alien to canonical tradition' (*AAS* 85 [1993] 1259).

[...] If the term 'person' in the first paragraph of can. 1097 were to be extended so much more widely as to include in its meaning also the psychic, moral and intellectual qualities of the subject, the second paragraph of the same canon would appear utterly useless, since it would not contain a different kind of error and 'it would render superfluous can. 1098, concerning fraud, which is considered by all a great novelty in the new Code' (U. Navarrete, o.c. 664).

[...] In canonical tradition and in the jurisprudence of Our Tribunal the referred to wider interpretation of the word 'person' is positively excluded.

IV. Types of Proofs Required

A. Clearly this canon will only rarely be applicable to marriages in western societies. Situations in which families play a very active role in arranging marriages or where personal contact between the contractants before marriage is highly restricted are infrequent and rare exceptions from ordinary circumstances. However, the canon articulates a declaration of principle concerning the defects of consent.

B. The error regarding the person one is marrying must influence matrimonial consent. Since marriage entails the gift of oneself to another specific person whom the contractant intends to marry, an error regarding the identity of the marital partner invalidates consent. Proof that this has occurred is noted in *coram* Funghini, April 1997, *Forum* 10 (1999) 349-401 (see III J above).

C. The criterion of identity is fundamental for the first paragraph of canon 1097 so that an error about the identity or about the identification of the partner results in the nullity of the marriage. For this reason an error about a quality which amounts to an error of person, according to the interpretation of Suarez, does not exceed the scope of the error in §1, since it firmly implies a certain, exclusive, and well restricted identity of the person: "Undoubtedly an error of person, as when a woman, while thinking and intending to marry the first-born son, contracts with another, invalidates marriage." (Coscius, *De sep. thori, lib.*I, cap. II, n. 2)

D. P. J. Viladrich in *Code of Canon Law Annotated* (Montréal: Wilson & Lafleur, 1993) 688:

> Since the very persons of the contracting parties as spouses are the object of consent and since the conjugal union between these persons is the bond, the error concerning the very person of the other contracting party substantially affects the object of consent, to the point that it does not really exist. Therefore, according to natural law, marriage does not exist either.

E. The error must be substantial about the person of the other spouse as we read in *coram* Stankiewicz, 28 April 1988 *RRDec.,* 80:275-285:

> When the error about the concrete identity of a person is substantial, it excludes consent or matrimonial will and invalidates the marriage, according to common doctrine, by natural right itself, not only by positive ecclesiastical right. For 'through a substantial error about the person of the other spouse the mutual matrimonial consent in the erring spouse is entirely prevented since the consent of the erring spouse is carried to a third person who is totally different from the other contractant; therefore through an error of this kind the validity of the marriage is altogether impeded by natural law' (F. X. Wernz - P. Vidal - Ph. Aguirre, *Ius matrimoniale* [Rome 1946], n. 467, 600).
>
> Clearly this is a question of an *impeding error* about the identity of the person whence the declaration of the will, which in marriage is made in consideration of a [specific] person, is directed to a person different than the one who is believed to be present.

Recent doctrine states the same according to which an error about the person applies to 'the physical individuation of the person, according to what the law prescribes in canon 1097, §1 *CIC*, an application which is certainly not frequent in today's matrimonial praxis' [...] For an error of person can be verified 'in marriages contracted by blind, deaf, mute persons or through a procurator, and in an even rarer case in the external identity between two persons' (P. A. Bonnet, *Introduzione al consenso matrimoniale canonico* [Milan, 1985], 70). (*RRDec.*, 80:277-278.)

F. Even if a contractant would be disposed to marry the person after the error in person was discovered, the consent given is still invalid according to *coram* Faltin, 9 May 1989 *RRDec.,* 81:333-347:

Since consent is an act of the will, an error in the person or in the spouse excludes the will of the one marrying. C. 1083, §1 [*CIC* 1917] states in an absolute fashion: 'Error concerning the person invalidates marriage'. It is a question of a substantial error to the extent that the matrimonial consent concerns a person different from the spouse with whom the wedding takes place. Since 'the will of the one in error is null' (cf. L. 20, Dig. XXXIX, 3), in the case of an error in the person, a marriage between the contractants does not arise by the nature of the law itself. 'It does not make a difference whether it is merely an accompanying error, that is, whether the one erring, once the error is detected, would be disposed to contract marriage with this person while he intended [to marry] that other [person] because this will is only hypothetical, but not real' (I. Chelodi – V. Dalpiaz, *Ius Matrimoniale*, 4th ed., [Trent, 1937], p. 137, n. 112). Rightly the norm of the old Code with regard to error of person is also ratified in the new Code of 1983 [...] (c. 1097, §1) because of an absence of true consent which is by natural law necessary for valid consent. (*RRDec.*, 81:335.)

G. Error as an assent to something false invalidates the act of the will as *coram* Funghini, 20 December 1989 *RRDec.,* 81:775-788 states:

To have a valid consent and a marriage that is in truth contracted it is required that the consent be placed between persons who are by law able to do so, do it with the right intention and full freedom of choice, in the legitimate form and also with a due understanding of its object. The latest condition is not verified where there is error, that is, an erroneous judgment of the matter or a false representation of it inasmuch as these do not correspond to reality. For error implies a discrepancy between comprehension and reality: 'it designates something false or a defined or particular fallacy which therefore has the appearance of a positive or probable content, but which is in fact negative' (S. Caramella, *Errore*, in *Enciclopedia Filosofica*, vol. II [1957], col. 30).

In our province the practical error is of interest because consent is an act of the will (c. 1081, §2) and 'an act of the will presupposes an appraisal or a judgment of anything on which it has a bearing' (S. Thomas, *Summa Theol.*, III, q. 51, art.1 ad 1).

An error, as 'an assent to something false' (cf. Boyer, *Cursus philosophiae*, vol. II, 2nd ed. [1939], 229) has juridical importance and weight inasmuch as it determines the formation and the expression of the will which in this matter is not brought to its effect because of that erroneous judgment or that false representation of reality which definitely and properly constitute an error. (*RRDec.*, 81:776-777)

An error of person invalidates a marriage (cf. c. 1083, §1), and this invalidity is based on natural law because it involves the substance of the contract which deals with a determined individual person, who is being considered in the mind [of the contractant], but not a different or other [person] who is entirely extraneous to the object of the contract. (*RRDec.*, 81:777)

H. The persons of the contractants truly belong to the substance of marriage according to a decision *coram* Stankiewicz, 22 July 1993 *RRDec.,* 85:590-600:

Since every human person errs, ecclesiastical law which is founded on natural law sets certain and definite limits to the efficacy of juridic error on account of the principle of the salvation of souls (c. 1752). This was done both to protect the liberty of the Christian faithful led into error against the irrevocable effect of marital consent under the influence of false knowledge, and to remove uncertainty about the validity of marriage when any error can be resolved by the duty of the office. Since marriage, or the 'intimate community of life and love between man and woman' (Second Vatican Council, *Gaudium et spes*, n. 48) consists in a community of persons, the persons of the contractants without doubt pertain to the substance of marriage. For this reason the choice of a certain person as spouse must be free not only from a grave extrinsic or intrinsic compulsion, but also immune from a false apprehension so that no one assents by error to celebrate marriage with a person other than the one who is present. For an error in the person of the spouse, although it is unilateral, truly impedes matrimonial consent when it concerns one of those who are the substance of marriage itself because it plainly includes two, namely 'the persons who bind themselves and their mutual strength to each other' (St. Thomas, *Commentum in lib. IV Sententiarum*, d. 30, q. 1, art. 2, in c.). Thus an error of person, when it is substantial, impedes by the very law of nature the value of marriage. C. 1097, §1 ratifies the power of this error when it states: 'An error of person invalidates marriage'.

Indeed it is debated whether a substantial error in the person turns out to be only improper because it does not directly vitiate marital consent, but only negatively excludes it, or whether it rather must be seen as an obstacle, that is, inasmuch as it falls into the declaration or the substance and consequently deflects the object of the declaration from the substantial object of consent. On the other hand, even if the concept of an epistemological error conveys a false judgment about some matter, it nevertheless under the juridic aspect properly induces a false knowledge and representation of a matter. Therefore an error constitutes in itself a defect of knowledge even as it affects at the same time marital consent which as an act of the will (c. 1057, §2) necessarily presupposes an act of the intellect. For indeed as the constant theological-canonical tradition holds, 'when an error impedes knowledge, a defect in the consent itself also follows, and consequently also [a defect] in the marriage; and thus the error has by natural law that which empties consent' (St. Thomas, *Commentum in lib. IV Sententiarum*, d. 30, q. 1, art. 1, in c.). In whatever way the juridic force of the error is considered, it remains certain that in the matrimonial contract such an error is substantial and as such exerts by the very nature of the matter a juridic efficacy which invalidates the marriage as the ecclesiastical law quoted above has acknowledged and ratified." (*RRDec.*, 85:592)

V. Related Issues

A. James H. Provost, "Error as Ground in Marriage Nullity Cases":

> Error is the false apprehension of a thing, or a false judgment of the mind. Over and above ignorance, error adds a fallacious judgment about the object that is willed. People who are in error know something, and know that they know something; but what they know is not correct, objectively speaking. In other words: what they know does not correspond to actual reality. (*CLSA Proceedings* 57 [1995] 308.)

B. Agustine Mendonça, "Error of Fact: Doctrine and Jurisprudence on Canon 1097":

> C. 126 (*CCEO* c. 933) which provide the general principles concerning the extent of the invalidating efficacy of error and ignorance, is pivotal to a proper understanding of c. 1097. (35) [...] The error which "is *objectively substantial*" concerns the substance of the act. According to this hypothesis, a juridic act is invalid because the error causes a defect of consent in relation to the very substance of the act considered *objectively*. Therefore, the object internally willed by the will is, because of the error, substantially different from the one indicated in the external manifestation of such an act. The substance of marriage consent is twofold: marriage itself and the persons of the spouses. [...] [I]f one is in error concerning the physical identity of the other party, consent would be invalid [since] the error concerns the substance of the marriage. [...] The law does not require in this case any intention to the contrary; rather error by itself invalidates the juridical act of consent. (*SC* 34:36)

C. S. Villegiante, "L'error in Persona," *ME* 125 (2000) 545, mentions that recent sentences – i.e. *coram* Defilippi, March 6, 1998; *coram* Turnaturi, June 18, 1998, and *coram* Defilippi, November 26, 1998, which are not yet published – show that the position of the Rota now "seems clear and definitive" in considering the "person as a subject of rights and obligations who is not only identified by physical criteria, but also by other elements and qualities which have much weight in the present Code."

Chapter VI

Sources For Canon 1097, §2

Error Concerning A Quality Of A Person

Marianne Burkhard, OSB, JCL

I. Pertinent Canons

A. See canon 1097, §2.

B. See the following allied canons: 1083, §2 1917 *CIC*, Canon 1055, §1; 1056; 1057, §1; 1057, §2.

II. Conciliar and/or Papal Teachings

Pope John Paul II, allocution to the Rota, 30 January 1993.

> Subjecting canon law to capricious or contrived interpretations, in the name of an ambiguous and indefinite *humanitarian principle*, would mean destroying the very dignity of man, even before the norm. [...] even as 'error about the quality of the person' can impugn the consent only when a quality, neither frivolous nor trivial, was 'directly and principally intended', that is, as Rotal jurisprudence has effectively asserted: 'when the quality is intended before the person' (*quando qualitas prae persona intendatur*). (English trans. from Woestman, *Papal Allocutions*, 226.)

III. Rotal Jurisprudence

A. Connection with "*error redundans*." Much of canonical jurisprudence regarding canon 1097, §2 addresses the question of its connection to c. 1083, §2, its predecessor in the 1917 code. Therefore it seems appropriate to quote one of the best such summaries at length as well as some other statements.

1. *Coram* de Lanversin, 7 July 1993 *RRDec.*, 85:536, nn. 8-9:

> Unlike the Old Code, which sees the 'quality of person' fully brought about in the identity of the person as considered

physically (cf. c. 1083), the New *Code of Canon Law* understands it in a loftier manner. Indeed if 'an error concerning a quality of a person', even though it is the cause of the contract, does not by itself invalidate marriage, it nevertheless does so if the quality is 'directly and principally intended' (cf. *CIC* 83 c. 1097) which is certainly the direct and principal means for choosing a person, and thus it is evident that it obtains the same effect as an error of person (cf. *CIC* 83 c. 1097, §1). This was even more evident in the formulation of *CIC* 17 c. 1083, §2 that spoke of an error of quality 'redounding [amounting] to an error of person'. [...]

'A subject intends *directly and principally* a quality of the person but is in error about the quality intended in this manner. Therefore, the defect considered in c. 1097, §2 is the error (an act of the intellect), but it rests on an intended quality (an act of the will). To err about a determined quality and to want such quality *directly and principally* are two acts which pertain to different human faculties' (Castaño, *Il sacramento del matrimonio*, vol. I [Rome, 1991] 147). (535-36, n. 6, 7)

Indeed, in the recently promulgated Code, the Legislator finally brought back the proper rule, the so-called third Alphonsian rule which, taken from Aquinas, speaks of an error of quality in substance, or redounding to an error of person, if consent was given directly and principally concerning a quality and less principally concerning the person; already a sentence *coram* Heard of July 21, 1941 (*RRDec.,* 33:533) speaks of this rule. In this sentence one must pay greatest attention to these words: 'While *CIC* 17 c. 1083 states that an error concerning a quality of a person would invalidate marriage whenever the error of quality redounded in an error of person and while it says nothing at all about the necessity of having a condition or a pact to prove this, the canon clearly insinuates that in the external forum an error of quality can turn into an error of person' (as quoted in *coram* Corso, May 12, 1987).

A person, or the identity of a person, at the present time is not exclusively constituted and identified and distinguished from others by bones but is composed of quite a few qualities and elements of a different order which in our age enjoy great esteem and which define, as they say, what is proper to a person. This is especially the case with regard to moral, social, spiritual, or religious qualities which are very often desired and which, as is obvious, cannot be of minimal importance; yet in the estimation of the subject they also cannot be accidental or extrinsic, but for the purpose of the contractant they are 'essential', otherwise they do not 'redound' to the person and do not identify the person as the one with whom marriage is to be contracted.

Following the doctrine of the Second Vatican Council (cf. *Gaudium et spes*, n. 61), rotal jurisprudence explicitly teaches: 'A person does not obtain his/her individuality solely or prevailingly from his/her physical identity, but from all those physical, moral, social qualities which make of every human being an individual distinct from all the others' (*coram* Pompedda, July 28, 1980, *RRDec.,* 71:550, n. 3).

2. *Coram* Stankiewicz, 28 April 1988 *RRDec.,* 80:276-282:

[...] the invalidating error about the concrete identity of a person can be compared with regard to its juridic effects to the *error-defect about a determining quality of the person*, that is with a case where the error about a quality, even an accidental one, amounts to an error of person. This comparison is at times really admitted notwithstanding the conceptual difference between the two errors, of which the first affects the declaration of the will and thus excludes consent, while the other affects the causal determination and by itself only affects the consent. But when this error concerns a determining quality of the person, it acquires the force of an invalidating error about the identity of the person in the juridic acts which are to be posited with regard to this person in the matrimonial contract: for then the person 'deprived in reality of that quality or that way of being which the [other] party attributed to him/her by error, *is not that* person for whom the other contractant took him/her when s/he made the declaration' (E. Betti, *Teoria generale del negozio giuridico* [Turin 1960] 411). (*RRDec.,* 80:278)

Therefore the norm of the new Code does more than receive the interpretation of the error redundans in the light of the third rule of St. Alphonsus (cf. *coram* [Stankiewicz], January 24, 1983, n. 7) or to make more evident the formulation of the abrogated c. 1083, §2, 1° (*coram* Corso, May 12, 1987, n. 6) because it substantially 'corresponds to the doctrine of St. Alphonsus' (*Communicationes* 15 [1983] 232), and directly speaks of the invalidating force of the error of quality when it is made the immediate and prevailing object of the will of one party, or when it is directly and principally intended by a party, and indeed does so independently from that [expression] 'that it does, or does not amount' to an error of person as, on the contrary, the old canon explicitly required (J. F. Castaño, "Il consenso e la forma canonica" in *Il nuovo Codice di diritto canonico* [Rome, 1983] 364). (*RRDec.*, 80:280)

Thus the error of quality directly and principally intended truly functions in the area of the autonomous contractual will because it makes sure that that which is objectively accidental (an accidental quality), subjectively and for the one acting becomes a substantial element and enters into the substance of the consent.

B. Definition of "error of quality" (cf. also the definitions of error under canon 1097, §1):

1. *Coram* Colagiovanni, 22 November 1983 *RRDec.,* 75:659; also in *ME* 113 [1988] 465-483:

   For an error as a false apprehension [of something] could be introduced from an ambiguity of the object itself (or, in the case of a spouse in marriage, the subject) in which the appearances of these qualities coexist with the objective lack of them (hence the erroneous deduction of the matter from its appearance: '*noumenos*' namely, 'from observation').

2. *Coram* Jarawan, 30 January 1988 *RRDec.,* 80:42:

   With regard to error 'of quality of person' one has to remember what has been observed in a decision *coram* Pompedda of July 22, 1985: 'Indeed a quality of a person, which in general is seen as something accidental, still can sometimes attain such great weight in the ethnic and social value system as well as a great value in the spiritual and religious realm, and even a most universal value at least in certain places and times, that it touches and penetrates the person him/herself and determines him/her in his/her individual identity'.

3. *Coram* Doran, 9 November 1989 (*ME* 116 [1991] 383, n. 6):

A person is not determined only by an external aspect or a name, but by any quality which distinguishes the person from others. An error about a quality thus will amount to an error of person 'if the one who wants to marry a certain person, who is also *determined by that quality*, is deceived' and marries another who offers him/herself for that [first] one (cf. Gasparri, *De Matrimonio*, vol. II, n. 793).

4. *Coram* Funghini, 20 December 1989 *RRDec.,* 81:777:

An error of quality becomes significant 'when the quality, erroneously attributed to the other party, is in some way very important for that person, and constitutes the reason or the motive why the one who errs wants the spouse and, as it were, directly desires the quality and chooses the person and resolves to marry her/him because s/he holds that the person possesses the desired quality. In such a case the object of consent is [...] lacking: the quality calls forth consent and in the mind of the contractant circumscribes it'.

C. An error may, or may not, be caused by deceit.

Coram Corso, 15 March 1989 (unpublished; excerpted in F. Della Rocca (ed.), "Massimario rotale" in *Diritto Matrimoniale Canonico*, IV [1995] n. 21:99-100, henceforth cited as *Massimario rotale*):

In a decision *coram* Serrano we read: 'But one who is led by a grave error, even though it may not necessarily have come from deceit, and who intends in the other something which s/he finds to be absent in reality: this one can, just as when handing over something false, be substantially deficient in matrimonial consent from accepting something false. The

> quality or circumstance, which as a condition according to his/her expectation one pursues as belonging to the other, is according to the mind of those marrying almost an object – even if it is something personal and is intended as an integral part of the person – on which 'the handing over and accepting of oneself' revolves'.
>
> What finally relates to the recognition of the error, [...] it is not necessary in the case of a quality which is lacking in the spouse that the person falsely showed the quality with or without deceit before the wedding, but [...] it suffices that the error be uncovered later from the revelation of the absence of that quality when the conjugal life has already begun. When the acts reveal a spouse who deceitfully, and indeed rationally, simulated qualities before the celebration of the marriage, then there is greater certitude that one can speak indeed of an error [...]

D. When an error of quality is caused by deceit, there is a close connection to canon 1098.

Coram Doran, 9 November 1989 (*ME* 116 [1991] 383, n. 6):

> [...] the new law granted invalidating force to an error, whether or not it be the result of deceit, about a quality directly and principally intended (c. 1097, §2 *CIC* 1983), or to an error about a quality 'which by its very nature can seriously disturb the consortium of conjugal life', provided that it be an error caused by deceit and that the deceit be perpetrated 'in order to obtain consent' (c. 1098 *CIC* 1983).

E. Error versus Condition.

Coram Doran, 9 November 1989 (*ME* 116 [1991] 381-382, n. 5):

> In this entire discussion error must not be confused with condition: the one in error has a quality in mind which, besides intending it directly, s/he also [intends] principally, that is especially and chiefly; the one setting a condition rather treats the quality exclusively. Therefore, if the error of quality is reduced to a condition *sine qua non*, then [...] 'the marriage is not invalidated because of an error, but because of a

condition to which the consent is bound' (F. Cappello, *Tractatus Canonico-Moralis: De Sacramentis*: vol. *De Matrimonio*, [Torino, 1950] 559, n. 587 bis).

F. Nature of Quality.

1. *Coram* Funghini, 20 December 1989 *RRDec.,* 81:777, n. 4:

   [...] the quality must not be something futile or frivolous and, if it is not absolutely grave, it must be valued as great by the one erring so that for him/her it constitutes something primary. But if, in a particular case, what strictly speaking for many does not reach the level of [something] substantial, so seduces or restricts the one erring, it is necessary that for him/her it forms the object of the contract inasmuch as it is before all else demanded in a spouse in order to marry him/her. Yet because a person is to be considered in his/her full dignity and real existence, all the moral, institutional, professional and social aspects of life greatly influence the determination of a person, such as e.g. their social group, education, professional training, health, and mental faculties, etc.

2. *Coram* Stankiewicz, 13 December 1990 *RRDec.,* 82:852, n. 11:

   Yet whatever can be said about the objective gravity of the quality which operates chiefly in fraudulent deception (cf. also c. 821 *CCEO*) and which, when lacking, can by its very nature disturb the partnership of conjugal life, such as the unknown sterility of the spouse, especially when the procreation of children is greatly desired by the other spouse or when local customs place fertility among the conditions of a valid marriage (cf. *c.* this *Ponens*, February 24, 1983, *RRDec.,* 75:50), it is certain that in the area of an invalidating error the quality must have so much weight and importance in the subjective estimation of the one in error that the existence of this quality in the spouse is directly and principally intended (c. 820, §2 *CCEO*), that is in preference of the person itself. Thus a quality truly required in a spouse and making the person whole enters into the object of consent in which the contractants' mutual giving and accepting each other in order to establish marriage actually disappears.

3. *Coram* de Lanversin, 7 July 1993 *RRDec.,* 85:536, n. 10:

> [...] it is clear that the qualities which identify a person as individual cannot be generic, external, foolish, or transitory in time, they cannot be among the more or less changing ones, the optional or elective ones; rather it is necessary that they have a certain objectivity and firmness, just as the substance of the person, indeed of the 'person as a totality', has (cf. *Gaudium et spes*, n. 61) and that they enter into that which constitutes the one so that from all of these qualities this person can be recognized as an individual.

4. *Coram* Funghini, 28 November 1990 *RRDec.,* 82:815-816, n. 3:

> The code does not determine the qualities that would amount to an error of person, neither by way of examples nor by saying anything about their special characteristics. According to the unanimous and most recent jurisprudence of this apostolic Tribunal it is no longer required that the quality of the other party be exclusively proper and constitute the only means of identifying the person who otherwise would be unknown.
>
> On the contrary, one must consider the personal qualities not only of a physical order, but also of a spiritual, intellectual, moral, social etc. order which, if they are not an absolute foundation [of marriage], certainly and gravely touch the matrimonial life in which the marriage *in facto esse* is being accomplished. These qualities, such as health, virginity, the ability to have children, intellectual ability, social status, education, profession, etc., must be taken into account not because they really change the concept of the person, but because these qualities constitute an 'identifying moment in the perception of marriage, not identifying the person for all, but for the only person who is of interest for the argument of our discussion, namely for the other contractant' (p. A. Bonnet, "Il consenso" in *Matrimonio canonico fra tradizione e rinnovamento* [1985] 182). Thus an error can revolve around a quality which truly influences the determination of a certain person, i.e. revolve around qualities 'which in themselves, or in the society in which we live, are greatly esteemed and

define persons' (*coram* Di Felice, March 26, 1977, *RRDec.,* 69:151). A merely accidental or frivolous quality, as is easy to see, is incapable of obtaining invalidating effects.

G. Directly and principally intended.

1. *Coram* Doran, 9 November 1989, as excerpted in *Massimario rotale* IV [1995] 48:189 (cf. also *ME* 116 [1991] 384, n. 9):

As St. Thomas teaches, 'intention, as its name denotes, means to *tend to something*: both the action of the mover and the movement of the thing moved tend to something, but that the movement of the thing moved tends to anything, proceeds from the action of the mover. Therefore intention belongs first and principally to that which moves to the end: hence we say that an architect or anyone, who is in authority, by his command moves others to that which he intends. Now the will moves all other powers of the soul to the end, as shown above [q.9, a.1]. Hence it is evident that intention, properly speaking, is an act of the will' (I-II, 12,1 in c; cf. II-II, 180,1 in c.) which is either explicit or implicit as we read in a decision in a case from Caracas *coram* Palestro of June 24, 1987, n. 6: 'An implicit act remains in the positive order insofar as it is contained in it again and again really and not presumptively, positively and not interpretatively though its substance does not appear directly and immediately in the manifestation of the contractant's consent' (cf. also a decision in a case from Naples *coram* Pompedda, of July 22, 1985, n. 15).

2. A decision *coram* de Lanversin, 7 July 1993 *RRDec.,* 85:537, n. 11, argues that if an error about a quality of a person is to have invalidating force, the following three elements must be present:

a) The quality in the person of the spouse must be 'intended' by the spouse who is in error, as the law explicitly requires. This is the case when the intended quality is specified by an act of the intellect and is drawn into [it] by an explicit, or at least implicit, act of the will. For the one who errs about the intended quality embraces it with his/her intention or with his/her will inasmuch as 'an intention is an act of the will' (Siwek, *Psychologia Metaphysica* [Rome, 1962] 437). Yet not any act of the will is sufficient [for this], but only the one in which a quality is directly and principally chosen.

b) The quality is 'directly' desired by the will when it constitutes the immediate object of the act of the will, but not any generic or mediate object which is contained in another object from which it can be deduced as from premises.

c) Finally the quality is 'principally' desired by the will when it is heeded in a particular manner before the person of the spouse, but not as an accessory or only incidentally such as something second to the substance of the person and only accompanying the person. If we explain the meaning of the adverb 'principaliter' in the words of St. Alphonsus in this way, it can be admitted that in such a case 'consent is given directly and principally to the quality and less principally to the person'.

3. *Coram* Stankiewicz, 28 April 1988 *RRDec.,* 80:281, n. 10:

[...] in the error about a quality directly and principally intended this quality is the object of the intention 'in its meaning of propositum – something which is proposed' and which the person who is in error and who consents 'out of error' relates to the 'quality of the person of the spouse' (J. F. Castaño, "*Il consenso*", p. 364). In this way the quality of the person of the spouse according to the intention of the one in error flows back into the substance, as it can clearly be deduced from the doctrine of St. Alphonsus which says in the 'third rule': 'But if consent is given directly and principally with regard to a quality, and less principally with regard to the person, then *the error of quality flows back into the substance*' (31, n. 1061). Thus the error of quality directly and principally intended truly functions in the area of the autonomous contractual will because it makes sure that that which is objectively accidental (an accidental quality), subjectively and for the one acting becomes a substantial element and enters into the substance of the consent.

H. Qualities Associated with Particular Cultures.

Coram Faltin, 26 May 1989 *RRDec.,* 81:379-88:

One needs to consider that among the qualities, which identify a person objectively in Indian society, the virginity of the woman is preeminent (cf. among other rotal sentences the decision *coram* Heard, June 23, 1941 in a case from Dinajpur). Note also that one must not confuse, as we have intimated above, a quality implicitly directly and principally intended, with a quality presumptively directly and principally intended. At any rate and in every case one must pay attention to the subjective evaluation of the contractant in whom the quality of the spouse identifying him/her as person must be so rooted and, as it were, incarnated that it is most difficult to distinguish a defect of consent from a moral or psychological incapacity of that person in error to think, act and behave in any other way; such a person thus wants to pursue this quality in all people so that s/he cannot want or act otherwise. (383-84, n. 10)

For according to the indigenous customs, the rooted traditions and the perennial culture of the people in Sri Lanka, 'the girl must be a virgin at the moment of the wedding', as can be deduced from the confessions of the parties and the declarations of all witnesses in this case. Indeed, the Respondent herself confessed candidly: 'According to our culture the good character of a girl is proven by her virginity'. Under the social-cultural aspect this quality of virginity is such an objectively essential element for the identification of the woman that it must be considered as implicitly directly and principally intended among the people of Sri Lanka who are part of the Indo-Pakistani culture. (385-86, n. 15)

It is clear that this is not a case of condition precisely because the Petitioner did not know that virginity was lacking in his spouse. For this reason 'he never set virginity as a condition for marriage'. While the quality of virginity in the spouse was not supposed by the man, it nevertheless was, according to the customs and culture of his people, a simple and necessary prerequisite, and therefore directly and principally intended. In other words, what is of interest here is the subjective estimation of the quality by the Petitioner and about which there is no doubt and which is evident from his reaction when he discovered that the girl was not a virgin. (*RRDec.*, 81:387, n. 18)

IV. Types of Proofs Required

A. *Coram* Stankiewicz, 19 December 1985, excerpted in *Massimario rotale* IV [1995] 188-189, n. 48:

> The quality [...] about which there was an error can be assessed in a twofold manner, i.e. according to an *objective* and a *subjective* criterion. The objective assessment of the quality can be done by using a triple measure, namely: a) of an individual and exclusive quality which belongs to the identification of the physical person and which was yet unknown; b) of a moral, social and juridic quality belonging to the individuation of the person as considered more completely and integrally, and indeed [belonging] to the personality; c) of a quality necessary to the fulfillment of the essential rights and obligations of the marriage also belonging to the identification of the person. Yet whatever can be said about the objective nature and gravity of that quality, be it with regard to the moral, social, or juridic aspect, or with respect to the requirements for a consortium of conjugal life, [of that quality] which identifies the physical person or the personality, it is at present certain that the quality in the person of the spouse must have so much weight in *the subjective assessment of the one in error* that it entered his/her very will, that is, it was *directly and principally* intended by that person in error (c. 1097, §2 *CIC* 1983).

B. *Coram* Stankiewicz, 28 April 1988 *RRDec.,* 80:281-282, n. 11:

> It will be for the judge to decide the importance which the contractant attributed to a determined quality in the other spouse since the direction of this contractant toward this quality derives from the prevalence of a subjective evaluation over the objective value of the desired quality. Such a quality may be desired 'directly and principally' more than the person him/herself who is, as it were, 'less principally' considered. For example in a certain case the quality of being a doctor was so required of the Respondent by the Petitioner that 'she wanted to marry the doctor rather than that man' (*coram* Di Felice, March 26, 1977, n. 10 in *RRDec.,* 69:154).

C. *Coram* Faltin, 26 May 1989 *RRDec.,* 81:383, n. 9, states that in assessing the quality one has to look at two hypotheses:

> [...] a) to what extent the quality is *subjectively* intended expressly, directly and principally; and b) to what extent the quality is intended directly and principally *objectively by the society and subjectively by the contractant,* and indeed is *implicitly* vehemently directly and principally intended. There can be no question when a physical, juridic, social or moral quality is *expressly* that is, directly and principally, intended, that is, insofar as it identifies the spouse *subjectively*. But the same can be said when the quality is imposed directly and principally *objectively* by society as [a quality] that specifically identifies a person, and is thus directly and principally intended by the contractant *subjectively* but *implicitly,* as presupposed naturally, according to the culture and traditions of the society. This is so because 'an implicit act remains in the positive order so that, although its substance does not appear directly and immediately in the expression of the contractant's consent, it is nevertheless *wholly contained in it, really and not presumptively, positively and not interpretatively*' (cf. *coram* Palestro, June 24, 1987, and *coram* Pompedda, July 22, 1985).

D. *Coram* Doran, 1 March 1990, as excerpted in *Massimario rotale* IV [1995] 231, n. 60, quoting *coram* de Lanversin, 20 March 1985:

> The proof of an error of quality 'which was directly and principally intended' is, as in all other cases based on defect of consent, *direct* and *indirect*: 'namely it is judged from the confession of the one in error, confirmed by credible witnesses; it can be derived from the behavior of the one in error at the time when s/he observed that the spouse lacked the quality which s/he had wanted to attribute to that same spouse and directly and principally intended in accordance with the principles which were explained.' Thus one has to examine the degree of importance which the aforementioned quality had in the mind of the one in error 'having considered all the collateral circumstances of the person and the place'.

E. *Coram* Stankiewicz, 13 December 1990 *RRDec.,* 82:852-853, n. 12:

The juridic proof of an error of quality of a person directly and principally intended is not easy because of the necessity that there be a manifestation in the external forum of either the error which is an internal act representing an erroneous judgment, or the absence of the required quality, the erroneous perception of which must not only be the cause of the matrimonial contract, 'but must be above all required directly and principally by the one in error by a positive act of the will'.

Yet such a proof is not impossible. Certainly it is the duty of the judge to evaluate, as is observed in a sentence *coram* de Lanversin, March 20, 1985, '[to assess and *discern* the quality] so long as it altered the personality, and [the judge must] establish in individual cases whether or not ignorance of that quality determined the error [...] These rules are to be observed in deciding this matter, i.e. *prudence*, that no facile laxity arise in explaining the road to divorce, and on the other hand to avoid rigorism which would be insensitive to the problems of conjugal life'. Certainly in order to declare the nullity of a marriage, the *lack of a quality* directly and principally intended does not suffice, rather it is necessary to prove the ignorance about this lacking quality 'in the act of choosing to offer consent', otherwise the error cannot be verified. 'And finally in estimating that error of quality amounting to an error of person, the judge can deduce it from the behavior of the one who claims to have fallen into error, especially [from his behavior] after having discovered his/her error after s/he had approached the altar'. [*coram* de Lanversin, March 20, 1985, *RRDec.,* 77:167-8.] (*RRDec.*, 82:852-853)

F. *Coram* Faltin, 26 May 1989 *RRDec.,* 81:384, nn. 10, 11:

Finally we think it is worth mentioning that, in order to declare a marriage invalid, it does not suffice to prove the lack of the quality directly and principally intended, but *it is necessary to prove ignorance of the lack of the quality in the act of choosing to give consent* (cf. *coram* de Lanversin, March 20).

The proof of an 'error of quality amounting to an error of person' is *direct* coming from the confession of the one in error and from confirmation of credible witnesses, and *indirect* deriving from the behavior exhibited by the one in error as soon as s/he has discovered in the spouse the lack of the quality 'directly and principally' intended by him/her.

G. *Coram* Doran, 9 November 1989, as excerpted in *Massimario rotale* IV [1995] 188-189 (cf. also *ME* 116 [1991] 381-89):

With regard to proof the decision *coram* de Lanversin of March 20, 1985, formulates the following principles: it is the duty of the judge to do a discretionary assessment of the quality which is in question, to assess the extent to which the personality was changed through the effect of that very quality, and to decide 'whether or not ignorance of that quality determined the error amounting to an error of person'. In deciding this matter the *prudence* of the judge is absolutely necessary so that 'there arise no easy laxity in explaining the road to divorce', and, on the other hand, one must also 'avoid rigorism which would be insensitive to the problems in conjugal life'. Obviously for juridically declaring the nullity of marriage it is not sufficient that the lack of the quality 'directly and principally' desired exist, but it is necessary to prove ignorance of the lack of this quality at the moment of consent, otherwise there would be no error. And in evaluating the error in the qualities of the persons as 'amounting to error of person' the judge can deduce them 'from the behavior of the one who contends to have fallen into error, particularly after having detected his/her error, after s/he had approached the altar'.

To have proof the mind of the one in error must be thoroughly examined, and it must be stated in what manner s/he determined or defined the person of the spouse through one or another quality.

The proof in marriage nullity cases based on 'error of quality directly and principally intended' is *direct* and *indirect*: the first [proof] derives from the confession of the one in error and confirmation from credible witnesses, while the indirect proof derives from the way the erring party behaved after s/he discovered that the quality he wanted did not exist in the spouse. The judge must also assess ('after having considered all the circumstances of the persons and place') the importance which the one in error attributed before the wedding by his/her judgment to the quality which s/he desired. In addition the judge must also examine either the firmness of the one in error (through which the aforesaid quality becomes the 'reason for marrying'), or his/her manner of behaving as soon as s/he realized the absence of the quality in the object. (cf. the decree of ratification *coram* Colagiovanni, March 25, 1983.)

V. Related Issues

A. In a very helpful article by Emilio Colagiovanni, "*Error personae or in qualitate personae*" (*ME* 122 [1997] 525-526), it is stated:

> We can say that error concerns not only the physical person, but also the 'personality' (cf. Colagiovanni, November 22, 1983; Stankiewicz December 19, 1983). 'A person considered in a more complete and full way, that is, the whole personality', as St. Thomas had already hinted (*Summ. Theol.* I, q.39, a.3, ad 4 4; I. q.29, a.4). If a marriage is contracted primarily, if not uniquely, *intuitu personae* [in consideration of a person] with certain qualities particularly esteemed by the contractant and in the cultural set of values, and the other party lacks that quality or qualities, matrimonial consent is null. It is indeed true that from a *philosophical* point of view qualities are accidental to a person, but *psychologically* 'one knows a person with and through his/her qualities' (*Summ. Theol. Suppl.*, q.51, a.2), and *socially* some qualities are most relevant given that they refer to the very high values which induce someone to do what is good (for him/her)' (*Summ. Theol.*, q.58, a.3). These qualities are the basis of the very *communion of life and love* that should be set up through marriage. This matrimonial communion is intended not only on the institutional level or according to social norms or requisites, but also, sometimes above all, according to the personal desires, intentions, imagination and ideals of the contractant. (cf. *coram* Agustoni, July 10, 1984)

This same article also contains a list of all the qualities found in specific rotal sentences. The qualities listed are: moral qualities; civil, juridical condition; educational-professional activity; qualities connected with virginity or the capacity to have children; particular social and civil qualities; physical or psychic good health or not having a specific disease; illegitimate birth, bad moral records in the family; a woman's housekeeping abilities; use or abuse of drugs, alcoholism; homosexuality, bisexuality, transvestitism; some such cases may be invalid on other grounds also, i.e. 1095, 2° and 3°, 1098 (*ME* 122:535-36).

B. K. Boccafola, "Deceit and Induced Error about a Personal Quality" (*ME* 124 [1999] 697f):

> Error about a personal quality, induced by deceit, can now be a ground of nullity of marriage.
>
> In our explanation above we referred to c. 125, §2 and noted that an act placed because of deceit [...] is valid unless the law makes some other provision. C. 1098 of the present Code is precisely the legal norm that makes just such an exception to the principle stated in c. 125, §2 with regard to the marriage contract. The Legislator in the New Code has now recognized and given precise juridic relevance to an error of quality caused by deceit. This juridic relevance established in c. 1098 is quite limited and subject to precise conditions [...]

C. R. Funghini, "*Errore sulla qualità della persona direttamente e principalmente intesa*" (*ME* 120 [1995] 67):

> Presupposing that *error* is a *false judgment* which is *absolute*, there is no doubt that a contractant who is intimately, though falsely, convinced of the existence of a determined quality cannot state a condition that this quality exist.

D. M. Hilbert, "*Error in qualitate personae,*" *Per 87* [1998] 434 (as quoted in A. Mendonça, "Error of Fact..." notes that the quality must be intended "knowingly and willingly;" therefore the word 'directly' "excludes interpretative will.")

E. A short discussion of culturally significant values is found in A. Mendonça, "The Importance of Considering Cultural Contexts in Adjudicating Marriage Nullity Cases with Special Reference to Southeast Asian Countries," *Forum* 7 [1996, 69-152] 82-102.

The values discussed are: family status or prestige, caste, age, virginity, offspring, dowry, conversion.

F. Canonical Equity: In cases coming from significantly different cultures canonical equity is often invoked:

1. Pope Paul VI, allocution to the Rota, 6 February 1973:

> This element [canonical equity] characterizes your jurisprudence in a very special way. The Church imposes on ecclesiastical judges the obligation of judging *according to what is good and equitable (ex aequo et bono)*. Your tribunal has made this obligation its own from the start, particularly in those cases that are entrusted to the *judgment of the Rota (arbitrio Rotae)*. Yours is an *equity informed by law (aequitas iure formata)*.
>
> The existing *Code* took on the requirements of mercy and humanity with the aim of providing a milder, more understanding justice. It speaks of 'natural equity' and 'canonical equity', thereby referring to the ultimate principle to which natural law and canon law will appeal. It spells out the import of the notion of *equity* and the function it seeks to carry out – equity here seeks a higher form of justice with a spiritual goal in mind. It softens the rigor of the law, but sometimes it also increases certain penalties. In all cases it distinguishes itself from purely positive law when the latter is unable to take particular circumstances into account. Finally, in conformity with the apostolic origins of Church law, it urges Christians to avoid judicial processes and to submit their cases to judges who will judge 'according to what is good and equitable'. (English trans. from Woestman, *Papal Allocutions*, 118-119.)

2. Pope John Paul II, allocution to the Rota, 17 February 1979:

> The ecclesiastical judge, therefore, will not only have to bear in mind that 'the primary requirement of justice is to respect the rights of the person', but will also have to look beyond this, in turn, for charity. (see also allocution of 26 February 1983, n. 2 [English trans. from Woestman, *Papal Allocutions*, 154 and 177].)

3. Pope John Paul II, allocution to the Rota, 28 January 1991:

Precisely because it is a reality that is deeply rooted in human nature, marriage is affected by the cultural and historical conditions of every people. They have always left their mark upon the institution of marriage. The Church, therefore, cannot prescind from the cultural milieu. I recalled this in my apostolic exhortation *Familiaris consortio* (n. 4): 'Since God's plan for marriage and the family touches men and women in the concreteness of their daily existence in specific social and cultural situations, the Church ought to apply herself to understanding the situations in within which marriage and the family are lived today in order to fulfill her task of serving'. (English trans. from Woestman, *Papal Allocutions*, 214-215.)

4. *Coram* Doran, 9 November 1989, as excerpted in F. Della Rocca, *Massimario rotale* IV [1995] 189 (see also *ME* 116 [1991] 381-85):

Finally we recommend to the judge to make use of 'canonical equity'. This blessed equity which is defined as that 'superior justice which in particular cases prudently mitigates juridic rigor' and is called *canonical* because this is 'the canonical legislator's humanity through which he benignly attempts to temper excessive rigor and prudently adapts the severity of the legal text to concrete cases' since 'principles and laws customarily express [things] very briefly and generally presuppose related concepts, and cannot consider the [specific] circumstances which demand some adjusting'. (Vermeersch-Creusen, *Epitome Iuris Canonici*, vol. I, 7th ed. [Mechelen, 1949] 129, n. 127, 2.)

5. *Coram* Faltin, 26 May 1989 *RRDec.,* 81:382-383, n. 8:

With regard to the 'error of quality amounting to an error of person' it is useful to recall that, when judging cases coming from distant regions, this Apostolic Tribunal is used to proceed to judge them 'in the light of canonical equity' (cf. *coram* de Lanversin, June 26, 1982; and *coram* Davino, March 26, 1987), having in mind c. 19 *CIC* so that from the highest law no great injustice may arise. When, however, equity according to the classical concept, is not opposed to the law, but rather when the law is defined as 'constituted equity', equity in this sense is the substance of law, 'namely the end which the law pursues' (cf. S. D'Angelo, "De aequitate in C.I.C." in *Periodica* 16 [1927] 210-224). There is certainly no one among ecclesiastical judges who would not know that justice is to be administered under the direction of equity [...] especially in marriage cases which concern error as treated in c. 1097, §2 of the present *C.I.C.* (and in c. 1083, §2,1° of the old Code) [...] Indeed in all things, but chiefly in law, equity is to be observed. (cf. D. 50, 17, 90)

6. J. J. Coughlin, OFM, "Canonical Equity," *SC* 30 [1996] 431, 433:

[…] unwritten equity constitutes a recognition that a specific application of the positive law may need a correction. The problem arises in that the legislator, faced with the requirement to fashion law in the best interests of society, cannot anticipate every concrete situation. Despite the benign intention of the legislator, the words of a certain statute, when applied to a specific set of circumstances, either impose impossible burdens or prove especially difficult. When there is a clash between a particular application of positive law and a significantly more just or charitable result, one must be able to presume that the legislator had no intention in such circumstances to require the specific observance of the enacted rule. An authentic appeal to unwritten equity involves a case in which the particular application of a law would be contrary to the will of the legislator. Pursuant to the view of St. Thomas Aquinas, this does not constitute an abrogation of law, but the correction of the application of law in certain circumstances. Thus, unwritten equity is not apart from the law; instead it always exhibits fidelity to the mind of the lawgiver.

[…] Consistent with the intention of the lawgiver, authentic canonical equity recognizes that the law itself is a structure intended to convey a deeper non-legal reality. In order to promote an ecclesiastical common good in which individual may flourish, canon law attempts to establish a legal order that fully corresponds to the faith claim of the dominion of Jesus Christ. [...] [C]anonical equity thus signifies a juridical instrument by which one vested with the sacred power of governance acknowledges the profound nature and end of canon law.

Chapter VII

Sources For Canon 1098

Dolus

John P. Donovan, JCL

I. Pertinent Canons

A. See canon 1098.

B. See the following allied canons: 6, §2; 9; 125, §2; 1055, §1; 1056; 1057, §1; 1057, §2; 1084, §3; 1096, §1.

II. Conciliar and/or Papal Teachings

A. Vatican Council II, *GS* 48:

Holiness of marriage and the family. The intimate partnership of life and the love which constitutes the married state has been established by the creator and endowed by him with its own proper laws: it is rooted in the contract of its partners, that is, in their irrevocable personal consent. It is an institution confirmed by the divine law and receiving its stability, even in the eyes of society, from the human act by which the partners mutually surrender themselves to each other; for the good of the partners, of the children, and of society this sacred bond no longer depends on human decision alone. (Flannery, *Vatican Council II*, 1:950.)

B. Vatican Council II, *GS* 49:

Married love is an eminently human love because it is affection between two persons rooted in the will and it embraces the good of the whole person; it can enrich the sentiments of the spirit and their physical expression with a unique dignity and ennoble them as the special elements and signs of the friendship proper to marriage. The Lord, wishing to bestow special gifts of grace and divine love on it, has restored, perfected, and elevated it. A love like that, bringing together the human and the divine, leads the partners to a free and mutual giving of self, experienced in tenderness and action, and permeates their whole lives. (Flannery, *Vatican Council II*, 1:952)

C. Pope John Paul II, in his 1984 allocution to the Rota, recommends the study of rotal jurisprudence as a guide for the accurate interpretation and application of canon 1098. He writes:

[...] the expert jurisprudence of the Rota could make a valuable contribution. [...] the further clarification of canon 1098 [...]. These important determinations, [...] should serve as direction and guidance to all the tribunals of the particular churches [...] (English trans. from Woestman, *Papal Allocutions*, 185.)

III. Rotal Jurisprudence

A. *Coram* Ragni, 27 April 1993 *RRDec.,* 84:288-306: *Dolus* can be negative by purposeful omission, positive by directed action, substantial if it involves an essential element or simply accidental due to a mistake. *Dolus* is utilized to create a false sense of reality, an image that is desired but not founded. Even though one is deceived, even simply, to be mistaken is to be lured into error in the consent. Consent based on a fallacy goes against the nature of the mutual commitment of the marital covenant.

Ragni refers to the Spanish commentary for further definition and clarification of *dolus.* Manipulation to obtain consent goes against one freely engaging in the marital bond. ["'*Aunque quien es enganado yerra, no deben confundirse error y dolo*', *profert commentator hispanicus in Código de Derecho Canonico*" (Eunsa, Pamplona 1983, 661), *qui sapienter collustrare prosequitur*: "*Mientras en el error suieto hace un iuicio falso del obieto y es el autor de la falta de adecuacion entre su idea y la realidad; en el dolo, en cambio, es un tercero quien elabora, mediante engano, una falsa realidad provocando asi en el suieto la percepcion en apariencia "verdadera" de un obieto en si mismo falso.*

De ahi que en el dolo exista una indigna manipulacion con mala fe por un tercero de la formacion del acto del entendimiento del suieto paciente, imprescindible para consentir, que "natura sua" debe corresponder al senorio del propio contrayente." c. Ragni, *RRDec.,* 85:290.]

B. *Coram* de Lanversin, 17 March 1993 *RRDec.,* 84:151-169: *Dolus* is defined as the truth having been deliberately kept from another in order to obtain the desired effect.

C. *Coram* Burke, 25 October 1990 *RRDec.,* 82:722-733, or see *SC* 26 [1992] 235-255 for an English translation: Burke clearly wishes to establish the unique nature of *dolus*, especially in relationship to the grounds of error before determining if there is cause for nullity. *Dolus* alters information necessary for valid consent. The perpetrator intends to marry but consents as one for whom the reality is other than that of his own person, which he suspects would not be acceptable to the other; thus, establishing a condition for the other party, not a condition of his own. The *dolus* itself then is not the sole difficulty; it is the lack of trust with the revelation, the imposed error, and imposed condition, which, when revealed, disturbs conjugal life.

The jurisprudence that Burke establishes is one that is reflective of the conciliar understanding of marriage and the evolution of the scope of understanding of the sacrament. For *dolus* to invalidate the understanding of marriage is one that is based on the covenant, self-giving, self-sacrificing, unconditional relationship that is to be reflective of each individual's relationship with God.

D. *Coram* Bruno, 19 November 1993 *RRDec.,* 84:673-682: Similar to previous jurisprudence, *coram* Bruno highlights important factors in understanding *dolus,* including the deliberate intention to deceive, in order to obtain consent; the distinction between *dolus* and the error of quality of person (c. 1097, §2); the quality of the object for which the *dolus* was perpetrated and the grave disruption of the married life. In highlighting these points which we have previously examined, *coram* Bruno warns especially about the seriousness of the quality.

Bruno observes that what may appear to be a trivial issue gives rise to a separation, may be seen as more serious at the moment of emotional upheaval. ("*Una certa soggettivita non si puo escludere psicologiacamente; non la escluse neppure un Consultore, il quale ebbe a rilevare (e nessuno lo contradisse), nella seduta del 18 maggio 1977: "Locutio adhibita in canone . . . non talis est ut excludat omnino qualitatem minoris momenti, quae tamen subiective consideratur maximi momenti" (Communicationes, 1977, p. 372, can. 299)" [Il Matrimonio nella nuova legislazione Canonica e Concordataria, p. 221, n. 636].*" *c.* Bruno, *RRDec.,* 85:676.) The act of *dolus* destroys consent, for it does not allow marriage to commence with a full cooperation and understanding that is reflective of the nature of marriage (cc. 1055, §1 & 1056). Ignorance of qualities of the marriage, although itself invalidating (c. 1096), is not the issue, but rather what is at issue is being kept in ignorance regarding a matter that would affect the marital life.

E. *Coram* Ragni, 27 April 1993 *RRDec.,* 84:288-306: *Dolus* is unique in that even though one party wants marriage, but deliberately chooses to manipulate, lie, and omit important qualities, so that the other party is led into a marriage that is not freely chosen. The investigation in determining for nullity is not one of how did the parties choose to live in error, condition or simulation, but rather, how has ignorance prevented them from engaging in the marriage they entered into. Ignorance imposed due to deception, rather than capacity undermines the union for the quality of trust; thus unity is not present. Once discovered, does a marriage exist? Is the trust and unity present? The importance of the issue for which the *dolus* may not be so grave to disrupt the union as the lack of trust, the manipulation exposed is what becomes disruptive. (Paolo Moneta. "*La qualita che per sue natura puo gravamente turbare il consorzio della vita coniugle.*" *ME* 120 [1995] 125.)

F. *Coram* Burke, 25 October 1990 *RRDec.,* 82:722-733, or see *SC* 26 [1992] 235-255 for an English translation: The responsibility of the judge is to demonstrate the seriousness of the error of quality and then to show the possibility and reason for intended deceit.

IV. Types of Proofs Required

A. *Coram* de Lanversin, 17 March 1993 *RRDec.,* 84:151-169, outlines four criteria to establish how *dolus* can be understood as invalidating consent per the realm of canon 1098:

1. *Dolus* must be in place at time of wedding;
2. *Dolus* must be in place to assure the obtaining of the consent of the unsuspecting party;
3. The *dolus* must be of the other party;
4. The defect of the quality that was present must be so grave that it disrupts the marital life, irreparably.

B. To evaluate *dolus* is to understand the substantial significance of the deceit imposed. It is purposely preventing another person to truly engage in marriage to its full capacity because of the malice of the other withholding information, trust, unity and self. Once discovered, it then disrupts the property of indissolubility, essential to marriage in accord with canon 1056.

C. *Coram* Burke, 25 October 1990 *RRDec.,* 82:722-733, or see *SC* 26 [1992] 235-255 for an English translation: To apply canon 1098 Burke stresses the gravity of the disruption to conjugal living, the gravity of the error of quality and the gravity of the deceit: ("It is not the deceit, but the concealed quality, or more concretely its potential for disturbance on married life, that must be grave.")

By stressing the importance of the gravity of the quality of error, rather than any quality at all, the dignity of a life commitment is upheld. The quality must be one that actually impacts one's understanding of marriage. Although one may be in error regarding an aspect of marriage, we look to how one is deceived about a constitutive element of marriage, as to how the consent was exchanged under false pretenses. The assumptions are that both parties have an equal understanding of marriage and that both parties establish between themselves a partnership of mutual sharing, support and nurturing.

V. Related Issues

A. Parties

1. *Coram* Bruno, 19 November 1993 *RRDec.,* 84:673-682: The Respondent is not necessarily the person who perpetrates the *dolus*. Someone else could victimize both the Petitioner and Respondent, keeping both in ignorance. Their ignorance of the matter, that when known would seriously disrupt their relationship, is what gives rise to the *dolus* that invalidates their consent. *Dolus*, committed by anyone, so that a man and woman will exchange consent is invalidating.

2. *Coram* de Lanversin, 17 March 1993 *RRDec.,* 84:151-169: When freedom is constrained by limitations due to deception, then the consent is not mutual, that is, one partner has an advantage, power to manipulate the other, the antithesis of mutual consent. To allow one

party to have correct knowledge while the other is led to false knowledge is to impose an injustice against freedom.

3. *Coram* Burke, 25 October 1990 *RRDec.,* 82:722-733, or see *SC 26* [1992] 235-255 for an English translation: When perpetrated by a third person, again the error of quality is imposed onto the unsuspecting person. The *dolus* itself then is not the sole difficulty; it is the lack of trust with the revelation of the imposed error, which, when revealed disturbs conjugal life.

B. Retroactivity

1. *Coram* Stankiewicz, 27 January 1994 *Per* 84 [1995] 529-552: Wedding date prior to 27 November 1983, affirmative decision.

2. *Coram* Stankiewicz, 30 January 1992 (*ME* 118 [1993] 529-537): Wedding date prior to 27 November 1983, affirmative decision. Stankiewicz refers back to the grave disruption of the conjugal life. Although not elaborated upon, the *dolus* undermined the essence of the relationship, which was not in doubt, thus allowing for the decision of nullity.

3. *Coram* Bruno, 19 November 1993 *RRDec.,* 84:673-682: As a juridic act, *dolus* alone is not invalidating, but through the concession of canon 1098 it can be used to petition for nullity (c. 125, §2). As a new canon, canon 1098 addressing consent, *coram* Bruno reminds us that it is not retroactive (c. 9).

> In our examination we are reminded by Montini that our interpretation of the law is to follow the tradition and spirit of the law (Gianpaolo Montini. "*La rilevanze del dolo nel matrimonio nella sue evoluzione storica.*" *ME* 120 [1995] 100; cf. c. 6, §2). However, canon 1098 is new, *dolus* as invalidating consent is new, and the definition of marriage as given in *GS* 48-49 sets a new understanding and tradition of marriage that challenges our interpretation.

4. Lawrence G. Wrenn, *Annulments*: 6th edition (Washington: CLSA [1996] 223): Wrenn provides a private response from the Code Commission dated, 8 February 1986 that states *dolus* is to be viewed as positive law, thus not retroactive. However, in his translation of the letter, it states:

> Given, however, the great variety of cases which the canon could embrace, one could not a priori rule out the possibility that some of those cases could involve nullity deriving from the natural law, in which case it would be legitimate to render an affirmative decision. It is therefore the task of the judge, who is in possession of all the possible facts, to determine whether the case at bar involves a type of error invalidating the consent by the disposition of Canon 1098 but by force of the natural law as was the case in certain sentences that predated the promulgation of the Code. (Wrenn, *Annulments* 223)

There appears to be differences of opinion among those who developed the *Code of Canon Law*; thus, there will be differences amongst judges. In the letter from the Code Commission we are however reminded, as every defender of the bond reminds a judge, that when in doubt, marriage does enjoy the favor of the law, c. 1060. Thus, where there is doubt, it is positive law, when there is obvious deceit it is natural law.

Chapter VIII

Sources For Canon 1099

DETERMINING ERROR: INDISSOLUBILITY

Gerald T. Jorgensen, PhD, JCL

I. Pertinent Canons

A. See canon 1099.

B. See the following allied canons: 126, 1055, §1; 1056; 1057, §1; 1057, §2; 1097, §1; 1097, §2.

II. Conciliar and/or Papal Teachings

A. Vatican Council II, *GS* 47:

The universal and ordinary magisterium sounded the alarm for Western culture: "Yet the excellence of [the institution of marriage] is not everywhere reflected with equal brilliance." [Paragraph continues on with examples.] (Flannery, *Vatican Council II*, 1:949.)

B. Paul VI, allocution to Rota, 9 February 1976, *AAS* 68 (1976) 205: Addressed the general deterioration of the institution of marriage in society.

C. John Paul II, ap. exhort., *FC*, 22 November 1981, n. 6 (*AAS* 74:87):

[...] signs are not lacking of a disturbing degradation of some fundamental values: a mistaken theoretical and practical concept of the independence of the spouses in relation to each other; serious misconceptions regarding the relationship of authority between parents and children; the concrete difficulties that the family itself experiences in the transmission of values; the growing number of divorces, the scourge of abortion; the ever more frequent recourse to sterilization; the appearance of a truly contraceptive mentality. (Flannery, *Vatican Council II*, 2:891.)

D. John Paul II, allocution to Rota, 28 January 1991, *AAS* 83: 948-949:

> [The cultural and historical conditions of every people] have always left their mark upon the institution of marriage. The Church, therefore, cannot prescind from the cultural milieu. I recalled this in my Apostolic Exhortation *Familiaris consortio*: 'Since God's plan for marriage and the family touches men and women in the concreteness of their daily existence in specific social and cultural situations, the Church ought to apply herself to understanding the situation within which marriage and the family have lived today in order to fulfill her task of serving'. [n. 4] [...]
>
> Contemporary culture [...] presents some aspects which cause concern [...]
>
> In particular, in the affluent and consumeristic western world, such positive aspects tend to be distorted by an immanentistic and hedonistic vision that undermines the real meaning of marital love [...]
>
> From such a mentality the misconception of the holiness of the institution of marriage often follows, not to speak of the rejection of the institution of marriage itself, which opens the way for the spread of free love.
>
> Even when it is accepted, the institution [marriage] is often deformed both in its essential elements and in its properties. This happens, for example, when marital love is experienced in egoistic self-centeredness, as a form of evasion, which tends to justify itself and be consumed in itself [...] (English trans. from Woestman, *Papal Allocutions*, 214-217.)

E. See also John Paul II, 2 February 1994, *Letters to Families* 39-43, 60-65 *passim*.

F. Address to Pontifical Council for the Family, 24 January 1997: divorce and remarriage is a most distressing problem and "a wound that is more widely affecting even Catholic environments." (*AAS* 89 [1997] 482)

G. John Paul II, allocution to Rota, 27 January 1997, *AAS* 89 (1997) 488:

At the root of this attitude [i.e., personalism means that when problems arise in marriage one should divorce] we see an *individualistic culture*, which is antithetical to true personalism. (English trans. from Woestman, *Papal Allocutions*, 242.)

H. John Paul II, allocution to the participants to the study week promoted by the Pontifical Institute for Studies on *Marriage and Family*, in *ME* 124 (1999) 448-451:

In comparison with 18 years ago when your academic journey began, the challenge posed by the secular mentality regarding the truth about the person, marriage and the family has in a certain sense become even more radical. It is not only a question of debating the individual moral norms of sexual and family ethics.

The image of man/woman proper to natural reason and, in particular, to Christianity is opposed with an alternative anthropology. The latter rejects the fact, inscribed in its corporeity, that the sexual difference is an identifying characteristic of the person; consequently the concept of the family founded on an indissoluble marriage of a man and a woman, as the natural and basic cell of society is critically challenged.

5 – In view of these challenges, the Church has no other option than to turn her gaze to Christ, the Redeemer of man and fullness of Revelation. As I had occasion to say in the Encyclical *Fides et ratio*: 'Christian Revelation is the true lodestar of men and women as they strive to make their way amid the pressures of an immanentist habit of mind and the constrictions of a technocratic logic' (n. 15). This guidance is offered to us precisely through the revelation of the foundation of reality, that is, of that Father who created it and maintains it in being at ever instant.

III. Rotal Jurisprudence

A. *Coram* Giannecchini, 18 December 1996, *ME* 123 (1998) 560-591:

> Provided that it does not determine the will, error about the unity or indissolubility or the sacramental dignity of marriage does not vitiate matrimonial consent (c. 1099).
>
> The human act, which is the only and necessary cause of such important effects and which no one can supply, must be endowed, without any doubt, with a proportionate knowledge and a free and unencumbered choice so that it can be an act of the intellect attaining, as a pre-requisite, its objective and an act of the will or a free and unimpeded decision by means of which the passage into the act of execution is either deliberate or not. Only through the intellect and the will is a man, indeed, master of his own acts. When the operation of the intellect, or of the will, is missing totally or partially, one can hardly speak of a human act.
>
> 4 – Not only in the case of total or partial simulation but also in the case of error about sacramental dignity, special attention is to be given to the positive act of the will, because error, which in itself is an act of the intellect, cannot invalidate marriage unless it influences and determines the will. And this is so because consent is essentially a human act.

B. In the above cited law section, Giannecchini seems to try to draw a distinction between what is meant by a "positive act of the will" in simulation and "determining the will" in error. He seems to argue that indeed "error determining the will" is essentially a "positive act of the will" that operates unknowingly as opposed to operating knowingly in simulation. A precise or fine distinction, to say the least, but for Giannecchini it has practical implications.

C. Furthermore, the above cited rotal decision is representative of the debate in the Rota as to whether error is an autonomous *caput nullitatis* or only a factor in some other grounds (e.g., the remote cause in simulation). See Donald M. Campbell, "Canon 1099: The Emergence of a New Juridic Figure?" *Quaderni Studio Rotale* 5 (1990) 35-72; James H. Provost, "Error as a Ground in Marriage Nullity Cases," *CLSA Proceedings* 57 (1995) 306-324; and Lynda A. Robitaille, "Simulation, Error Determining the Will, or Lack of Due

Discretion? A Case Study," *SC* 29 (1995) 397-432 for a review of the issues and insights into this debate. Canonical science and jurisprudence do appear to be converging on the existence of error as an autonomous *caput nullitatis*, given canons 126 and 1099 and the understanding of marriage demanded in canons 1055 and 1057.

D. *Coram* Stankiewicz, 25 April 1991, *ME* (1993) 377-382 and in *RRDec.,* 83:280-290, of which the law section is translated in Lawrence Wrenn, *Law Sections*, (Washington: CLSA, 1994) 41-47, appears to best articulate the law regarding canon 1099 (determining error) and using it as an autonomous *caput nullitatis*. Although Giannecchini did not cite it, many other rotal auditors (e.g., see Defilippi below) frequently cite it in their decisions addressing partial simulation of indissolubility or determining error.

Since, indeed, error determining the will in its assent to the principles of divorce demands a state of certainty, a firmness of mind and exclusion of anything containing the appearance of anything to the contrary, the will determined by error deliberately does not tend toward development of a direct and immediate exclusion of indissolubility by positive act of will because it does not consciously perceive the objective reality of canonical matrimonial order. This property, by a false judgment of the intellect, does not preserve anything of the essence of marriage such that it must logically be excluded. For that reason, the will determined by error is directed toward another object, essentially different from the essential formal object of matrimonial consent by substituting in this manner, although unknowingly, its own schema of a merely dissoluble marriage formed according to the principles of error in place of the schema of the essential properties of marriage. (cf. Decision before the undersigned *ponens* 26 June 1987, *Romana* No. 5)

E. As long as error remains invincible, error about indissolubility determines the will by directing consent toward a marriage that is dissoluble. (See also A. Stankiewicz, "L'errore di diritto nel consenso matrimoniale e la sua autonomia giuridica, *Per* 83 [1994] 635-668.)

F. *Coram* Defilippi, 22 November 1996, *RRDec.,* 88:749-750, n. 7.

Exclusion of the good of the sacrament, as we have seen eloquently written in a case before Pompedda, 'from the psychological point of view can come about on two grounds. Either the one contracting marriage positively and directly excludes permanence, even though he wishes to contract marriage; or the contracting party positively and directly anticipates and intends marriage without indissolubility, since he recognizes it only as a matrimonial custom or only accepts it as such' (*coram* Pompedda, 17 July 1989, *RRDec.,* 81:508s, n. 4).

Canon 1101, §2 treats of the first hypothesis while the second is covered by canon 1099, from which it is concluded that error 'concerning the indissolubility of marriage', if 'it determines the will vitiates matrimonial consent'. Now that error, which, at one time, most called 'theoretical' relevant to solubility of marriage, today often becomes 'practical', inasmuch as it enters into the very sphere of the total personality, as they say, or in the vernacular 'the frame of reference'. Therefore a basis for a defective consent can sometimes be found in the erroneous conviction itself of the one contracting marriage (cf. *coram* Colagiovanni, unpublished decision of 27 May 1986).

[...] In reality, in these cases, following the doctrine of canon 1099 *CIC*: 'there can be no hesitation to infer from this error some presumption of a defect of consent flowing from the intellect into the will' (*coram* Ewers, 24 February 1968, *RRDec.,* 60:126, n. 2). Therefore, 'it seems the principle should be retained, namely that the more error is accepted and fostered in one's very heart and soul, the more readily is there a presumption of the exclusion of an essential property. The will, which is like a blind faculty of the soul, ordinarily follows the representation of the intellect. The will is deflected from the object presented to it by the intellect with more difficulty to the extent that the adherence of the intellect to that same object is more conscious, more internalized and stronger. Sometimes it happens that a certain truth or error becomes like a new nature of a man, and so it pulls his will irresistibly' (*coram* Pompedda, 23 January 1971, *RRDec.,* 63:54, n. 5) (*coram* de Lanversin, 15 June 1992, *RRDec.,* 84:352s, nn. 11s).

Now, it can happen that error 'so penetrates and influences the personality, so to speak, of the one contracting marriage, that sometimes he opposes what is in his mind or sometimes doesn't do or carry out what the mind might want. In this case error can be said to lead to the nullity of the marriage, not so much in itself but rather because of the will, which has brought about its own defect' (*coram* Felici, 17 December 1957, *RRDec.,* 49:844, n. 3).

Therefore, to put it correctly, in these cases also the nullity of matrimony is to be attributed formally to the act of the will, which is directed to an object, which, because of substantial error, is perceived by the intellect in a way discordant with the doctrine of the Church.

For, as our most excellent Dean clearly teaches us, there can be an 'error specifying the object': 'This happens when the consent of the marrying party is directed to the object in as much as the object is basically changed by such error; in other words the error is the object of the will of the marrying party. Such an error cannot fail to falsify and destroy the consent if the quality upon which rests the error itself cannot be reconciled with the authentic object of matrimonial consent' (M.F. Pompedda, *Mancanza di fede e consenso matrimoniale*, in *Studi di Diritto matrimoniale canonico*, [Milano, 1993], 438). In this case, 'the will determined by error is directed to following an object essentially different from the formal essential object of matrimonial consent, thus substituting, even though unknowingly, its own concept of matrimony, formed according to the attractiveness of the error, in place of the essential properties of matrimony' (*coram* Stankiewicz, 25 April 1991, *RRDec.,* 83:284, n. 8).

IV. Types of Proofs Required

A. Error is a defect of the intellect. More specifically, it is a false judgment about or a mistaken assessment of an object (in this case, the object of marriage). The result of this erroneous judgment can be a state of subjective certitude grounded in the error. People in error often feel quite certain of what they know and harbor no doubt about it. However, their certitude does not change the objective reality.

B. The central fact to be proved is the existence of a deeply rooted error about marriage that determined the party's will.

C. However, unlike simulation, error *does not* require a positive act of the will (i.e., an intention excluding indissolubility from consent). Error involves a fundamentally poisoned consent.

D. The judge must find in the acts of the case, i.e., the facts, circumstances, and indices gathered through instruction of the case, sufficient proof that the party held deep-rooted error about the nature of marriage and that this error poisoned the party's matrimonial consent.

E. Either direct or indirect proofs or, more commonly, a combination of both can be used to establish the existence of error that vitiates matrimonial consent. The judge will have to rely on the behavioral and sometimes verbal expressions of the party.

F. Through the behavioral and sometimes verbal expressions of the party, the judge will have to discern the extent of the influence of contemporary secular culture on the party's attitude toward marriage. To the extent that the party has absorbed the values and attitudes of the divorce culture, he will be prone to enter marriage that he deems less than indissoluble. Social scientists have identified a number of variables that, taken individually and together, are more or less strong predictors of divorce; these variables can serve as indices of the existence of determining error or simulation. In cases involving error about indissolubility, judges may not be able to reach moral certitude without the use of presumptions formulated by the judge. (See Gerald T. Jorgensen, "Culture and Error *Non Simplex* – Not So Rare," *CLSA Proceedings* 62 [2000] 153-216.)

V. Related Issues

A. Canon 126 pivotal to a proper understanding of canon 1099.

1. This norm contains three distinct hypotheses in relation to the invalidating efficacy of error. The first hypothesis deals with error that is *objectively substantial (error which concerns the substance of the act)*. According to this hypothesis, a juridic act is invalid because the error causes a defect of consent in relation to the very substance of the act considered *objectively*. Therefore, the object internally willed by the will is, because of the error, substantially different from the one indicated in the external manifestation of such an act. The substance of marriage consent is twofold: marriage itself and the person of the spouses. If one errs in regard to marriage itself, or any

of its essential elements, the act of consent would be invalid. The error [...] is objectively substantial. The law does not require in this case any intention to the contrary; rather error by itself invalidates the juridical act of consent (Mendonça, "Error of Fact," *SC* 34 [2000] 36).

2. The error "determining the will" concerning the essential properties of marriage [i.e., unity – this is *not* the *consortium totius vitae* or the *bonum coniugum*; it is the aspect of one spouse, although some commentators have broadened this aspect of marriage to include the notion of the obligation of marital fidelity, however, rotal jurisprudence seems to hold that conjugal fidelity is an essential element of marriage *not* a property – and indissolubility] or the sacramental dignity [no agreement among rotal auditors as to whether this is marriage itself, an essential element of marriage, or an essential property of marriage] (c. 1099; *CCEO* c. 822) constitutes another application of error which amounts to a condition *sine qua non* of canon 126 (*CCEO* c. 933) [or where the law makes some other determination, as mentioned by c. 126]. In this figure, the error concerning an essential element of marriage [property as specified in law] – which *in se* has no invalidating efficacy, since it does not necessarily follow that the contractant applies it to his or her concrete marriage, – influences the will in such a way that it determines the object of conjugal consent, by circumscribing it to fit his or her own erroneous idea(s) of the marriage. (Mendonça, "Error of Fact," *SC* 34 [2000] 38-39). {What appears in brackets, [...], are the contributor's comments, not direct quotes from Mendonça.}

B. Simple Error

1. The 1917 code stated that simple error about the properties of unity and indissolubility did not invalidate consent (c. 1084). Simple error is that which remains in the intellect but does not influence the will. Thus simple error and valid consent coexist.

2. Thomas P. Doyle, "Title VII: Marriage," in his commentary on canon 1099 in J. Coriden et al. (eds.), *Code of Canon Law: A Text and Commentary*, CLSA (New York: Paulist Press, 1985) 782:

> This coexistence is based on the presumption that all Christians have a general intention to marry according to the mind of Christ. [...] Simple error, is therefore, understood to

mean false notions about marriage which are superceded by the acceptance of true Christian marriage. [...] The law now refers to error in a general way, no longer qualifying it as 'simple'. It admits that it may well influence the will, since it implicitly distinguishes between error which remains in the intellect and that which influences the will [...] If the error is such that it precludes not only an awareness but also an acceptance of the true nature of marriage, then it could well influence the person to choose a model of marriage contrary to Christian marriage. Thus consent would be invalid (Doyle, 782).

3. The jurisprudential presumption of "simple error" was first articulated by Benedict XIV (1791) – presumption of *error simplex* (*De Synodo Diocesana* 1, 13, c. 22, nn. 3 and 8 as cited in *Codicis Iuris Canonici Fontes*, v. 4, n. 1050, ed. Petri Cardinal Gasparri).

C. Rotal jurisprudence addressing, if not the non-existence of the presumption of "simple error," at least, the almost complete erosion of it:

1. *Coram* Pompedda, 23 January 1971, *RRDec.,* 63:54:

    In our judgment it is not a legitimate conclusion from canon 1084 [*CIC* 1917] to say there exists a presumption in favor of marriage for those people who, perhaps largely because of their religious beliefs or secular education, are laboring under a misunderstanding of the essential properties of marriage. This is especially true since such a presumption is arrived at only by gratuitously conjecturing to a second presumption, namely, that it never occurs to such people, when they enter marriage, to apply their intellectual error to their intention. It would seem, therefore, as regards both Catholics and others, that the principle should be retained that, the more deeply and radically an error is ingrained and endorsed, the easier it is to establish a presumption in favor of an essential property of marriage being excluded.

2. *Coram* Pinto, 6 November 1972, *RRDec.,* 64:673:

In our day it is not possible to presume that with a general and prevalent intention the parties will have willed to contract marriage according to divine institution while they obstinately persevere in their errors even though they know sufficiently well the doctrine of the Church.

3. *Coram* Huot, 22 April 1982, *RRDec.,* 74:194:

Most certainly in the case of people of sound mind, marriage is presumed to be contracted according to the law of nature and society; but we must admit that in the case of some people who profess no religion, and who from their youth have been steeped in errors, this common presumption must be reduced to little or nothing.

4. *Coram* Faltin, 16 April 1997, *ME* 123 (1998) 255-257:

Finally, dealing with and deciding about these matters, one must examine carefully the circumstances as well as the events both of place and time which preceded, accompanied and followed the celebration of marriage in which certain sure facts took place, and other evidences or complements as well pursuant to canon 1679.

10 – To the preceding observations, given the particular aspect of this case, it is appropriate to add that in our times 'we cannot exclude cases in which the conscience of even some Christian people is so distorted by ignorance and invincible error that they sincerely believe that they can contract a valid marriage while excluding the sacramental aspect from it' (see *Propositiones Commissionis Internationalis* [Motions of the International Commission], 1977, in *Civiltà Cattolica*, Prop. EV, 6, 363, No. 471).

We read the following statement correctly and appropriately written: 'Once it was reasonable to hold (presume) that Chris-tians, living as they were in a relatively closely-knitted society, could have a minimum of faith, and as a result to have a minimum of intention of contracting [marriage] by doing what the church does; however, this presumption today doesn't seem to be valid any longer [...].' (See M.F. Pompedda, *Fede e Sacramento del matrimonio*

[Faith and the Sacrament of Marriage], in *Quaderni Studio Rotale* [Essays on the Rota], II, p. 57.)

In fact, we have some decisions of Huot. which state: 'In our times one cannot assume that those who continue stubbornly in their errors, although they know the church's doctrine sufficiently, would want with a general and prevalent intention to contract a marriage just like God instituted it, [...] it can hardly be expected that one approaching marriage while fixed in a state of rebellion against God's very authority would generally want to give a true matrimonial consent out of a religious motivation [...].' (See Rota decisions, together with *coram* Pinto, 6 November 1972, *RRDec* 64:637 [should be 673]; ibid. 1971: 596; *coram* Huot, 10 November 1987, No. 6, ibid. File No. 14, 632; *coram* Serrano, 18 April 1986, File No. 14,000, ad 5 toward the end.)

D. Thomas P. Doyle, O.P. provides a helpful analysis of process of consent to illustrate how error can influence the will. (See Doyle, 782-783.)

E. Barbara Whitehead, *The Divorce Culture*, (New York: Alfred A. Knopf, 1997) 76-77:

The logic of expressive divorce also suggested that relationships themselves – especially relationships that are binding or permanent – are risky investments. The most reliable form of investment becomes the investment in the self. The logic of expressive divorce argued not only for building one's own psychological capital, therefore, but also for keeping it 'liquid'. A self not tied down by permanent bonds and obligations was a self that could take advantage of new opportunities as they came along (Whitehead, 76-77).

F. Barbara Whitehead, *The Divorce Culture*: 44:

In the history of American divorce the last third of the twentieth century marks a time of profound discontinuity and rapid change. Indeed, the cultural fault line, the B.C. and A.D. of American divorce, can be drawn somewhere in the mid- to late 1960s. Before that time, divorce was contained within a system of marriage and subject to its jurisdiction. After that time, divorce moved outside the government of marriage and established its own institutional jurisdiction over family relationships. Before the mid-1960s, divorce was viewed as a legal, family, and social event with multiple stakeholders; after that time, divorce became an individual event defined by and responsive to the interests of the individual (Whitehead, 44).

G. John Witte, Jr., *From Sacrament to Contract: Marriage, Religion, and Law in the Western Tradition* (Louisville, KY: Westminster John Knox Press, 1997):

> The early enlightenment ideals of marriage as a permanent contractual union designed for the sake of mutual love, procreation and protection is slowly giving way to a new reality of marriage as a 'terminal sexual contract' designed for the gratification of the individual parties (Witte, 209).

H. Barbara Whitehead, *The Divorce Culture*:

> Divorce has become so pervasive that many people naturally assume it has seeped into the social and cultural mainstream over a long period of time. Yet this is not the case. Divorce has become an American way of life only as the result of recent and revolutionary change. [...] the divorce rate [...] continued its upward climb until the early 1980s, when it stabilized at the highest level among advanced Western societies. As a consequence of this sharp and sustained rise, divorce moved from the margins to the mainstream of American life in the space of three decades. [...] In the new conception of divorce, (a) strain of eighteenth-century political thought mingled with a strain of twentieth-century psychotherapeutic thought. Divorce was *not only an individual right but also a psychological resource* (emphasis added). [...] the conception of divorce as both an individual right and an inner experience merged with and reinforced the new ethic of obligation to the self. [...] Divorce in America is not unique, but what we have made of divorce is uniquely American. [...] Compared with other Western societies, Americans have a strong tradition of divorce (Whitehead, 3-13).

I. In a recent article, the rotal auditor Serrano argued that a judge cannot just consider the choice to marry as an intellectual decision but must overcome the limits of rationalism or strict voluntarism.

Serrano asserted a need to consider not only the autonomy of the act of the will, but also its historicity, i.e., what goes before it, the personal biographies of the persons involved, the cultural context of the persons involved. Serrano stated that a judge must place a great emphasis on the person's attitude before marriage and study who this person is in terms of education, environment, prematrimonial circumstances, etc. (J. M. Serrano Ruiz, "El acto de voluntad por el que se crea o frustra el consentimiento matrimonial," *REDC* 51 [1994] 567-589.)

J. Robert Bellah et al., *Habits of the Heart: Individualism and Commitment in American Life* (Berkeley: University of California Press, 1985) 107:

> For the classical utilitarian individualist, the only valid contract is one based on negotiation between individuals acting in their own self-interest. For the expressive individualist, a relationship is created by the full sharing of authentic feelings. But both in hard bargaining over the contract and in the spontaneous sharing of therapeutically sophisticated lovers, the principle is basically the same. No binding obligations and no social understanding justify a relationship. It exists only as the expression of choices of the free selves who make it up. And should it no longer meet their needs, it must end (Bellah, 107).

Chapter IX

Sources For Canon 1099

DETERMINING ERROR: UNITY

Ronny E. Jenkins, JCD

I. Pertinent Canons

A. See canon 1099.

B. See the following allied canons: 126; 1055, §1; 1056; 1057, §1; 1101, §1; 1101, §2.

II. Conciliar and/or Papal Teaching

A. Pius XI, *Casti connubii*, n. 20, 31 December 1930, *AAS* 22 [1930] 546-547:

Wherefore, conjugal faith, or honor, demands in the first place the complete unity of matrimony which the Creator Himself laid down in the beginning when He wished it to be not otherwise than between one man and one woman. And although afterwards this primeval law was relaxed to some extent by God, the Supreme Legislator, there is no doubt that the law of the Gospel fully restored that original and perfect unity, and abrogated all dispensations as the words of Christ and the constant teaching and action of the Church show plainly. With reason, therefore, does the Sacred Council of Trent solemnly declare: "Christ Our Lord very clearly taught that in this bond two persons only are to be united and joined together when He said: 'Therefore they are no longer two, but one flesh'. [Conc. Trid., Sess. xxiv.]

B. Vatican Council II, *GS* 48:

By their very nature, the institution of matrimony itself and conjugal love are ordained for the procreation and education of children, and find in them their ultimate crown. Thus a man and a woman, who by their compact of conjugal love 'are no longer two, but one flesh' (Mt 19:ff), render mutual help and service to each other through an intimate union of their persons and of their actions. Through this union they experience the meaning of their oneness and attain to it with growing perfection day by day. As a mutual gift of two persons, this intimate union and the good of the children impose total fidelity on the spouses and argue for an unbreakable oneness between them. (Flannery, *Vatican Council II*, 1:950.)

C. John Paul II, allocution to the Rota, 24 January 1981, *AAS* 73 [1981] 228-234:

It is well known how, since the beginnings of its magisterium, the Church – confirmed by the word of the Gospel (cf. Mt. 19:5; 5:32) – has always taught and confirmed explicitly the precept of Jesus on the unity and indissolubility of marriage, without which there can never be a secure family, the healthy and truly vital cell of society. (English trans. from Woestman, *Papal Allocutions*, 166.)

D. John Paul II, allocution to the Rota, 30 January 1993, *AAS* 85 [1993] 1256-1260:

Thus, to give an example, it would could cause serious harm to the stability of marriage and so to its sacred nature, if the fact of simulation was not formulated concretely on the part of the alleged simulator in a 'positive act of will' (*actus positivus voluntatis*, c. 1101, §2); or if the so-called *error of law (error iuris*) regarding an essential property of marriage or its sacramental dignity did not acquire such intensity as to condition the act of will, thus causing the consent to be null (see c. 1099). (English trans. from Woestman, *Papal Allocutions*, 226.)

E. John Paul II, allocution to the Rota, 1 February 2001, *AAS* 93 [2001] 360-365:

To present consent as the following of a cultural model or one of positive law is not realistic and risks needlessly complicating the investigation of matrimonial validity. It is a question of seeing whether the persons, in addition to identifying each other's person, have truly grasped the essential natural dimension of their married state, which implies, as an intrinsic requirement, fidelity, indissolubility and potential fatherhood/motherhood as goods that integrate a relationship of justice. (English trans. from Woestman, *Papal Allocutions*, 264.)

F. John Paul II, allocution to the Rota, 1 February 2001, *AAS* 93 [2001] 360-365:

The essential properties, unity and indissolubility, are also inscribed in the very being of marriage, since in no way are they laws extrinsic to it. Only if marriage is seen as a union involving the person in the realization of his natural relational structure, which remains essentially the same throughout his personal life, can it withstand the changes of life, the efforts and even the crises through which human freedom often passes in living its commitments. But if the marital union is thought to be based only on personal qualities, interests or attractions, it obviously is no longer seen as a natural reality but as a situation dependent on the current perseverance of the will in relation to the continuance of contingent facts and feelings. Certainly, the bond is caused by consent, that is, by an act of the man and the woman's will, but this consent actualizes a power already existing in the nature of man and woman. Thus, the indissoluble force of the bond itself is based on the natural reality of the union freely established between man and woman. (English trans. from Woestman, *Papal Allocutions*, 263.)

G. John Paul II, *FC* 19:

The gift of the spirit is a commandment of life for Christian spouses and at the same time a stimulating impulse so that every day they may progress toward an ever richer union with each other on all levels – of the body, of the character, of the heart, of the intelligence and will, of the soul – revealing in this way to the church and to the world the new communion of love, given by the grace of Christ. Such a communion is radically contradicted by polygamy. This, in fact, directly negates the plan of God which was revealed from the beginning, because it is contrary to the equal personal dignity of men and women, who in matrimony give themselves with a love that is total and therefore unique and exclusive. As the Second Vatican Council writes: 'Firmly established by the Lord, the unity of marriage will radiate from the equal personal dignity of husband and wife, a dignity acknowledged by mutual and total love'. (Flannery, *Vatican Council II*, 2:829.)

H. *Catechism of the Catholic Church,* nn. 1644-1645:

The love of the spouses requires, of its very nature, the unity and indissolubility of the spouses' community of persons, which embraces their entire life: 'so they are no longer two, but one flesh'. They 'are called to grow continually in their communion through day-to-day fidelity to their marriage promise of total mutual self-giving'. This human communion is confirmed, purified, and completed by communion in Jesus Christ, given through the sacrament of Matrimony. It is deepened by lives of the common faith and by the Eucharist received together. 'The unity of marriage, distinctly recognized by our Lord, is made clear in the equal personal dignity which must be accorded to man and wife in mutual and unreserved affection'. Polygamy is contrary to conjugal love which is undivided and exclusive. (*Catechism of the Catholic Church,* nn. 1644-1645.)

III. Rotal Jurisprudence

A. *Coram* Stankiewicz, 21 April 1983, *RRDec.,* 75:178, n. 2:

By its very nature conjugal love demands an exclusive unity of the spouses because in the natural order it brings about a more profound, more complete, and more intimate relationship in which a person can take part perpetually and stably. Since conjugal love involves a *total relation* of the spouses, the intimate union of marriage imposes total fidelity on the couple and argues for an unbreakable oneness between them (*GS,* 48). Even more, unity and indissolubility receive a special firmness in Christian marriage because of the sacrament (1917 code c. 1012, §2; 1983 code c. 1056). ([translation: E. Pfnausch])

B. *Coram* Colagiovanni, 20 July 1984, *RRDec.,* 76:487, n. 5:

Clearly, the influence of simple error concerning the unity and indissolubility or sacramental dignity of marriage does not vitiate matrimonial consent, as is stated in canon 1099. The new formulation of the code removes the previous phrase, 'even if it is the cause of the contract', and inserts the words: 'so long as it does not determine the will'. In this way, the new code receives the common jurisprudence of the preponderance of the influence of error, which is in the mind, and which determines the will in such a way that consent itself is vitiated by the effect [of the error on the will].

C. *Coram* Bruno, 19 December 1984, *RRDec.,* 76:649, n. 4:

The peculiar distinction between simple error and obstinate error [*pervicax*] rooted in the mind should be forgotten [...] Someone is influenced by obstinate error when the error enters the sphere of the will, causing the person to implicitly will what the mind presumes. The will is deprived of its particular faculty of considering and coming to judgment, which generally works in a harmonious collaboration with the intellect and so generally avoids error.

D. *Coram* Masala, 19 February 1985, *RRDec.,* 77:107-108, n. 5:

A positive act of the will is not to be confused with error "concerning the unity and indissolubility or sacramental dignity of marriage," which, "so long as it does not determine the will, does not invalidate matrimonial consent (c. 1099)." As an intellectual act, error – which resembles the truth – always influences the operation of the will since the will is moved by an object it has previously known. [...] We admit that it can happen "that error so penetrates and attracts the person that the one exchanging consent knows nothing else than what he or she thinks, can act in no other way than how the mind wills. In this case the error can be said to lead to the nullity of marriage, not so much because of the error itself, but rather due to the will which is vitiated by the error. Nevertheless, this positive will is not to be presumed, but is to be proven by valid and rational arguments."

E. *Coram* Pompedda, 22 July 1985, *RRDec.,* 77:396, n. 3:

Error, which is false knowledge of some object or fact, can be examined as a defect of will in juridic acts. Error can be essential (or substantial) or non-essential. Non-essential error is directed at the qualities of an object that hardly undermine the [...] motive of the act. Essential error, which renders the act itself null, takes place when it concerns the juridic act in its totality, or some constitutive element of the same act.

F. *Coram* Fiore, 19 October 1990, *RRDec.,* 82:699, n. 9:

> This mind set, so rooted in the Respondent that it becomes as if second nature, seems to be the direct or proximate cause of simulation, as the jurisprudence of Our Apostolic Tribunal has frequently taught. In other words, error, which so imbues the Respondent, determines the will, and so vitiates matrimonial consent according to the norm of canon 1099 of the current code of canon law.

G. See *Rotal Jurisprudence* section of the other section on canon 1099.

IV. Types of Proofs Required

Proof of error concerning the unity of marriage follows the general proof requirements for all error cases, with a few exceptions. See *Types of Proofs Required* section of the other section on canon 1099.

V. Related Issues

A. Rotal jurisprudence concerning this ground is extremely sparse since few cases have been heard by it on error of unity. Nevertheless, the ground should not be avoided for that reason alone. There are an increasing number of marriages in the United States involving persons from countries or cultures that permit or even promote polygamy at least as a right (whether or not it is ever used). So it is important to recall that for the invalidity of consent to result a person need not even have the intention of exercising his right to marry more than one spouse. The reservation of the right is sufficient to invalidate.

B. "Serial polygamy" as invalidating. That is, a person who has been in several marriages, all subsequent to the prior one, is not necessarily excluding the property of unity. Still, it is important to understand the mindset of a person who enters serial marriages. If his or her intention is to enter another marriage while, at least before God's eyes, the previous bond is still valid; a type of violation of unity may be involved.

C. Rotal auditors and canonists would argue that, in effect, there is little distinction between determining error and simulation. That is, invalidating error amounts to an act of the will by which an essential property of marriage, here unity, is excluded from consent. Simulation results in the same thing, and by the same means (an act of the will). Others would argue that determining error as described in canon 1099 is an autonomous ground, not only by definition of the code, but by the actual process at work in a person influenced by determining error. It is not merely another type of simulation, but a distinct operation of the will at work. The most prominent proponent of the autonomy of error is Stankiewicz. For practical purposes, a tribunal needs not be overly concerned with this debate. It should be concerned, however, with determining whether or not a positive act of the will did occur in cases alleging nullity of marriage due to either determining error or simulation. With simulation, the positive act of the will is knowingly posited. With error determining the will the positive act of the will is *not* knowingly or consciously posited.

D. Another issue of (lesser) debate is whether or not error and simulation are compatible grounds of nullity. Can a tribunal use both grounds on the same person? Or must they be used subordinately? The Rota itself formulates the grounds in both ways. A lower grade tribunal may do so as well.

Chapter X

Sources For Canon 1101, §2

Total Simulation

Margaret A. Ramsden, SFCC, JCL, with
Gerald T. Jorgensen, PhD, JCL

I. Pertinent Canons

A. See canons 1101, §1 and 1101, §2.

B. See the following allied canons: 1055, §1; 1055, §2; 1056; 1057, §1; and 1057, §2.

C. Although the law only implies a distinction between "total" and "partial" simulation, jurisprudence has traditionally differentiated between these two types of simulation. Total simulation occurs when the content of marital consent itself (cc. 1055, §1; 1057) is excluded through "a positive act of the will." Partial simulation occurs when some essential property or element of marriage is excluded through "a positive act of the will." Total simulators may be aware that a marriage does not exist while partial simulators may believe that a subjectively defined marriage does exist.

II. Conciliar and/or Papal Teachings

A. Total simulation occurs when an expression of consent exists simultaneously with a positive act of the will excluding the object or content of consent. John Paul II, in his 1999 allocution to the Rota, describes consent as "choice" and "commitment." He writes:

> This consent is nothing other than the conscious, responsible assumption of a commitment through a juridical act by which, in reciprocal self-giving, the spouses promise total and definitive love to each other. They are free to celebrate marriage after having chosen each other with equal freedom, but as soon as they perform this act they establish a personal state in which love becomes something that is owed, entailing effects of a juridical

nature as well. (English trans. from Woestman, *Papal Allocutions*, 251.)

B. Total simulation results from "a positive act of the will" excluding the content of consent or the marriage itself in its essential nature. As Pope John Paul II, in his 1997 allocution to the Rota, teaches:

> *Marriage* certainly has an *essential nature*, described in canon 1055, which pervades the entire teaching concerning marriage, as can be seen in the concepts of 'essential property', 'essential element', 'essential rights and obligations of marriage', etc. This essential reality is a possibility open in principle to every man and woman; indeed, it represents a true vocation for the great majority of the human race. (English trans. from Woestman, *Papal Allocutions*, 243.)

III. Rotal Jurisprudence

A. With total simulation, there is a "conscious" exclusion "of a commitment" and, therefore, "a juridical act" does not exist.

1. *Coram* Egan, 19 July 1984, *RRDec.,* 76:477-484:

> [...] The difference between the two is that one is fictitious consent (total simulation), while the other is incomplete consent. One who elicits a totally simulated consent, unlike a partial simulator, cannot ignore the fact that he/she acts invalidly. Whereas, a person who simulates only partially, unlike the former, almost always has in mind that he/she consents to some form of marriage. (Mendonça, *Rotal Anthology*, 143.)

2. *Coram* Colagiovanni, 15 December 1982, *RRDec.,* 74:638-645: "[...] In total simulation there is no consent; whereas in partial simulation the consent is present, but it is limited or distorted." (Mendonça, *Rotal Anthology*, 140.)

B. *Coram* Ragni, 19 July 1983, *RRDec.,* 75:471:

> [...] total simulation can occur:
> a) when the contracting party has the intention of not contracting, which is to say he puts on an act while

manifesting (in which case the substance of the contract is destroyed);

b) when the contracting party consents to marriage solely and exclusively for personal reasons (*ob fines operantis*) absolutely extraneous to the *finis operis*, that is, to marriage itself;
c) when the very cause of the marital contract (that is, the mutual handing over of the perpetual and exclusive *ius in corpus*) is excluded because, if the contracting party exclusively intends another covenant essentially different from marriage, the contract itself collapses;
d) when the dignity of the sacrament is excluded from the contract;
e) when the contracting party wishes to substitute for the notion of Christian marriage a concept which really excludes it, or even if he excludes the permanent society between a man and a woman to procreate children.

C. *Coram* Serrano, 11 December 1981, *RRDec.,* 73:625:

But it can happen that someone in celebrating marriage intends other objects, extrinsic to marriage, in other words, *fines operantis*: whether honorable, such as in order to establish peace between families, to preserve honor, to preserve health, or base, such as from a vicious greed for riches, for vain glory, or from lust. Such objects extrinsic to marriage can really be found in the mind of the contracting party in two ways: 1) the extrinsic end can be had as a secondary end, more or less as a reason for deciding to marry, although without it the marriage would not take place. In this case the will to achieve this extrinsic end [...] does not exclude the substance of marriage [...]; 2) The extrinsic end can be had as a principal and final cause of contracting towards which the party principally and exclusively directs himself; and, therefore, it excludes the intention of contracting, which is to say it excludes marriage itself [...]. With a very serious disordering [of nature], the extrinsic end is preferred to the essential end [of marriage], and consent to the marriage itself is lacking, which cannot exist on this hypothesis [*igitur*] [...] and it is a case of total simulation.

D. *Coram* Faltin, 18 January 1988, *RRDec.,* 80:3-6:

[...] Nor is there required in the simulator either an evil intent, i.e., bad faith in causing deception or intentional divergence, i.e., conscious deformity between the internal will and the external declaration. It is sufficient that the contractant internally and effectively wishes not to contract marriage. This can be done for a variety of reasons but the reasons should be at least subjectively and proportionately grave, and may include fear pressed upon the subject, that is to say, force by which the subject is compelled to agree to celebrate the unwelcomed nuptials [...]

In the case of consent vitiated by total simulation 'the knowledge and intent to simulate is necessary; but it is not necessarily required that the simulator be aware of the juridic effects', that is to say, the nullity of the marriage brought about by the simulated consent (see from the decision of 17 July 1983 *coram* Fiore, n. 3). (Wrenn, *LS*, 52.)

E. *Coram* Bruno, 26 February 1988, *RRDec.,* 80:167-168:

In total simulation marriage itself is rejected and the defect of consent results in the nonexistence of the juridic act.

In partial simulation, on the other hand, one does not reject marriage, which one wills, but the consent is vitiated by a positive exclusion of an essential property or element of marriage, which invalidates the marriage. [...] (Wrenn, *LS*, 69.)

F. *Coram* de Lanversin, 31 July 1990, *RRDec.,* 82:678:

Total simulation arises not only by the exclusion of marriage itself, or of the other party, but also by including elements which radically contradict those of the community of life and love established by the Creator's laws.

G. *Coram* Palestro, 27 May 1992, *RRDec.,* 84:282, n. 5:
Whoever totally simulates has no intention of contracting a marriage, but whoever excludes some good on the contrary wants to contract marriage, but intends marriage as conceived by him or herself, namely, the person's object is something other that the object toward which by its nature matrimonial consent is directed.

H. *Coram* Ragni, 19 July 1993, *RRDec.,* 85:471:

If the contracting party should wish to substitute for the notion of Christian marriage a concept which really excludes it [i.e., Christian marriage], or even if he or she excludes the permanent society between a man and a woman for the purpose of procreating children, [the consent is invalid].

I. *Coram* de Lanversin, 17 March 1993, *RRDec.,* 85:153-155:

6. Total exclusion, that is, total simulation, concerning the marriage contract is addressed at the same time with partial simulation by can. 1101, §2 *CIC*, which states: 'But if one or the other or each party, by a positive act of the will, excludes marriage itself or any essential element of marriage or any essential property, the person contracts invalidly'.

Concerning the manner of expression in can. 1101, §2, also one should not forget that in total simulation the one contracting, advisedly and knowingly intends to establish an appearance, while in reality the person excludes marriage itself. However, in partial simulation the person hopes for and wants some type of marriage (a pseudo-marriage) which is adjusted to his or her pleasure and many times does not know of the nullity being perpetrated. (Cf. *coram* Ragni, sentence issued on 1 March 1993.)

From the above is derived the fact that total fiction can be directed toward the marriage itself in as much as the one getting married in no way wants within him or herself to be married, but wants some other advantage (i.e., wealth, some help, freedom from parents, etc.), having thus rejected entirely the matrimonial institute in a direct way. On the other hand, the one who rejects all the essential elements or goods of marriage (*bonum sacramenti, bonum fidei, bonum prolis*), taken all together or conjunctively, perpetrates partial simulation. [...]

8. The solid jurisprudence of Our Forum holds for total simulation that the *finis operis* cannot be excluded by the *finis operantis* without by that very fact corrupting the essence of the contract if indeed the will of the contractant does not intend in any way the *finis operis* but only the *finis operantis*, implicitly excluding

the former (cf. *coram* Lefebvre, decision issued on 12 March 1960, *RRDec.*, 52:171, n. 2).

However, someone who merely proposes to himself or herself a *finis* different from the *finis operis*, does not vitiate the consent and therefore does not render the marriage invalid, unless, at the same time by a positive intention absolutely excludes the *finis operis*. *Finis operantis*, which differ from the *finis operis*, are legitimate as long as they are not opposed to it.

For this reason, someone who wants marriage as a means to pursue ends is not by that very fact to be said as having simulated consent. For a cause for simulation which is both grave and proportionate is to be investigated – a cause which the contractant must have held as prevailing over contracting marriage correctly. [...] because by the very fact the contractant intends to contract marriage, unless he expressly excludes the required end, he correctly intends to make that marriage in virtue of it and implicitly.

In the other hypothesis the contractant moves toward and regards that end, principally excluding the marriage itself or regards the celebration as a vain ritual devoid of all value or as a rite not producing a marriage. In this case, with consent for the marriage itself lacking, this marriage does not exist (cf. *coram* Funghini, sentence issued 14 October 1992, ibid., pp. 450 ff., n. 2). [...]

10. Nevertheless, presumptions can be overcome and, as the approved jurisprudence of Our Apostolic Tribunal teaches, to prove simulation in any process, at least three things are required: the confession of the simulator, a cause which is proportionately grave, a set of circumstances both before and after marriage, which support it (cf. *coram* Ewers, decision issued 19 April 1972, *RRDec.*, 64:181).

J. *Coram* de Lanversin, 18 February 1984, *RRDec.,* 76:100, n. 4:

For that reason it must be said that in canonical total simulation (which many times takes an unilateral form), as in the absolute simulation of the civil lawyers (cf. E. Perego, *La simulazione nel matrimonio civile*, [Milan, 1980] 92 ff.) there is completely absent the will for marriage (since there is present the will to reject it), while in partial simulation there is present a certain matrimonial will which is atypical (that is a pseudo-matrimonial will), which is openly in opposition to the substance of marriage as founded by the laws of the Creator. But this pseudo or atypical matrimonial will is not able to produce a valid conjugal bond, since it pulls away from marriage some essential good, that is the good of children, of fidelity or of the sacrament (*coram* Stankiewicz, 29 January 1981, *RRDec.,* 74:47, n. 5).

IV. Types of Proofs Required

A. *Coram* Faltin, 16 April 1997, *ME* 123 (1998) 254-255:

9 – As far as the proof of simulation is concerned, there is absolutely no doubt that to prove in the external forum the existence of a simulated contract, due to the exclusion of marriage itself or the rejection of some essential property of marriage or the denial of some essential element of the marital union, is rather difficult since there is a contrary presumption expressed in canon 1101, §1. Since this is at least a presumption 'by law', the simulation of consent must be proved with convincing arguments, free from any prudent and reasonable doubt.

The proof of a simulation ordinarily begins with the admission of the simulating person given not so much in a judicial setting but more particularly outside of it, which admission may be given to trustworthy witnesses at an unsuspected time or was made known plainly by the manner of acting or behaving of the one who was responsible for the simulation. In fact, sometimes deeds have more value than words, without, however, overlooking the disposition, character and personality traits of the same person, together with his/her religious, moral and socio-cultural education and so on.

In reality, the proof becomes still more difficult, but not impossible, when the admission of the simulating person is lacking, namely, when the simulating person, although he/she has been properly and lawfully summoned, disdaining the authority of the church, has refused to stand before the tribunal both of the first instance or of appeal.

In such situation, one must investigate the motivating cause, which led the contracting person to simulate the action as he/she is said to have done. Such cause must be serious and proportionate to the cause leading to the contract.

Finally, dealing with and deciding about these matters, one must examine carefully the circumstances as well as the events both of place and time which preceded, accompanied and followed the celebration of marriage in which certain sure facts took place, and other evidences or complements as well as pursuant to canon 1679.

B. *Coram* Burke, 19 October 1995, *ME* 123 (1998) 605-607:

17 – *Proof of Simulation.* The following elements should converge to constitute juridic proof of exclusion: a) the confession of the person simulating, made at a period which is not to be considered suspect; b) the *explanation* of the simulation, drawn from the causes both of simulating and of contracting, with due consideration for the particular position of the simulator; c) the *confirmation* of the simulation, coming from the antecedent, concomitant and subsequent circumstances, and borne out by credible witnesses or trustworthy documents (cf. *coram* Pinto, 9 April 1973: *RRDec.,* 65:361).

18 – Even if there is a confession by the alleged simulator, the weight of this is obviously undermined if it has not backing from other sources; and particularly if it is contradicted by the other party.

At the same time it is the judges' duty to weigh apparent contradictions: between evidence given by witnesses, between what one party asserts and another denies, or between different statements of the same party. At times what seem to be inconsistencies may, on careful examination, find a plausible explanation in the peculiarities of character, difficulties in expressing self, etc. The core meaning must be sought, so as to see if apparent contradictions can be reconciled at a deeper level. The credibility or sincerity of the parties and witnesses is of course of importance, and testimonials can help in establishing this. But it is from adequate pondering of the Acts that the judge must arrive at his final conclusions.

C. *Coram* Giannecchini, 18 December 1996, *ME* 123 (1998) 572-575, n. 9:

[I]f the following can be had: 1°) the confession of the alleged simulator, mainly an extrajudicial one, confirmed by trustworthy witness; 2°) a proportionally grave reason for simulating clearly distinct from the reason for contracting; 3°) and, in addition, favorable circumstances that are specific, clear, and pressing as well as antecedent, concomitant, and subsequent to the marriage.

Then the proof of simulation is possible because all those elements taken together can form moral certitude in the mind of the judge about the fictitious or insufficient consent given.

Be it noted in that regard that: a) the judicial confession of the simulator himself if furnished with its constitutive notes and qualities, can have, since the new Code, the force of full proof, from the new Code (cf. cc. 1535-1536), but only when other elements are added to corroborate that confession. Serious consideration is to be given to the character and wit, the training, education, and the reasons for acting of the one confessing, as well as to his credibility, all of which provides a measure of the alleged confession weight (cf. *coram* Rogers, 26 January 1971, *RRDec.,* 63:61, n. 3); b) In what refers to the witnesses' depositions, we are warmed by one decision *coram* Pompedda that, besides their knowledge and credibility, "it is to be always kept in mind that deeds, surely, are more eloquent than words, but above all that the memory lapse of words, or assertions disconnected from the circumstances is of no value. Circumstances, indeed, explain the words and make them clear while providing the motive and adding the proof to the assertions (*coram* Pompedda, Romana, 13 February 1987, n. 6, unpublished); c) In what refers to the apt and grave cause for repudiating the perpetuity of the bond, it must be noted that it is easier to find it in the one who avers absolute freedom or in the recusant of any obligation when added, above all, to the repudiation of the teaching of the Church about marriage and to a style of life imbued with a hedonistic spirit cut off from morality. However, for those who foster a secular education, as they say, without any acrimony towards the teaching of the Church, which they know but do not approve of or accept, 'the obstacle for proof (is to be found) in getting through the transition from abstract convictions to the positive act of the will' (*coram* Pompedda, 23 April 1985, *RRDec.,* 77:217, n. 5) [this may be a case where canon 1099 is the more appropriate *caput nullitatis* to be considered].

D. *Coram* Stankiewicz, 29 May 1992, *RRDec.,* 84:314:

Direct proof arises from the extra-judicial confession by the simulator personally, offered in a non-suspect time to the other party and witnesses worthy of belief, correctly confirmed by all these later in the trial.

E. Even without direct proof, simulation can be proven. Rotal jurisprudence has consistently held that it sometimes happens that the alleged simulator's behavior is far stronger evidence than any verbal confession could be (cf. *coram* Felici, 24 April 1956, *RRDec.,* 48:403; *coram* Serrano, 31 March 1979, *RRDec.,* 71:148-157; *coram* Serrano, 27 November 1981, *RRDec.,* 73:592; *coram* Ragni, 19 July 1983, *RRDec.,* 75:467).

F. Antoni Stankiewicz, "De iurisprudentia Rotali recentiore circa simulationem totalem et partialem," *ME* 122: 189-234, 425-436.

However, those who think otherwise are at least forced to admit that nevertheless the distinction under its psychological aspect can have some importance: for the one who totally simulates, that is, as is better stated excludes marriage itself, is well conscious of his act of nullity since he so thoroughly does not want the marriage. The person, who partially simulates and excludes one or more of the essential goods of marriage, is able to think he is contracting marriage, since in someway his will is directed toward marriage. However, what must be avoided is that 'a merely psychological criterion' used in canonical simulation must not be confused with psychological or psychiatric simulation (ICD-9-CM V65.20) or with fictitious disturbances (DSM-IV 300.16; 19) with which experts in psychological and psychiatric matters deal.

After considering the above, one can understand why rotal jurisprudence *requires a consciousness of simulation in the case of total simulation* (emphasis mine) but does not do so in the case of partial simulation. For, the person who partially simulates, excluding the good of children, of fidelity, or of the sacrament, 'many times does not know that he or she is contracting invalidly. While the person who excludes marriage itself has the point of view that he or she is not giving matrimonial consent', (*coram* De Jorio, 29 April 1964, *RRDec.,* 56:314, n. 7) that is, 'the person must necessarily in the act of contracting be conscious of the fiction; otherwise, the person is feigning now and not earlier' (*coram* Pinto, 30 July 1969, *RRDec.,* 61:903, n. 5; *coram* Egan, *RRDec.,* 76:479, n. 4).

In other words, 'the person who simulates marriage itself by that very fact must know that he or she is contracting a null marriage,' (*coram* Pucci, 23 March 1966, *RRDec.,* 58:175, n. 10) while, 'the awareness of simulating can be absent in partial simulation' (*coram* Ferraro, 11 November 1980, *RRDec.,* 72:719, n. 7; *coram* Agustoni, 22 March 1983, *RRDec.,* 75:131, n. 3). [...] (See William H. Woestman, OMI, ed., *Simulation of Marriage Consent.* [Ottawa: St. Paul University, 2000] 171-211.)

G. As indicated in the rotal decisions quoted at the beginning of this section, the judge must assess the motive for simulation and for the marriage. According to the rotal auditor Serrano, the judge must consider not only the autonomy of the act of the will, but also its historicity, i.e., what goes before it, the personal biographies of the persons involved, the cultural context of the persons involved, the person's attitude before marriage, and who the person is in terms of education, environment, prematrimonial circumstances, etc. [cf. J. M. Serrano Ruiz, "El acto de voluntad por el que se crea o frustra el consentimiento matrimonial," *REDC* 51 (1994) 567-589.]

H. Furthermore, recent rotal jurisprudence has noted that the fact that persons stay in a union or even "work" on the union does not mean they did not simulate against marriage itself or some essential element of marriage (cf. *coram* Funghini, 17 April 1991, *RRDec.,* 83:246-247).

I. *Coram* Stankiewicz, 21 April 1983, *RRDec.,* 75:182:

In order to obtain proof of this with moral certitude, in addition to the simulator's confession, which is confirmed by trustworthy witnesses, one should consider the force of the pre-nuptial intention in the light of the post-nuptial behavior with respect to that intention [...] And one should examine whether there was proportionate reason for the simulation. Likewise, actions, which the law sometimes deems to be more eloquent than words, are to be taken into account.

V. Related Issues

A. Beal, John P. "The Substance of Things Hoped For: Proving Simulation of Matrimonial Consent," *Jur* 55 (1995) 745-793.

B. Johnson, John G. "Total Simulation in Recent Rotal Jurisprudence," *SC* 24 (1990) 383-425, includes a model law section starting on page 423.

C. Woestman, William H. *Simulation of Marriage Consent: Doctrine, Jurisprudence, Questionnaires* (Ottawa: St. Paul University, 2000).

D. Wrenn, Lawrence "Total Simulation," [from the decision *coram* Faltin issued on 18 January 1988, *RRDec.,* 80:3-6], *Law Sections* (Washington: CLSA, 1994) 49-53.

Chapter XI

Sources For Canon 1101, §2

Partial Simulation: Intention Against Children

Richard Soseman, JCL and Brian Rejsek, JCL
with Clarence Hettinger, Gerald T. Jorgensen PhD, JCL
and John P. Donovan, JCL

I. Pertinent Canons

A. See canons 1101, §1 and 1101, §2.

B. See the following allied canons: 1055, §1; 1056; 1057, §1; 1057, §2; 1061, §1, and 1096, §1.

C. Thus, in the grounds presented here, the marriage contract is deprived of its substantial formal object and so is necessarily injured in its being and consequently disappears. A marriage willed without offspring in its principles would be some kind of institute substantially different from that which the Creator willed and established and which the Church protects. Vatican Council II, relating firm Catholic teaching, taught this again.

II. Conciliar and/or Papal Teachings

A. Vatican II, *GS* 50:

> "marriage and married love are by nature ordered to the procreation and education of offspring." (Flannery, *Vatican Council II*, 1:953.)

B. Pope Paul VI, encyclical *Humanae vitae*, 25 July 1968, stated:

> [...] [H]usband and wife, through that mutual gift of themselves [in marriage], which is specific and exclusive to them alone, seek to develop that kind of personal union in which they complement one another in order to co-operate with God in the generation and education of new lives [...].

This love is above all fully *human* [...] It is not, then, merely a question of natural instinct or emotional drive. It is also, and above all, an act of the free will, [...].

And finally this love is *creative for life*, for it is not exhausted by the loving interchange of husband and wife, but also contrives to go beyond this to bring new life into being. 'Marriage and married love are by their character ordained to the procreation and bringing up of children. Children are the outstanding gift of marriage, and contribute in the highest degree to the parents' welfare'. [*GS* 50 (*AAS* 58 [1966] 1070-1072).]

Married love, therefore, requires of husband and wife the full awareness of their obligations in the matter of responsible parenthood [...]

Responsible parenthood, moreover, in the terms in which we use the phrase, retains a further and deeper significance of paramount importance which refers to the objective moral order instituted by God, – the order of which a right conscience is the true interpreter. (Flannery, *Vatican Council II*, 2:400-402.)

C. John Paul II, allocution to the Rota, 24 February 1981, "The Magisterium and Jurisprudence of the Tribunals of Apostolic See Protect the Family," stated:

The Church, therefore, also with its law and the exercise of its *judicial authority* can and must safeguard the values of marriage and the family to promote human persons and foster their dignity. (English trans. from Woestman, *Papal Allocutions*, 169.)

D. John Paul II, 22 November 1981, ap. exhort., *FC* 18-20 stated:

The family, which is founded and given life by love, is a community of persons: of husband and wife, of parents and children, of relatives. Its first task is to live with fidelity the reality of communion in a constant effort to develop an authentic community of persons [...].

The love between husband and wife [...] is given life and sustenance by an unceasing inner dynamism leading the family to ever deeper and more intense *communion*, which is the foundation and soul of the *community* of marriage and the family.

19. The first communion is the one which is established and which develops between husband and wife: by virtue of the covenant of married life, the man and the woman 'are no longer two but one flesh' [Mt 19:6; cf. Gen 2:24] and they are called to grow continually in their communion through day-today fidelity to their marriage promise of total mutual self-giving [...].

Such a communion is radically contradicted by polygamy: this, in fact, directly negates the plan of God which was revealed from the beginning, because it is contrary to the equal personal dignity of men and women who in matrimony give themselves with a love that is total and therefore unique and exclusive [...].

20. Conjugal communion is characterized not only by its unity but also by its indissolubility: 'As a mutual gift of two persons, this intimate union, as well as the good of children, imposes total fidelity on the spouses and argues for an unbreakable oneness between them' [*GS* 48]. (Flannery, *Vatican Council II*, 2:828-829.)

E. This teaching was repeated by John Paul II, 28 January 1982 address to the Rota, "Consent Makes Marriage, Its Defense by the Church":

The Council saw marriage as a covenant of love (see *GS* 48). This covenant is 'freely and consciously chosen, whereby man and woman accept the intimate community of life and love willed by God himself' (*FC* 11) [...].

Love is essentially a gift. Speaking of the act of love the Council envisages an act of giving, which is one, decisive, irrevocable because it is a total giving which wants to be and remain mutual and fruitful. [...]

[...] Marriage consent is an act of the will which signifies and involves a mutual giving which unites the spouses between themselves and at the same time binds them to the children which they may eventually have, with whom they constitute one family, one single home, a 'domestic Church' (*LG* 11). [English trans. from Woestman, *Papal Allocutions*, 172.]

F. John Paul II, allocution to the Rota, 30 February 1986, "The Human and Ecclesial Meaning of Marriage," stated:

> This is why Christian marriage is a sacrament making a kind of consecration to God (see *GS* 48). It is a ministry of love, which, through its testimony, makes visible the meaning of the divine love and the depth of conjugal gift lived in the Christian family. It is a commitment of paternity and maternity. The source of that is the reciprocal love of the divine persons; it is the most perfect and unrivalled image. This mystery will affirm itself and realize itself in every participation in the Church's mission, and it is in the Church that Christian spouses have to give proof of love and testify to love which they live between them, with and for their children, in that fundamental and irreplaceable ecclesial cell – the Christian family. (English trans. from Woestman, *Papal Allocutions*, 188-189.)

G. In the 1992 *Catechism of the Catholic Church*, concerning the Sacrament of Matrimony, we read:

> n. 1661 The sacrament of Matrimony signifies the union of Christ and the Church. It gives spouses the grace to love each other with the love with which Christ has loved his Church; the grace of the sacrament thus perfects the human love of the spouses, strengthens their indissoluble unity and sanctifies them on the way to eternal life (cf. Council of Trent: *DS* 1799).

> n. 1664 Unity, indissolubility and openness to fertility are essential to marriage. Polygamy is incompatible with the unity of marriage; divorce separates what God has joined together; the refusal of fertility turns married life away from its 'supreme gift', the child (*GS* 50, §1).

IV. Rotal Jurisprudence

A. *Coram* Funghini, 16 April 1986, *RRDec.,* 78:260-261:

This presumption (contrary to the petition for a declaration of nullity) will be very grave if the wife should have begotten not once but twice. Against this it is worth very little in the judicial forum to attribute the cause of the two conceptions to error and not to the will.

This is so not only because the presumption for the will stands in the external forum and for this reason the fact itself, i.e., two children, constitutes a strong argument in favor of the assumption. Just as sleeping witnesses cannot be used to prove an assertion which can be demonstrated as certain and true only through witnesses, so also an error of the will or of the human act, i.e., of the person, where a proof is to be set up about the same act. For when the scope of the whole question is to clarify a posited act of the will excluding offspring – what, in other words, was the will about undertaking offspring, if from it offspring was born – the judge cannot immediately believe in the error and attribute to it the power to remove the obstacle which directly signifies that will, otherwise it will be almost impossible for the judge to settle the matter in accordance with the truth. For everything can be attributed to error; not everything, however, which is attributed to error has force in a trial, especially in our case where, with the admission of error, the whole matter is easily confused and the judge cannot establish a distinction or a difference and say what is to be attributed to error or what in truth is to be attributed to the will. Add to this, since the error in the case coincides with the order established by nature and God, namely since it speaks of ordination to offspring to which marriage and conjugal acts are ordained by their nature, it [error] is to be given very little or rather no importance in our law unless it is clear from other sources and with certainty that there was another will, which seems to be entirely difficult.

> An individual rejects the good of offspring who decides through a positive act of the will that all offspring is to be excluded from the marriage to be entered. For through this positive exclusion the intrinsic ordination to the generation and education of offspring stated in canon 1013, §1, is denied.

Offspring certainly is not of the essence of marriage in regard to its effect, i.e., in regard to its real existence as a fruit of marriage, since it can be lacking not only through human will but also because of a natural defect; and in this case 'sterility neither impedes nor invalidates marriage' (c. 1068, §3).

It can, however, be lacking also because of the depraved human will and in this case attention is to be given to the well-known distinction, constantly received by the approved authors and jurisprudence, between the exclusion of offspring in its principles, i.e., between the exclusion of the right to acts *per se* apt for the generation of offspring and the exclusion of the exercise of the recognized and accepted right.

Generation is excluded in both cases, but matrimonial consent is infected only by the former. 'We contend that the spouse-to-be', it is read in a sentence *coram* De Jorio, 'who in entering marriage has the firm will to place or to allow no conjugal act, does not yield or accept the right to the body ordained to acts *per se* apt for the generation of offspring and that he contracts invalidly on this ground. On the contrary, an individual who would decide to place and allow conjugal acts, even though after a long time or on infertile days, is to be judged to have yielded and accepted the right but to have circumscribed its exercise, its use, within quite narrow limits, which is not sufficient to void matrimonial consent'.

B. *Coram* Funghini, 12 November 1986, *RRDec.,* 78:607:

Since matrimonial consent is the act through which both contractants yield and accept the perpetual and exclusive right to the body for acts *per se* apt for the generation of offspring, one contracts invalidly who in manifesting consent has the firm will not to place or allow any such act.

But the intention to postpone offspring or to limit the number of children does not fall under this censure because, in such case, the right to offspring is not denied and the required ordination to offspring is not in any way excluded even though the exercise of the right is limited.

Besides, the fact that offspring was not begotten can very well be compatible with an existing intention for offspring; for its absence is not to be attributed solely to human bad will since offspring can be lacking in spite of the spouses' vehement desire because of a natural defect which renders one or the other sterile.

C. *Coram* Giannecchini, 24 February 1987, *RRDec.,* 79:62:

Supported by the natural law, ecclesiastical law establishes that no one can contract a valid marriage if he should have presumed to exclude offspring. Evidently it is not a matter in the case about the fact of offspring or of the conception and birth of offspring but about the good of offspring, as they call it, i.e., about the right to be exchanged between the parties for acts *per se* apart for the generation of offspring. It is then a matter of offspring in its principles because marriage cannot exist without the intention of offspring and if anything contrary of this nature would be expressed in the consent which makes a marriage it would not be a true marriage.

D. *Coram* Stankiewicz, 29 October 1987, *RRDec.,* 79:598, 600-601:

Christian spouses through matrimonial consent, i.e., through an act of the will, mutually yield and accept one another in order to constitute a marriage (c. 1057, §2), i.e., the partnership of the whole of life which by it natural characteristics is ordered to the good of the spouses and to the generation and education of offspring (c. 1055, §1). By means of this ordination, especially 'to offspring to be procreated through some sexual cooperation' (c. 1096, §1), the conjugal partnership differs essentially from the other human partnerships and is individuated among the rest of juridical businesses. For this reason ordination to offspring undoubtedly enters into the irrevocable covenant of marriage through which the spouses-to-be, while they perfect the personal and full mutual donation, are united and bound to one another with a perpetual and exclusive bond with the offspring that might be procreated especially because, 'according to God's proposal marriage is the foundation of the great community of the family because the very institute of marriage and conjugal love are destined for the procreation and education of offspring in which they are consummated' (John Paul II, Apostolic Exhortation, *Familiaris consortio,* n. 14). [...]

6 – According to the jurisprudence of Our Forum, the temporary exclusion of offspring induces a narrowing of the conjugal right in the following cases:

a) If the temporary exclusion of offspring concurs with the will to exclude indissolubility, viz., when a spouse-to-be preserves the choice to break off the bond for some hypothesis and meanwhile decides to beget no offspring. For then the presumption stands for the exclusion of the right to conjugal acts *per se* apt for the generation of offspring or the good of offspring. Besides, this exclusion through a resolutive condition turns out to be perpetual and gives not only a presumption but even certainty to the exclusion of offspring.

b) If the temporary exclusion of offspring is made in the form of a condition, viz., if it is opposed to consent as a condition, which by its nature limits consent and consequently the conjugal right itself. For, since through a condition not only the use but also the right is always and necessarily excluded, marriage is vitiated in its substance not only of the use in perpetuity but also if it is excluded for a time. Indeed, since the right flowing from matrimonial consent is exclusive and perpetual by its very nature and for this reason does not admit limits, a condition to interrupt it even most briefly or even only for an act suffices for entirely destroying it.

c) If offspring is rejected through a pact between the spouses-to-be to avoid offspring even for a time. For a pact always enters into consent and vitiates it if it is contrary to the substance of marriage; nor is it bound to special forms since for the essence of a pact it is necessary that consent be had to the same opinion whether elicited by both contractants at the same time or determined by the proposal of one to which the other freely accedes and positively consents.

d) If the exclusion of offspring is accomplished through a positive act of the will having the force of a condition, because it itself also takes on the nature of a condition and begets the same effects as it. Therefore if there is certainty about this positive act of the will having the force of a condition, it is useless to inquire whether the right was refused only for a time or in perpetuity.

E. *Coram* Funghini, 7 July 1993, *RRDec.,* 85:522:

The mere delay of the procreation of offspring to a more favorable time for the spouses so that, for example, during the interim they might be able to establish a career or to have successful marriage or to recover good health or to prepare a more comfortable home, etc., is not enough to reject children. Bearing in mind the distinction between the right and the exercise of the right [...], in this case one ought to say that there is question about abuse or the incorrect use of the right legitimately handed over and accepted. Summarizing in short the principle, the doctrine and the jurisprudence [...]: 'the intention against the procreation of offspring can invalidate the marriage only when the contractant intends perpetually, or for a determinate or indeterminate amount of time, or hypothetically and conditionally to abstain completely from acts of themselves apt for the procreation of offspring fulfilled in a human manner, denying the right to them or deciding to complete them immorally, frustrating its ordination, using the right according to their own judgment'. (*coram* Palestro, decision of 29 January 1986, *RRDec.,* 78:78, n. 7.)

F. *Coram* de Lanversin, 26 January, 1994, *RRDec.,* 86:51:

When the exclusion of the good of offspring is invoked, a distinction is to be made in the first place between the true denial of the right in its principles and the intention to have children in the future, after certain circumstances have been verified. The former is the absolute refusal to the partner of the right to offspring, i.e., a determinate and prevailing intention – a positive act of the will having been elicited, a condition sometimes having been expressed – to bar, perpetually and absolutely children from the marriage here and now to be entered, so that the manifested consent is stripped of ordination to offspring, which is an intrinsic and essential mark of marriage itself (c. 1055, §1); the latter, however, directly regards rather the manner of acting and of using that right exchanged with the partner. One intention enters into consent and limits and invalidates it; the other is added to consent and remains external to it and cannot kill it.

For this reason, as often as there certainly is clarity about the purpose of the spouse-to-be to exclude children from the marriage absolutely and for an indefinite time, consent narrowed, i.e., vitiated, by this purpose or condition is not able to bring about the sacrament of marriage.

G. *Coram* Burke, 15 December 1994, *RRDec.,* 86:721:

The question of the exclusion of children '*ad tempus*' must be considered carefully. If this temporary exclusion is made by a mutual agreement between the parties, although the acting on the intention is left to a later time, it does not invalidate the marriage because the intention of children exists. Such an agreement will not always be prudent for the ultimate stability in addition to the happiness of the conjugal partnership. This, nevertheless, presupposing the use of means that are licit, in very many cases can correspond to that 'responsible paternity' which is explained in more recent teaching from the magisterium. [...]

On the contrary, if there is a unilateral exclusion of children for an indeterminate time (which certainly can become absolute if certain conditions are not met), then consent given is inadequate. Such an exclusion contaminates the nature of the self-giving of the spouse, and violates the right of the other party to find a spouse who is open to the possibility of procreating children. A great injury is inflicted upon the person, who enjoying the capacity of having children and desiring them would be obliged to remain under such an invalid bond.

H. *Coram* Stankiewicz, 24 July 1997:

But with the new legislation on marriage, which defines psychic incapacity in a more precise way (c. 1095), one may hold that not every kind of incapacity to give the matrimonial consent carries with it the incapacity of simulation, unless we deal with the incapacity arising from lack of a sufficient use of reason (c. 1095, §1), which simply makes a person incapable of a human act, that is both conscious and free [...].

Concerning the purpose of marriage to be the procreation of children (see can. 1055, §1), we are rightly taught that 'fecundity is a specific gift, a special mission of marriage because conjugal love by its nature is meant to be fecund', and 'a child is not added extrinsically to the mutual love of the spouses; the child emanates from the essence of this very love, being its fruit and completion'. (*CCC*, 2366)

For this reason, 'the Church, who 'stands for life' (John Paul II, Apostolic Exhortation *Familiaris Consortio*, 30) teaches that 'it is necessary that every use of marriage should be in itself directed to the procreation of human life'.' (Paul VI, Encyclical *Humanae Vitae,* 11) In fact, 'this doctrine, which has been proclaimed frequently by the teaching of the Church, if founded on the indissoluble bond decreed by God, which no man has the power to break, between the meaning of unity and the meaning of procreation, both of which are included in the conjugal act'. (ibid. 12) Therefore, the spouses, 'called to be givers of life, share in the creative power and paternity of God' (see Eph 3, 14-15; Mt 23, 9); they 'know that, in the task of transmitting and rearing human life, which is to be considered as their special mission, they are collaborators of God's love and, as it were, his interpreters', from which work 'they will fulfill their task with human and Christian responsibility'. (*GS* 50; *CCC*, 2367)

What should be said of the case of spouse who, when they are about to enter marriage, prompted by anxiety over the transmission of new life or other reasons, decide to avoid the birth of children for a set period of time when exercising the right to the act of conjugal life, while maintaining the power of separating of their own will the principle of unity of conjugal acts from the principle of procreation? To carry out this intention is not beyond their powers, unlike, for instance, the attempt of changing the natural purpose for procreation of the marriage institution, which they cannot accomplish directly, unless they reject the very marriage communion that has children as its purpose. (c. 1096, §1; *coram* the underwritten *Ponens*, Decision of 7 March 1991.) But in a temporary exclusion of procreation, one must always explore whether the temporary postponement of children has limited the very conjugal right, at least for a time, or whether it has only diverted the right fully given and accepted from its correct use by way of a temporary abuse thereof. Indeed, the denial of the integral right or duty to conjugal acts that are in themselves suitable to the procreation of children, to which marriage is intended of its very nature and by which the spouses are made one flesh (c. 1061, §1), namely perpetually united on account of the perpetuity of the marriage bond (c. 1134), affects the matrimonial consent and makes it invalid. This, however, is not achieved by a simple curtailment of the exercise of the right or duty thereof, which therefore becomes simply an abuse and does not affect the validity of consent.

IV. Types of Proofs Required

A. *Coram* Palestro, 29 January 1986, *RRDec.,* 78:79:

The proposal, i.e., the firm will, which an individual might have brought in giving consent, not to generate offspring, i.e., neither to place nor to allow on his own body acts *per se* apt for the generation of offspring until he has tested the stability of conjugal life, invalidates marriage or at least suspends its validity if the very yielding and accepting was delayed but it does not invalidate if the use, i.e., the exercise, of the granted and accepted right was denied for a time.

But it is indeed a difficult matter to distinguish one from the other. However, the burden of proving that a positive act of the will was elicited by which the yielding of the right to conjugal acts, i.e., acts *per se* apt for offspring was postponed, lies on the Petitioner all the more because 'marriage enjoys the favor of the law'; for which reason one is to stand for the validity of the marriage until the contrary is proved.

B. *Coram* Colagiovanni, 8 July 1986, *RRDec.,* 78:430:

Of itself, the exclusion of the very right to offspring even if for a time invalidates matrimonial consent, but it must be fully proved that the simulator precisely and directly willed to deny that right to the marriage and/or to the partner. This is indeed not gathered only from general words but from very strict arguments taken from the confession of the simulator, from the confirmation of the depositions of witnesses, and most importantly from a motive grave enough and apt for denying such a right even temporarily.

C. Scholarly Opinion: Antonio Royo Marín, *Teología Moral II, Los Sacramentos* (Madrid: BAC, 1984) 587-588.

Consent, in order to be valid and legitimate, must fulfill certain conditions and posses certain qualities. The fundamental ones include four: it must be true, or internal, deliberate and free, mutual, and externally manifested. The internal will of the contracting parties must truly exist, and precisely ordered to that which constitutes the essence itself of the contract, that is, to give and accept the right over their own bodies ordered to the acts in themselves apt for the generation of children. Therefore, if consent should be directed exclusively toward another object, no true marriage would exist. These ends which are secondary or extraneous to marriage do not invalidate it unless they are unique and exclusive, that is, when marriage is contracted only for them, excluding its primary and essential object. This internal consent is always presumed by law when an external manifestation has been produced. Because of this, it is not enough to manifest in the external forum, even through oath, that one did not have the intention to contract marriage, it is necessary to prove this lack of intention, which is very difficult in practice. It is understood that the person who simulates contracting marriage without having the intention to contract it commits a most grave sin against truth and justice, unless they have done this for a most grave cause.

D. Scholarly opinion: Paulo Moneta, *"Matrimonio" in Il Diritto nel Mistero della Chiesa. vol. III.* 2nd ed. (Rome: Pontificia Universitá Lateranense, 1992) 241-242:

Nullity is more easily recognized when the exclusion of offspring is made in a conditional form, such as when it is proposed to have a child only after achieving a certain level of harmony or of confidence in their conjugal life or also to the gaining of a certain economic position. The generation of children is remanded, in these cases, to an undetermined time, being subordinated to the attainment of a situation, which may also never come into being. The proposal not to have children can, therefore, in fact reveal itself as perpetual and carry with it a negation of the *ordinatio ad prolem* applied to the entire married life. Also a simple temporal limitation of children (which happens, for example, in the case of those who do not intend to have children for the first years of marriage, or who propose to have a single child, excluding for the rest of the conjugal life other offspring) can assume an importance which invalidates marriage when it can be demonstrated that effectively, for the period of time under consideration, there existed the will to deny to the other party in an absolute mode the right to demand the completion of acts in a way normally open to the generation of children. Certainly, in similar cases, it is not easy, concretely, to determine when there is an exclusion of the right, and not simply of the use or exercise of this right. As we have already pointed out, this deals with a very abstract but distinctive criteria, which is difficult to reduce in human and psychological reality as a concrete matrimonial will: this is moreover strictly tied to a concept of marriage which privileges the contractual concept of the rights and duties of marriage which the spouses must reciprocally confer on each other, rather than the profound nature of interpersonal communion which arises between them.

V. Related Issues

A. Distinction between denial of the right itself, and the abuse of the right in Antoni Stankiewicz, "*De Iurisprudentia Rotali Recentiore circa simulationem totalem et partialem,*" *ME* 122 (1997) 501:

1. Sometimes among Rota decisions one can find a statement about the uselessness of the aforesaid distinction: "the distinction between the exclusion of the right and the exercise of this right, which was very highly influential among the learned, more so, however, in jurisprudence, affords no usefulness for deciding cases in which the marriage was accused of nullity on the grounds of the exclusion of the good of offspring by one or both parties.

2. Certainly this distinction used to be opposed by some, especially under the old code, namely, that "it rested on neither natural nor canon law and was foreign to the mind of St. Thomas, who distinguished only between intention and fact," even that "Sanchez was led into error by the words, 'because the existence of a thing does not depend on its use'."

3. Moreover, such a distinction "is an abstract concept, which cannot constitute an instrument for measuring the swayings and modifications of the human will;" "it is a circumlocution whereby the judge persuades himself that he has judged correctly," and "a criterion deduced from it fails when the use of the right is excluded perpetually."

Chapter XII

Sources For Canon 1101, §2

Partial Simulation: Intention Against Fidelity

Ronny E. Jenkins, JCD

I. Pertinent Canons

A. See canons 1101, §1 and 1101, §2.

B. See the following allied canons: 1055, §1; 1056; 1057, §1.

II. Conciliar and/or Papal Teaching

A. Pius XI, *Casti connubii*, n. 19, 31 December 1930, *AAS* 22 [1930] 546:

> The second blessing of matrimony which We said was mentioned by St. Augustine, is the blessing of conjugal honor which consists in the mutual fidelity of the spouses in fulfilling the marriage contract, so that what belongs to one of the parties by reason of this contract sanctioned by divine law, may not be denied to him or permitted to any third person; nor may there be conceded to one of the parties anything which, being contrary to the rights and laws of God and entirely opposed to matrimonial faith, can never be conceded.

B. Pius XI, *Casti connubii*, n. 20, 31 December 1930, *AAS* 22 [1930] 546-547:

> Wherefore, conjugal faith, or honor, demands in the first place the complete unity of matrimony which the Creator Himself laid down in the beginning when He wished it to be not otherwise than between one man and one woman. And although afterwards this primeval law was relaxed to some extent by God, the Supreme Legislator, there is no doubt that the law of the Gospel fully restored that original and perfect unity, and abrogated all dispensations as the words of Christ and the constant teaching and action of the Church show plainly. With reason, therefore, does the Sacred Council of Trent solemnly declare: "Christ Our Lord very clearly taught that in this bond two persons only are to be united and joined together when He said:

'Therefore they are no longer two, but one flesh'." [Conc. Trid., sess. xxiv.]

C. Vatican Council II, *GS* 48:

> By "its" very nature, the institution of matrimony itself and conjugal love are ordained for the procreation and education of children, and find in them their ultimate crown. Thus a man and a woman, who by their compact of conjugal love "are no longer two, but one flesh" (Mt 19:ff), render mutual help and service to each other through an intimate union of their persons and of their actions. Through this union they experience the meaning of their oneness and attain to it with growing perfection day by day. As a mutual gift of two persons, this intimate union and the good of the children impose total fidelity on the spouses and argue for an unbreakable oneness between them. (Flannery, *Vatican Council II*, 1:950.)

D. Vatican Council II, *GS* 48:

> Christ the Lord abundantly blessed this many-faceted love, welling up as it does from the fountain of divine love and structured as it is on the model of His union with His Church. For as God of old made Himself present to His people through a covenant of love and fidelity, so now the Savior of men and the Spouse of the Church comes into the lives of married Christians through the sacrament of matrimony. He abides with them thereafter so that just as He loved the Church and handed Himself over on her behalf, (6) the spouses may love each other with perpetual fidelity through mutual self-bestowal. (Flannery, *Vatican Council II*, 1:950.)

E. John Paul II, 1999 allocution to the Rota, 21 January 1999, *AAS* 91 [1999] 622-627, n. 3:

> *Amor coniugalis,* therefore, is not only and not primarily a feeling, but is essentially a commitment to the other person, a commitment made by a precise act of will. It is this commitment which gives *amor* (love) the quality of *coniugalis* (conjugal). Once a commitment has been made and accepted through consent, love *becomes* conjugal and never loses this character. Here the fidelity of love, which is rooted in the freely assumed

obligation, comes into play. (English trans. from Woestman, *Papal Allocutions*, 250.)

F. John Paul II, *FC* 19:

19. The first communion is the one which is established and which develops between husband and wife: By virtue of the covenant of married life, the man and woman 'are no longer two but one flesh' (*Mt.* 19:6 and cf. *Gen.* 2:24) and they are called to grow continually in their communion through day-today fidelity to their marriage promise of total mutual self-giving. (Flannery, *Vatican Council II*, 2:829.)

G. *Catechism of the Catholic Church*, n. 1611:

Seeing God's covenant with Israel in the image of exclusive and faithful married love, the prophets prepared the Chosen People's conscience for a deepened understanding of the unity and indissolubility of marriage. The books of Ruth and Tobit bear moving witness to an elevated sense of marriage and to the fidelity and tenderness of spouses. Tradition has always seen in the Song of Solomon a unique expression of human love, insofar as it is a reflection of God's love – a love "strong as death that many waters cannot quench."

H. *Catechism of the Catholic Church*, nn. 1646-1647:

By its very nature conjugal love requires the inviolable fidelity of the spouses. This is the consequence of the gift of themselves that they make to each other. Love seeks to be definitive; it cannot be an arrangement 'until further notice'. The 'intimate union of marriage, as a mutual giving of two persons, and the good of the children, demand total fidelity from the spouses and require an unbreakable union between them'. The deepest reason is found in the fidelity of God to his covenant, in that of Christ to his Church. Through the sacrament of Matrimony the spouses are enabled to represent this fidelity and witness to it. Through the sacrament, the indissolubility of marriage receives a new and deeper meaning.

III. Rotal Jurisprudence

A. *Coram* Funghini, 23 October 1991, *RRDec.,* 83:604:

The intention of not being faithful wounds and offends not only the good of the spouses, but impedes the consortium of the whole of life. And it does this not because the spouse sinfully uses his or her sexual faculty, but because when giving consent, the spouse does not hand over entirely to the other that to which he or she has an exclusive and perpetual right.

B. *Coram* Turnaturi, 18 April 1996, *RRDec.,* 88:340:

Generally, the good of fidelity is excluded when one or both of the contractants positively reject the obligation to be faithful to the other, or when they do not assume the obligation in this way. Nor is it necessary that the spouses hand over the *ius in corpus* to a third party. It is enough for them to refuse to hand over the exclusive right to the other spouse by reserving to him or herself the right to commit adultery.

IV. Types of Proofs Required

A. As with all simulation cases, there are four elements of proof required when using the ground of an exclusion of the *bonum fidei*: confession of the simulator(s), witness corroboration, motive for the simulation, and circumstantial evidence before, at the time of, and after consent.

B. See *Types of Proofs Required* sections in other partial simulation "Sources."

V. Related Issues

A. When deciding cases based on an exclusion of fidelity, one should keep in mind the development of jurisprudence on the issue over the past several decades. There has been a notable broadening of the applicability of this ground to concrete situations. The change is expressed well in a decision *coram* Stankiewicz of 21 April 1983, *RRDec.,* 75:179-180, who writes:

A major question is whether, for the exclusion of fidelity, it is necessary that the right to sexual acts be given to a third party, besides one's spouse; or whether it suffices that there be a positive refusal to hand over to one's spouse the exclusive power over the body; likewise, whether it is sufficient that a person proposes to reserve the right to commit adultery or to have sexual relations with whomever he wishes.

The jurisprudence handed down in the interpretation of this ground of nullity generally required that there be a positive act of the will by which the exclusive right to the body, which belongs only to the spouse, is handed over to a third party. Thus it would not be sufficient for nullity that a person intends to violate with others the exclusive conjugal right, or that he intends to continue with a particular third party a love affair that was already going on before the wedding. [...]

But a more recent jurisprudence 'in the light of an equitable interpretation of the notion of the *bonum fidei* no longer requires, as it did in the past, that by a positive act of the will the exclusive right to the body be conceded to a third person besides the spouse [citing Parisella]'. [...] In other words: to exclude the *bonum fidei* it is not required 'that the right be given to a lover'; but it suffices that the obligation of maintaining fidelity be rejected (*coram* Pinto, October 20, 1978, n. 7). [Private translation]

B. Another important element of jurisprudence on the *bonum fidei* is that a simple intention to commit adultery does not invalidate a marriage. This is because the intention to commit adultery, however odious and morally objectionable, does not necessarily exclude the obligation to fidelity so much as abuse the fulfillment of it. Adultery is a sin. As such it is not necessarily invalidating of consent. (See Stankiewicz decision cited immediately above in letter A – n. 5, 180-181.)

C. See Ronny E. Jenkins, "Faithful in All Things Conjugal: Recent Developments in the *Bonum Fidei*," *CLSA Proceedings* 61 (1999) 179-194.

Chapter XIII

Sources For Canon 1101, §2

PARTIAL SIMULATION: INTENTION AGAINST THE GOOD OF THE SPOUSES

Ronny E. Jenkins, JCD

I. Pertinent Canons

A. See canons 1101, §1 and 1101, §2.

B. See the following allied canons: 1055, §1; 1056; 1057, §1; and 1057, §2.

II. Conciliar and/or Papal Teaching

A. Vatican Council *GS* 48, *AAS* 58 (1966) 1067-1068:

> By its very nature the institution of marriage and married love are ordered to the procreation and education of the offspring and it is in them that it finds its crowning glory. Thus the man and woman, who "are no longer two but one" (Mt. 19:6), help and serve each other by their marriage partnership; they become conscious of their unity and experience it more deeply from day to day. The intimate union of marriage, as a mutual giving of two persons, and the good of the children demand total fidelity from the spouses and require an unbreakable unity between them. (Flannery, *Vatican Council II*, 2:950.)

B. John Paul II, allocution to the Rota, January 27, 1997:

> In a vision of authentic personalism, the Church's teaching implies the affirmation that marriage can be established as *an indissoluble bond* between the persons of the spouses, a bond essentially ordered to the good of the spouses themselves and of their children. Consequently, that conception of the conjugal union which would put this possibility in doubt and lead to a denial of the existence of marriage whenever problems arise in

the shared life of the spouses, would clash with a true personalist dimension. At the root of such an attitude we see an *individualistic culture*, which is antithetical to a true personalism [...] (English trans. from Woestman, *Papal Allocutions*, 242.)

C. John Paul II, allocution to the Rota, February 1, 2001:

The Church's Magisterium and canonical legislation abound with references to the natural character of marriage. In *Gaudium et spes* the Second Vatican Council, after first stating that 'God himself is the author of marriage and has endowed it with various benefits and ends' (n. 48), addresses several problems of conjugal morality by referring to 'objective criteria drawn from the nature of the human person and of his acts' (n. 51). For their part, both of the Codes I promulgated affirm in their definition of marriage that the '*consortium totius vitae*' is 'by its very nature ordered to the good of the spouses and the procreation and education of children' (*CIC*, c. 1055; *CCEO*, c. 776, §1). (English trans. from Woestman, *Papal Allocutions*, 260.)

D. John Paul II, allocution to the Rota, February 1, 2001:

[...] Marriage and the family are inseparable, because the masculinity and femininity of the married couple are constitutively open to the gift of children. Without this openness there could not even be a good of the spouses worthy of the name. (English trans. from Woestman, *Papal Allocutions*, 263.)

E. John Paul II, ap. exhort., *FC* 19:

This conjugal communion sinks its roots in the natural complementarity that exists between man and woman and is nurtured through the personal willingness of the spouses to share their entire life project, what they have and what they are: For this reason such communion is the fruit and the sign of a profoundly human need. But in the Lord Christ God takes up this human need, confirms it, purifies it and elevates it, leading it to perfection through the sacrament of matrimony: the Holy Spirit who is poured out in the sacramental celebration offers Christian couples the gift of a new communion of love that is the living and real image of that unique unity which makes of the church the indivisible mystical body of the Lord Jesus. (Flannery, *Vatican Council II*, 2:29.)

III. Rotal Jurisprudence

A. NOTE:

There are no cases judged to date in the Rota based on an exclusion of the good of the spouses. When the Rota has spoken of the *bonum coniugum* it has done so in cases concerning the inability to assume the essential obligations of marriage, one of which is the good of the spouses. This does not mean that lower tribunals cannot use the ground of simulation against the good of the spouses.

When using the ground of an exclusion of the good of the sacrament, general rotal jurisprudence on simulation of consent should be followed. However, since there are no rotal decisions that have actually judged a case on simulation of the bonum coniugum there is very little jurisprudence available on the matter. Consequently, relevant sections from other law sections on simulation should be consulted. Still, the Rota has addressed the notion of the good of the spouses in cases judged on other grounds; namely, the inability to assume an essential obligation of marriage. The following citations are taken from cases based on an inability to assume, and not from rotal decisions addressing exclusion of the good of the spouses.

B. *Coram* Bruno, 16 December 1988, *RRDec.,* 80:747, n. 3:

Some essential rights and obligations [of marriage] can be drawn out of canons 1012-1013 (cf. cc. 1055-1056 of the new code), but it is difficult to establish a list. Among them can be counted: a) the *ius in corpus* for the procreation and education of children; b) the good of fidelity and the sacrament, which are essential properties of marriage; c) the good of the spouses, which, in light of the Second Vatican Council finds a place in the new code, and is clearly in harmony with the former theological and canonical doctrine.

C. *Coram* Funghini, 23 October 1991, *RRDec.,* 83:604, n. 5:

In order for there to be true and valid consent, it is necessary that a giving and receiving [of persons] takes place which is mutual, integral, total, indivisible, without any reservation with respect to either its quality or the time and intensity of it, interpersonal, and irrevocable. Therefore, if this is intentionally missing or if the giving [of self] is defective, consent is vitiated. The intention of not being faithful not only wounds and offends the good of the spouses, but it also impedes the consortium of the whole of life.

D. *Coram* Jarawan, 24 November 1993, *RRDec.,* 85:696, n. 2:

The parties, from the moment of the celebration of the marriage, must be ready to assume the essential obligations of perpetuity and fidelity, to hand over to one another the right to acts per se apt for the generation of children, and also be suitably strong for promoting the good of the spouses, which is an essential element of marriage entailing the ability of joining with one's future spouse in an interpersonal relationship that is at least tolerable.

E. *Coram* Ragni, 6 February 1996, *RRDec.,* 88:95, n. 5:

As far as the essential obligations of marriage are concerned [...] they are expressed in the current *Code of Canon Law* in this way: a) exclusive and perpetual consortium of life (c. 1056); the good of the spouses (c. 1055, §1); c) the consortium of life between a man and a woman who are capable by law (cc. 1055 and 1057); the generation and education of children, or the good of children (cc. 1055, §1 and 1101, §2). It should be noted here that according to traditional doctrine the essential obligations of marriage are contained in the threefold goods of marriage (children, sacrament and fidelity). In the current code, however, one also finds the good of the spouses (c. 1055, §1), which includes several elements including the right to a communion of life.

F. *Coram* Turnaturi, 14 March 1996, *RRDec.,* 88:240, n. 22:

The capacity to assume the conjugal obligations does not concern only the three essential goods of marriage; namely, fidelity, children, and sacrament, but also the ability to establish a consortium of the whole of life directed at the good of the spouses, which is an essential element of marriage entailing the intra personal psychic capacity of establishing an interpersonal relationship with one's partner that is at least tolerable.

G. *Coram* Bruno, 17 May 1996, *RRDec.,* 88:390, n. 6:

The good of the spouses embraces the acceptance and fulfillment of all the obligations that make real the intimate conjoining and integration of persons in mutual assistance in the spiritual, material and social order such that a true conjugal life can be established and peacefully and progressively carried out.

H. *Coram* Huber, 3 July 1996, *RRDec.,* 88:497, n. 5:

Not a few authors call on the teaching of the Second Vatican Council when trying to establish what are the essential elements of the right to a communion of life. The Council defined marriage as an intimate community, the giving of two persons one to the other. From this description of marriage it can be difficult to draw out the essential elements of the right to a communion of life. Yet, these elements seem to be handed down to us through this text: 'Thus a man and a woman, who by their compact of conjugal love 'are no longer two, but one flesh' (Mt. 19:ff), render mutual help and service to each other through an intimate union of their persons and of their actions. Through this union they experience the meaning of their oneness and attain to it with growing perfection day by day (*Gaudium et spes*, n. 48). There is no one who considers the notion of 'mutual help' to include only assistance in matters domestic and sexual. Rather, it is a question of that profound assistance which leads the spouses to realize a better and more blessed life, and a union in which each one completes the other.

I. *Coram* López-Illana, 10 October 1996, *RRDec.,* 88:606, n. 12:

A key moment in establishing and carrying out the good of the spouses is the capacity of the spouses to engage in sexual relations in a way skillfully described and thoroughly taught by the Supreme Pontiff, John Paul II, with these words: 'Consequently sexuality, by means of which man and woman give themselves to one another through the acts which are proper and exclusive to spouses, is by no means something purely biological, but concerns the innermost being of the human person as such. It is realized in a truly human way only if it is an integral part of the love by which a man and a woman commit themselves totally to one another until death. The total physical self-giving would be a lie if it were not the sign and fruit of a total personal self-giving, in which the whole person, including the temporal dimension, is present: If the person were to withhold something or reserve the possibility of deciding otherwise in the future, by this very fact he or she would not be giving totally'. (*Familiaris consortio*, n. 11.)

J. *Coram* Boccafola, 12 December 1996, *RRDec.,* 88:796-797, n. 5:

After the Second Vatican Council, the teaching was solidified which requires [of the spouses] not only the capacity to assume the three obligations [of marriage] but also the ability to enter and sustain a consortium of life directed at the good of the spouses. This obligation has been considered by some to be a fourth good (cf. Pinto), and by others to be an essential element in line with c. 1101, n. 2.

IV. Types of Proofs Required

A. NOTE:

The proof of exclusion of the good of the spouses should follow the required proof for all simulation cases. Consequently, a confession is necessary. The confession should be corroborated by witness testimony. A motive for simulating must be demonstrated. Finally, circumstantial evidence before, at the time of, and after consent must also argue in favor of the alleged simulation. Since the Rota has not judged cases based on the exclusion of the good of the spouses, there is no rotal jurisprudence available that addresses any specific aspects of proving the ground. Consequently, it is necessary to consult jurisprudence on proving other types of simulation and apply those principles to this specific ground. What follows, then, are very general notions about proving simulation. Other sections of this work will provide more sources.

B. *Coram* Colagiovanni, 17 January 1984, *RRDec.,* 76:18-19, n. 4:

It may be difficult to prove [an inner intention] in the external forum since judicial knowledge of an internal act must be well founded through logical arguments, through indubitable and unequivocal facts, through circumstances, presumptions, *adminicula* and *indicia*, all taken together and made at once into a coherent structural argument.

C. *Coram* Funghini, 16 January 1991, *RRDec.,* 83:23, n. 9:

Proof of simulation is difficult since it requires investigation of internal facts which reside in the heart of the one alleged to have simulated, and since it is a question of overcoming opposing presumption established by law (c. 1086, §1 and c. 1014). The weightiest proof arises out of a judicial confession, corroborated extrajudicially by credible witnesses from a non-suspect time and reported by them in a tribunal. Additionally, a grave and adequate motive for simulating is necessary, which should be distinct from the motive for contracting the marriage. Circumstantial evidence prior to, at the time of and subsequent to the marriage is necessary. It should be consistent with the statements and arguments of the Petitioner. Such evidence should also render the simulation morally certain and not merely possible or probable.

D. *Coram* Davino, 18 April 1991, *RRDec.,* 83:270, nn. 4-5:

The proof of simulation in the external forum is difficult since a contrary presumption stands in the way. The necessity arises, then, that the simulation or limitation of the consent be proven with invincible arguments. In this way, proof first arises out of the confession of the simulator. The confession should not be simply judicial (which does not supply full proof) but also extra judicial (from a non-suspect time) and corroborated by credible witnesses. If the confession is lacking or inconsistent, it will be more difficult to prove the existence of the external manifestation of the act of the will that vitiated the consent. Careful investigation into a grave and proportionate motive should be made.

Chapter XIV

Sources For Canon 1101, §2

Partial Simulation: Intention Against Indissolubility

Gerald T. Jorgensen, PhD, JCL

I. Pertinent Canons

A. See canons 1101, §1 and 1101, §2.

B. See allied canons 1055, §1; 1055, §2; 1056; 1057, §1; and 1057, §2.

C. Although the law only implies a distinction between 'total' and 'partial' simulation, jurisprudence has traditionally differentiated between these two types of simulation (see *coram* de Lanversin, 18 February 1984, *RRDec.,* 76:100). Total simulation occurs when the content of marital consent itself (canons 1055, §1; 1057) is excluded through 'a positive act of the will'. Partial simulation occurs when some essential property or element of marriage is excluded through 'a positive act of the will'. Total simulators may be aware that a marriage does not exist while partial simulators may believe that a subjectively defined marriage does exist. For example, a person can partially simulate by excluding the perpetuity of the bond, that is to say, the *bonum sacramenti*. Either kind of simulation invalidates the marriage.

II. Conciliar and/or Papal Teaching

A. Vatican Council II, *GS* 48:

> It [marriage] is an institution confirmed by the divine law and receiving its stability, even in the eyes of society, from the human act by which the partners mutually surrender themselves to each other; for the good of the partners, of the children, and of society this sacred bond no longer depends on human decision alone. For God himself is the author of marriage and has endowed it with various benefits and with various ends in view: [...]. (Flannery, *Vatican Council II*, 2:950.)

B. Vatican Council II, *GS* 50:

But marriage is not merely for the procreation of children: its nature as an indissoluble covenant between two people and the good of the children demand that the mutual love of the partners be properly manifested, that it grow and mature. Even in cases where despite the intense desire of the spouses there are no children, marriage still retains its character of being a whole manner and communion of life and preserves its value and indissolubility. (Flannery, *Vatican Council II*, 2:954.)

C. See *Conciliar and/or Papal Teaching* section for "Sources for Canon 1099: Determining Error – Indissolubility" for additional resources.

III. Rotal Jurisprudence

A. *Coram* Defilippi, 16 February 1998, *ME* 126 [2001] 110-111:

Even if the marriage about which nullity is alleged was celebrated under the regime of the regime of the abrogated Code (and therefore a judgment would need to be formally made according to that Code), yet recourse to the Code in force at the moment was legitimate since the norm which is in force today, both in reality and in substance, hardly differs from the previous and may perhaps be clearer.

B. *Coram* Faltin, 16 April 1997, *ME* 123 [1998] 252-255:

7 – The legal principles to be invoked to explain the doctrine of simulation are found already in the Roman law. Iavolenus in fact teaches: 'In all matters where power of [personal] control is exchanged, the intentional intervention of both parties is required, in fact … no matter what the reason for entering the contract, unless the wills of both give their assent, it is impossible to bring to fruition what is being initiated' (D. 44, 7, 55). From this principle, Gaius correctly concludes concerning marriage: 'A simulated wedding is of no value whatever' (see D. 23, 2, 30).

8 – These principles of Roman law, inherent in natural law itself, not even the ecclesiastical legislation, which we are using here, can overlook or abrogate when it establishes that a valid contract cannot subsist if the consent of a contracting party is simulated or feigned, namely when all the external things seem to be regularly present,

while instead the inner will of the contracting party refuses to accept the obligations which stem from the very contract.

This law determines that, in order to have a marriage between the parties, a consent 'properly manifested between persons legally capable, that no human power can substitute, is required [...] whereby the husband and the wife give and receive to and from each other in order to establish the marriage' (cf. canons 1057; 1055, §1, together with *Romana coram* the undersigned *Ponens* on 21 October 1989 in *RRDec.,* 81:606, n. 4). Therefore, even if 'the inner intention to consent is presumed to be in conformity with the words or the signs used in the celebration of a wedding', legitimately and with reason the Legislator has determined to established the principle that the marriage is invalid 'if one or both of the parties, by a positive act of the will, exclude marriage itself or an essential element or an essential property of marriage' (canon 1101, §§1-2). From this there follows already that 'a feigning or simulation of marriage consent takes place when the contracting party does indeed properly utter the words expressing the consent, but he/she does not mean them internally' (cf. Gasparri, *De Matrimonio*, vol. II, n. 814). This simulation may be about 'marriage itself', [...] in such case we have total simulation; or [it may be about] 'some essential element or some essential property of marriage', and in such case we have a simulation, which is called partial in the sense that by acting in this manner he/she wants to enter a contract, but rejects some obligations deriving from the contract (cf. *coram* Bruno, 21 March 1980, *RRDec.,* 72:200-201).

C. *Coram* Burke, 19 October 1995, *ME* 123 (1998) 603:

13 – Simulated consent where, despite the apparent external acceptance of marriage in its integrity, some essential and constitutive element or property is fully and deliberately excluded in a person's intention is obviously inadequate to establish a true marriage. 'While the simulator professes by words or external signs to accept the marital covenant, he or she by internal intention rejects some essential element of the alliance. This interior rejection of the covenant means that he does not really give himself to the other party in a total conjugal donation. The simulator consents at most to a partial donation of his or her sexuality, by excluding either the perpetuity of the gift, or its uniqueness, or its procreative orientation. Such a cut-down and mutilated self-gift is ineffectual for constituting

marriage. Whoever gives himself to another partially, does not give himself maritally to him or her' (decision of 12 December 1988, *coram* the undersigned, *RRDec.,* 80:737).

D. *Coram* Defilippi, 22 November 1996, *RRDec.,* 88:749, n. 7:

7 – Exclusion of the good of the sacrament, as we have seen eloquently written in a case before Pompedda, 'from the psychological point of view can come about on two grounds. Either the one contracting marriage positively and directly excludes permanence, even though he wishes to contract marriage; or the contracting party positively and directly anticipates and intends marriage without indissolubility, since he recognizes it only as a matrimonial custom or only accepts it as such' (*coram* Pompedda, 17 July 1989, *RRDec.,* 81:508s, n. 4).

Canon 1101, §2 treats of the first hypothesis while the second is covered by canon 1099.

E. *Coram* Ewers, 28 July 1969, *RRDec.,* 61:896:

According to the constant jurisprudence of our Tribunal, whenever a person reserves to him or herself, by a positive act of the will, the faculty or liberty or possibility of obtaining a divorce, that person excludes, by that very fact, the perpetuity of the bond. [...]

Similarly the intention either to enter a dissoluble marriage or to contract marriage as an experiment vitiates the sacred covenant; for the joining of man and woman which is entered only for a time, is not and should not be called a marriage.

F. *Coram* Pompedda, 23 January 1971, *RRDec.,* 63:53-54:

[Indissolubility can be excluded] because the spouse, knowing the true doctrine on marriage, nevertheless contracts it with the understanding that he has the option, albeit hypothetical, of dissolving the bond and recovering his former status of full freedom.

G. *Coram* Pompedda, 23 January 1971, *RRDec.,* 63:53-54:

[Indissolubility can be excluded] because the party formulates his own doctrine on marriage [realizing or not that it contravenes the official teaching of the Church on indissolubility], a doctrine from which the idea of indissolubility is absent, and to which he adheres totally with both intelligence and willpower, so that when marrying he meant to celebrate marriage in that very manner and not otherwise.

H. *Coram* Palestro, 5 April 1989, *RRDec.,* 81:237:

The enduring jurisprudence of Our Forum holds that for simulation a positive act of the will is required; it must prevail, either absolutely or hypothetically, actually or at least virtually continuing up to the expression of consent, directly or indirectly, explicitly or implicitly expressed by which the parties wish not to undertake the marital covenant or, in celebrating it, exclude some essential element or property.

It is sufficient, however, that the party reserves to himself the right to dissolve the bond at some time without positively intending that the bond will be de facto dissolved; neither is it required that the party intends to seek a civil divorce or begin a process for an annulment so that he might enter a new marriage since it is enough that he considers marriage as not having any limitation except as he thinks of himself as bound. Nor is it necessary that there be an absolute intention of somehow dissolving the bond since the exclusion of *bonum sacramenti* which invalidates marriage is also present when the will is conditioned by rescinding the bond because something might happen; e.g., if love or harmony are absent, or conjugal life becomes unhappy.

I. *Coram* Davino, 19 July 1991, *RRDec.,* 83:493:

[According to our constant jurisprudence] it is well to remember in *coram* Filipiak of March 23, 1956 [*RRDec.,* 48:256] marriage is not only null because of an absolute exclusion of indissolubility, but also by hypothetical exclusion, that is limiting it by some hypothesis, e.g., infidelity, even if the party neither knows nor foresees that the conjugal bond will truly be broken.

J. *Coram* Burke, 19 October 1995, *ME* 123 [1998] 603, 605:

15 – *Positive and present act of the will.* The nub of the question of simulation is the actual mind of the person: whether by a positive act of the will he really excluded an essential aspect of the marital self-

donation. 'Among the presumptions which our Apostolic Tribunal has always used in looking for moral certainty that there was a positive act provoking a null marriage, an important place must be held by those which more closely touch the dispositions of mind of the person going through the ceremony. In other words, [...] examining the intention of the alleged simulator, considering his or her judicial or extra-judicial confession, or from an analysis of the cause of exclusion, with special attention to the character of the person, or from the circumstances, one seeks to discern whether or not he or she really gave himself to the other in entering the conjugal alliance' (*coram* Serrano, 6 December 1988: *RRDec.,* 80:724).

K. *Coram* Faltin, 26 May 1989, *IE* 2 [1990] 183:

[I]ntended by the contractant *subjectively* but *implicitly*, that is to say naturally [...]. The reason for this admission is that 'an implicit act remains in the positive order insofar as *it is really and not presumptively, positively and not interpretatively, contained wholly* in the act of consent even if its substance does not appear directly and immediately in the manifestation of a person's consent'.

IV. Types of Proofs Required

A. 9 – As far as the proof of simulation is concerned, there is absolutely no doubt that to prove in the external forum the existence of a simulated contract, due to the exclusion of marriage itself or the rejection of some essential property of marriage or the denial of some essential element of the marital union, is rather difficult since there is a contrary presumption expressed in canon 1101, §1. Since this is at least a presumption 'by law', the simulation of consent must be proved with convincing arguments, free from any prudent and reasonable doubt.

The proof of a simulation ordinarily begins with the admission of the simulating person given not so much in a judicial setting but more particularly outside of it, which admission may be given to trustworthy witnesses at an unsuspected time or was made known plainly by the manner of acting or behaving of the one who was responsible for the simulation. In fact, sometimes deeds have more value than words, without, however, overlooking the disposition, character and personality traits of the same person, together with his/her religious, moral and socio-cultural education and so on.

In reality, the proof becomes still more difficult, but not impossible, when the admission of the simulating person is lacking, namely, when the simulating person, although he/she has been properly and lawfully summoned, disdaining the authority of the church, has refused to stand before the tribunal both of the first instance or of appeal.

In such situation, one must investigate the motivating cause, which led the contracting person to simulate the action as he/she is said to have done. Such cause must be serious and proportionate to the cause leading to the contract.

Finally, dealing with and deciding about these matters, one must examine carefully the circumstances as well as the events both of place and time which preceded, accompanied and followed the celebration of marriage in which certain sure facts took place, and other evidences or complements as well as pursuant to canon 1679 (*coram* Faltin, 16 April 1997, *ME* 123 [1998] 254-255).

B. 17 – *Proof of Simulation*. The following elements should converge to constitute juridic proof of exclusion: a) the confession of the person simulating, made at a period which is not to be considered suspect; b) the *explanation* of the simulation, drawn from the causes both of simulating and of contracting, with due consideration for the particular position of the simulator; c) the *confirmation* of the simulation, coming from the antecedent, concomitant and subsequent circumstances, and borne out by credible witnesses or trustworthy documents (cf. *coram* Pinto, 9 April 1973, *RRDec.*, 65:361).

18 – Even if there is a confession by the alleged simulator, the weight of this is obviously undermined if it has not backing from other sources; and particularly if it is contradicted by the other party.

At the same time it is the judges' duty to weigh apparent contradic-tions: between evidence given by witnesses, between what one party asserts and another denies, or between different statements of the same party. At times what seem to be inconsistencies may, on careful examination, find a plausible explanation in the peculiarities of character, difficulties in expressing self, etc. The core meaning must be sought, so as to see if apparent contradictions can be reconciled at a deeper level. The credibility or sincerity of the parties and witnesses is of course of importance, and testimonials can help in establishing this. But it is from adequate pondering of the Acts that the judge must arrive at his final conclusions (*coram* Burke, 19 October 1995, *ME* 123 [1998] 605, 607).

C. [I]f the following can be had: 1°) the confession of the alleged simulator, mainly an extrajudicial one, confirmed by trustworthy witness; 2°) a proportionally grave reason for simulating clearly distinct from the reason for contracting; 3°) and, in addition, favorable circumstances that are specific, clear, and pressing as well as antecedent, concomitant, and subsequent to the marriage.

Then the proof of simulation is possible because all those elements taken together can form moral certitude in the mind of the judge about the fictitious or insufficient consent given.

Be it noted in that regard that: a) the judicial confession of the simulator himself if furnished with its constitutive notes and qualities, can have, since the new Code, the force of full proof, from the new Code (cf. cc. 1535-1536), but only when other elements are added to corroborate that confession. Serious consideration is to be given to the character and wit, the training, education, and the reasons for acting of the one confessing, as well as to his credibility, all of which provides a measure of the alleged confession weight (cf. *coram* Rogers, 26 January 1971, *RRDec.,* 63:61, n. 3); b). In what refers to the witnesses' depositions, we are warmed by one decision *coram* Pompedda that, besides their knowledge and credibility, 'it is to be always kept in mind that deeds, surely, are more eloquent than words, but above all that the memory lapse of words, or assertions disconnected from the circumstances is of no value. Circumstances, indeed, explain the words and make them clear while providing the motive and adding the proof to the assertions' (*coram* Pompedda, Romana, 13 February 1987, n. 6, unpublished); c) In what refers to the apt and grave cause for repudiating the perpetuity of the bond, it must be noted that it is easier to find it in the one who avers absolute freedom or in the recusant of any obligation when added, above all, to the repudiation of the teaching of the Church about marriage and to a style of life imbued with a hedonistic spirit cut off from morality. However, for those who foster a secular education, as they say, without any acrimony towards the teaching of the Church, which they know but do not approve of or accept, 'the obstacle for proof (is to be found) in getting through the transition from abstract convictions to the positive act of the will' (*coram* Pompedda, 23

April 1985, *RRDec.,* 77:217, n. 5) [this may be a case where canon 1099 is the more appropriate *caput nullitatis* to be considered] (*coram* Giannecchini, 18 December 1996, *ME* 123 [1998] 572-575, n. 9).

D. Direct proof arises from the extra-judicial confession by the simulator personally, offered in a non-suspect time to the other party and witnesses worthy of belief, correctly confirmed by all these later in the trial (*coram* Stankiewicz, 29 May 1992, *RRDec.,* 84:314).

E. Even without direct proof, simulation can be proven. Rotal jurisprudence has consistently held that it sometimes happens that the alleged simulator's behavior is far stronger evidence than any verbal confession could be (cf. *coram* Felici, 24 April 1956, *RRDec.,* 48:403; *coram* Serrano, 31 March 1979: *RRDec.,* 71:148-157; *coram* Serrano, 27 November 1981, *RRDec.,* 73:592; *coram* Ragni, 19 July 1983, *RRDec.,* 75:467).

F. [In fact,] a confession [...] need not always be made in words but may also be made by facts, which are sometimes more eloquent than words. In order for facts to be probative, however, they should be multiple, certain, univocal, and concurrent, and they should provide a basis, along with the rest of the acts and proofs, for the judge to prudently conclude that the contractant did not wish to bind him or herself by an indissoluble bond (*coram* Palestro, 26 October 1988, *RRDec.,* 80:567).

G. Without doubt the lack of an explicit confession regarding (the essential element or property or marriage itself) excluded on the part of the alleged simulator, renders proof more difficult but not impossible. For it can be supplied by complexity of concurring presumptions and indices which the jurisprudence of this Tribunal has elaborated in such causes.

a) Since often the ultimate or as it were root cause for any kind of simulation may be the malice of the alleged simulator, one needs to give great attention to his/her education, character, worthiness, personality. (cf. *coram* Ewers decision 10 June 1976 in *RRDec.,* 68:452, n. 2.) It could happen that a certain subject, because of his/her own psychological constitution, diagnosed by experts in psychiatry or psychology themselves, might be unfamiliar with those things included in the obligation to conjugal fidelity (or other essential element or property).

b) One needs to look into whether the alleged simulator maybe hostage to a liberal mentality, to corrupt or libidinous morals and indeed to too great a proclivity toward sex [...]

c) One needs to gather what had been the cause of contracting of marriage, namely, whether the alleged simulator genuinely fell in love with the other spouse, or whether it was merely love of a carnal or erotic kind. [...]

d) One needs to consider whether he or she, to whom is attributed the exclusion of fidelity (or any other essential element or property), shows himself/herself to be infected with moral and religious agnosticism and with intolerance toward any kind of bond. [...] From this behavior one can infer that the obligation had been excluded at least on the grounds of error specifying the object of the will. [...]

g) In these kinds of cases one needs to recall that the truth emerges not from one or other element but from the whole complexus of the cause (*coram* Rogers, decision 19 December 1964, in *RRDec.,* 41:956, n. 6). For from all the arguments considered at once we can arrive at that complexus of indices which according to the moral certainty of the Judges (can. 1608) cannot be explained except by an exclusion of (the essential element or property) from the very beginning (*coram* Defilippi, 16 February 1998, *ME* 126 [2001] 118-120).

H. As indicated in the rotal decisions quoted at the beginning of this section, the judge must assess the motive for simulation and for the marriage. According to the rotal auditor Serrano, the judge must consider not only the autonomy of the act of the will, but also its historicity, i.e., what goes before it, the personal biographies of the persons involved, the cultural context of the persons involved, the person's attitude before marriage, and who the person is in terms of education, environment, prematrimonial circumstances, etc. [cf. J. M. Serrano Ruiz, "El acto de voluntad por el que se crea o frustra el consentimiento matrimonial," *REDC* 51 (1994) 567-589]. If the evidence considered together convinces the judge(s) beyond 'any prudent and reasonable doubt' that the perpetuity of the bond of marriage was not the object of the alleged simulator's consent, it would justify an affirmative decision on grounds of partial simulation.

I. Furthermore, recent rotal jurisprudence has noted that the fact that persons stay in a union or even 'work' on the union does not mean they did not simulate against marriage itself or some essential element of marriage (cf. *coram* Funghini, 17 April 1991, *RRDec.,* 83:246-247, n. 2).

J. In order to obtain proof of this with moral certitude, in addition to the simulator's confession, which is confirmed by trustworthy witnesses, one should consider the force of the pre-nuptial intention in the light of the post-nuptial behavior with respect to that intention. [...] And one should examine whether there was proportionate reason for the simulation. Likewise, actions, which the law sometimes deems to be more eloquent than words, are to be taken into account (*coram* Stankiewicz, 21 April 1983, *RRDec.,* 75:182).

K. In rendering a decision, therefore, judges ought to investigate and weigh carefully [...] prudently and seriously [...] each individual case, taking into consideration the views regarding marriage and the customs and mores of the place. The judge should not only examine the words by which the Contractants manifest their mind but should also weigh the facts which have to do with the very expression of the consent or the way in which the consent is expressed, and from that the judge should determine the exact nature of the intention and whether it is established with moral certitude that there was indeed present an improper intention directly or indirectly, explicitly or implicitly manifested of not consenting to a perpetual bond.

That positive intention of not consenting to a perpetual bond, however, must proceed from a cause that is at least subjectively grave. Certainly one grave cause for excluding the *bonum sacramenti* can be the very character of the simulator and his or her preoccupation with cupidity and freedom. This perverse character points the more strongly towards the exclusion of the *bonum sacramenti* if, during the courtship period, facts or circumstances emerge which give rise to a suspicion that the marriage would not turn out well, since this constitutes an external or mixed cause of simulation (*coram* Palestro, 26 October 1988: *RRDec.,* 80:566-567).

V. Related Issues

A. See definitions of error under "Sources for Canon 1097, §1." The same definitions apply here, as error concerning the indissolubility of marriage can be a motive for simulation. As indicated above and in "Sources" for canon 1099, to prove simulation a proximate cause is necessary to transfer the error into a positive act of the will to exclude indissolubility. However, as indicated immediately above in the quote from the decisions *coram* Palestro (26 October 1988, *RRDec.,* 80:566-567) and *coram* Faltin (26 May 1989 in *IE* 2 [1990] 183) that positive act of the will can be implicit and can be proven indirectly.

B. See issues on culture, marriage, and indissolubility under the *Related Issues* section of "Sources for Canon 1099: Determining Error – Indissolubility". The same concepts, ideas, and material can be applicable here as well.

C. Divorce has become so pervasive that many people naturally assume it has seeped into the social and cultural mainstream over a long period of time. Yet this is not the case. Divorce has become an American way of life only as the result of recent and revolutionary change. [...] The divorce rate [...] continued its upward climb until the early 1980s, when it stabilized at the highest level among advanced Western societies. As a consequence of this sharp and sustained rise, divorce moved from the margins to the mainstream of American life in the space of three decades. [...] In the new conception of divorce, a strain of eighteenth-century political thought mingled with a strain of twentieth-century psychotherapeutic thought. Divorce was *not only an individual right but also a psychological resource* [emphasis added]. [...] The conception of divorce as both an individual right and an inner experience merged with and reinforced the new ethic of obligation to the self. [...] Divorce in America is not unique, but what we have made of divorce is uniquely American. [...] Compared with other Western societies, Americans have a strong tradition of divorce (see Barbara Whitehead, *The Divorce Culture*, 3-13).

D. 9 – But a positive erroneous assent determining the will according to object specified by the error operates autonomously as long as the invincible error remains. If the firmness of mind concerning the sole aspect of a pseudo-dissoluble marriage is affected by the appearance of something opposite as perceived by the contractant, then the loss of the state of certitude induces now a conscious divergence between the internal will and the objective reality of the order of canonical matrimony which must be expressed in an external declaration at the time of the contract, on account of which the theories of divorce deeply rooted in the mind of the contractant can become the proportionate and serious reason, either proximate or remote, of the reflex action of exclusion of indissolubility by a positive act of will which, likewise, renders marriage invalid (cf. canon 1102, §2).

Nevertheless, this exclusion of indissolubility of marriage, which takes on the figure of partial simulation, must be necessarily completed by a positive act of the will, that is, by an act truly elicited, not only presumed, whether explicit or implicit, which nonetheless must virtually persevere at the time of the giving of the matrimonial consent (cf. Decision before Colagiovanni, 27 May 1986, No. 4, SRRD LXXVIII, Pg. 344). But it is not necessary that the contractants decide that the bond will absolutely be broken because it is enough that he or she vindicate for himself the faculty of dissolving a marriage, if the case presents itself, that is, if love should disappear or the conjugal life become unhappy, and so on (*coram* Stankiewicz, 25 April 1991, *RRDec.,* 83:285; also in *ME* [1993] 377-382).

Chapter XV

Sources For Canon 1101, §2

PARTIAL SIMULATION: INTENTION AGAINST SACRAMENTALITY

Lawrence G. Wrenn, JCD

I. Pertinent Canons

A. See canons 1101, §1 and 1101, §2.

B. See the following allied canons: 1055, §1; 1055, §2; and 1099.

II. Conciliar and/or Papal Teachings

A. Vatican Council II, *GS* 48:

> Christ the Lord abundantly blessed this many-faceted love, welling up as it does from the fountain of divine love and structured as it is on the model of His union with the Church. For as God of old made Himself present to His people through a covenant of love and fidelity, so now the Savior of men and the Spouse of the Church comes into the lives of married Christians through the sacrament of matrimony. He abides with then thereafter so that, just as He loved the Church and handed Himself over on her behalf, the spouses may love each other with perpetual fidelity through mutual self-bestowal.
>
> [...] Authentic married love is caught up into divine love and is governed and enriched by Christ's redeeming power and the saving activity of the Church. Thus this love can lead the spouse to God with powerful effect and can aid and strengthen them in the sublime office of being a father or a mother.
>
> [...] For this reason, Christian spouses have a special sacrament by which they are fortified and receive a kind of consecration in the duties and dignity of their state. By virtue of this sacrament, as spouses fulfill their conjugal and family obligations, they are penetrated with the spirit of Christ. This spirit suffuses their whole lives with faith, hope, and charity. Thus they increasingly advance their own perfection, as well as their mutual

sanctification, and hence contribute jointly to the glory of God. (Flannery, *Vatican Council II*, 1:950-951.)

B. Pope John Paul II, *FC* 68:

Precisely because in the celebration of the sacrament very special attention must be devoted to the moral and spiritual dispositions of those being married, in particular to their faith, we must here deal with a not infrequent difficulty in which the pastors of the Church can find themselves in the context of our secularized society.

In fact, the faith of the person asking the Church for marriage can exist in different degrees, and it is the primary duty of pastors to bring about a rediscovery of this faith and to nourish it and bring it to maturity. But pastors must also understand the reasons that lead the Church also to admit to the celebration of marriage those who are imperfectly disposed.

The sacrament of Matrimony has this specific element that distinguishes it from all the other sacraments: it is the sacrament of something that was part of the very economy of creation; it is the very conjugal covenant instituted by the Creator 'in the beginning'. Therefore the decision of a man and a woman to marry in accordance with this divine plan, that is to say, the decision to commit by their irrevocable conjugal consent their whole lives in indissoluble love and unconditional fidelity, really involves, even if not in a fully conscious way, an attitude of profound obedience to the will of God, an attitude which cannot exist without God's grace. They have thus already begun what is in a true and proper sense a journey towards salvation, a journey that the celebration of the sacrament and the immediate preparation for it can complement and bring to completion, given the uprightness of their intention.

On the other hand it is true that in some places engaged couples ask to be married in church for motives which are social rather than genuinely religious. This is not surprising. Marriage, in fact, is not an event that concerns only the persons actually getting married. By its very nature it is also a social matter, committing the couple being married in the eyes of society. And its celebration has always been an occasion of rejoicing that brings together families and friends. It therefore goes without saying that social as well as personal motives enter into the request to be married in church.

Nevertheless, it must not be forgotten that these engaged couples, by virtue of their Baptism, are already really sharers in Christ's marriage Covenant with the Church, and that, by their right intention, they have accepted God's plan regarding marriage and therefore at least implicitly consent to what the Church intends to do when she celebrates marriage. Thus, the fact that motives of a social nature also enter into the request is not enough to justify refusal on the part of pastors. Moreover, as the Second Vatican Council teaches, the sacraments by words and ritual elements nourish and strengthen faith: that faith towards which the married couple are already journeying by reason of the uprightness of their intention, which Christ's grace certainly does not fail to favor and support.

As for wishing to lay down further criteria for admission to the ecclesial celebration of marriage, criteria that would concern the level of faith of those to be married, this would above all involve grave risks. In the first place, the risk of making unfounded and discriminatory judgments; secondly, the risk of causing doubts about the validity of marriages already celebrated, with grave harm to Christian communities, and new and unjustified anxieties to the consciences of married couples; one would also fall into the danger of calling into question the sacramental nature of many marriages of brethren separated from full communion with the Catholic Church, thus contradicting ecclesial tradition.

However, when in spite of all efforts, engaged couples show that they reject explicitly and formally what the Church intends to do when the marriage of baptized persons is celebrated, the pastor of souls cannot admit them to the celebration of marriage. In spite of his reluctance to do so, he has the duty to take note of the situation and to make it clear to those concerned that, in these circumstances, it is not the Church that is placing an obstacle in the way of the celebration that they are asking for, but themselves.

Once more there appears in all its urgency the need for evangelization and catechesis before and after marriage, effected by the whole Christian community, so that every man and woman that gets married celebrates the sacrament of Matrimony not only validly but also fruitfully (Flannery, *Vatican Council II*, 2:872-874).

C. Pope John Paul II, allocution to the Rota, 1 February 2001, n. 8:

8. In drawing to a close, I would like to dwell briefly on the relationship between the natural character of marriage and its sacramentality, seeing that there have been frequent aspects of marriage which include theological, pastoral and canonical proposals that are foreign to tradition, such as the attempt to require faith as a prerequisite for marriage.

Shortly after the start of my pontificate, following the Synod of Bishops on the family which discussed this topic, I addressed it in *Familiaris Consortio*, writing in 1980: 'The sacrament of matrimony has this specific element that distinguishes it from all the other sacraments: It is the sacrament of something that was part of the very economy of creation; it is the very conjugal covenant instituted by the Creator' (n. 68: *AAS* 73:163). Consequently, the only way to identify the reality that was linked from the beginning with the economy of salvation and that in the fullness of time is one of the seven sacraments of the new covenant in the proper sense is to refer to the natural reality presented to us by Scripture in Genesis (1:27; 2:18-25). This is what Jesus did in speaking about the indissolubility of the marital bond (cf. Mt19: 3-12; Mk10: 1-2), and what St. Paul did in explaining the nature of the 'great mystery' which marriage has 'in reference to Christ and the church' (Eph 5:32).

Matrimony, moreover, while being a 'sign signifying and conferring grace', is the only one of the seven sacraments that is not related to an activity specifically ordered to the attainment of directly supernatural ends. For the ends of marriage are not only predominantly but properly '*by its very nature*' the *good of the spouses* and the procreation of offspring (*CIC*, can. 1055).

A different viewpoint would consider the sacramental sign to consist in the couple's response of faith and Christian life; thus it would lack an objective consistency allowing it to be numbered among the true Christian sacraments. To obscure the natural dimension of marriage, therefore, with its reduction to a mere subjective experience, also entails the implicit denial of its sacramentality. On the contrary, it is precisely the correct understanding of this sacramentality in the Christian life that spurs us to a new estimation of its natural dimension.

On the other hand, to introduce requirements of intention or faith for the sacrament that go beyond that of marrying according to God's plan from the 'beginning' [...] in addition to the grave risks that I mentioned in *Familiaris Consortio* (no. 68, loc. cit. pp. 164-165): Unfounded and discriminatory judgments, doubts about the validity of marriages already celebrated, particularly by baptized non-Catholics, would inevitably mean separating the marriage of Christians from that of other people. This would be deeply contrary to the true meaning of God's plan, in which it is precisely the created reality that is a 'great mystery' in reference to Christ and the Church. (English trans. from Woestman, *Papal Allocutions*, 265-266.)

III. Rotal Jurisprudence

A. *Coram* Ragni, 30 May 1996, *RRDec.,* 88:411-414:

Since the argument deals with the exclusion of sacramentality in the act of manifesting matrimonial consent, the ground of nullity is based on paragraph 2 of canon 1101 which states that 'they contract invalidly if one or both parties by a positive act of the will exclude some essential element of marriage'. The sacrament of marriage is, for any baptized Christian, the marriage itself celebrated according to canonical norms, that is to say, the marriage which 'has been raised by Christ the Lord to the dignity of a sacrament between the baptized' (canon 1055, §2).

Consequently, keeping in mind the theology of the Church as handed down to us, the exclusion of sacramental dignity, carried out at the altar of God by a spouse through a positive act of the will, is an automatic rejection, that is to say, an exclusion of both the marriage and the sacrament, because that act renders matrimonial consent null and renders the entire act of marrying null in the same way in which an exclusion of the goods of fidelity, children and indissolubility destroys the entire marriage.

Therefore proof of a positive exclusion of the sacramentality of marriage is obtained by the same means as the proof of an exclusion of the above-mentioned goods: namely, through a judicial and extra judicial confession of the simulator, confirmed by circumstances that are antecedent to, concomitant with and subsequent to the celebration, confirmed by testimonies that are credible and given at a non-suspect time, and based on a proportionate cause for simulating.

If, therefore, these cornerstones are lacking, other motives or reasons or suppositions of a different kind are in no way able to supply for them.

Nevertheless, with a view towards clarifying the argument of the sacramentality of marriage, to which even today not all authors and jurists admit there is a full and generally accepted solution, the following conclusions, given in two modern esteemed commentaries on the present *Code of Canon Law*, seem germane.

> I. Aloysius Chiappetta, in his commentary, *The Code of Canon Law*:
>
> > Chiappetta notes that 'the inseparability of the contract of marriage and of its intimately connected sacrament, having become in the Church a 'common teaching' in accord with the position of Cardinal Bellarmine (*De Sacramento Matrimonii*, 1. I, Chapter 6) has been discussed in our time by many theologians and canonists in order to determine both its doctrinal and its pastoral character. Taking this into account, some conferences of bishops and ecclesiastical universities formally requested the Commission for the Revision of the Code to undertake an investigation of the problem, while others advised a suppression of the same canon (§2)', i.e. canon 1012, §2, *CIC* 1917.
> >
> > The consultors [see *Communicationes* (1977) 190, n. 1] were of the opinion that it was not within their competence to settle a theological-juridic question of such importance ... but unanimously decided to retain unchanged in the new Code canon 1012, §2 of the Pio Benedictine Code but added immediately: this in no way impedes a theological investigation from being undertaken but means only that

changes in a matter so delicate and serious for the life of the Church ought not to be made until the magisterium publicly issues its decision' (*Communicationes* [1977] 190, n. 1).

In the face of further entreaties, the consultors did not recede from their position since they had wished to follow 'the traditional doctrine affirmed many times by the pontifical magisterium, which is *properly considered a certain Catholic doctrine* [...] and which cannot be changed by the law through present day discussions unless through an explicit declaration of the authentic magisterium of the Church' (*Communicationes* [1983] 222, canon 1008, §2). And keeping in mind the inseparability, for baptized people, of the marriage contract and the marriage sacrament, and the several documents of the Roman pontiff (i.e. the *Syllabus* of Pope Pius IX, n. 66; the encyclical *Arcanum divinae sapientiae* of Pope Leo XIII, and, finally the apostolic exhortation, *Familiaris consortio* of Pope John Paul II, n. 68), the above mentioned Commentary adds: 'the principal of the inseparability of the matrimonial contract from the sacrament is incorporated into the formal declaration of the International Theological Commission of December 1977' (*Enchiridion VAT*, vol. 6, 360-363, n. 471; 384-387, and n. 495-496), repeating once again: 'without doubt this principal is to be considered 'Catholic doctrine, theologically certain' through the constant teaching of the pontifical magisterium', although the author unexpectedly concludes that we are still awaiting 'an authentic definition' (L. Chiappetta, *op. cit.* Edizioni Dehonianae, Naples, 1988, vol. II, 168, note 3), while, on the contrary, there are already many authentic declarations – in both conciliar and post conciliar documents of the magisterium of the Church, such as: The pastoral constitution, *Gaudium et spes*, December 7 1965, nn. 47-52; *Ordo celebrandi matrimonium* of the Sacred Congregation of Rites, March 19, 1969; From the International Theological Commission *Sixteen theses of Christology on the sacrament of marriage*, December 6, 1977, *Enchiridion VAT*, vol. VI, 352-358. From the International Theological Commission, *On Christian marriage*, December 6, 1977: *Enchiridion*

> *VAT*, vol. VI, 370-396; From the Synod of Bishops 1980, *On the duties of the Christian family*, October 24, 1980, *Enchiridion VAT*, vol. VII, 660-740; and *Nuntius*, October 25, 1980 ibid 742-759; besides the above mentioned exhortation *Familiaris consortio*, November 22 1981; and also what is commonly referred to as the *List of Rights of the Family*, October 23, 1983, in *Communicationes* 15 [1983] 140-152, and likewise keeping in mind other pontifical documents of great importance, such as the encyclical *Casti Connubii* of Pope Pius IX, December 31, 1930 and M.P. *Crebrae allatae sunt* of Pope Pius XII (for the Oriental Churches) of February 22, 1949.
>
> II. The teaching on sacramentality in the Spanish language commentary (BAC, Madrid 1983) is proposed in a more fitting and conclusive way. This commentary proposes two particular conclusions: 'a) the incorporation of the natural institute (marriage) into the supernatural order of grace in the case of the baptized means that sacramentality is not an accidental or extrinsic element but pertains to the very nature of marriage. Insofar as it is a sacrament it is a sensible sign that signifies grace; b) the inseparability between the contract and the sacrament of marriage for the baptized consists in the impossibility of separating those two realities when the marriage is between Christians'. Consequently 'if there is not a valid contract, there is no sacrament; and if there is no sacrament, there is no contract'.

Finally this commentary offers the conclusion: 'in practice the key question has to do with the pastoral matter about the existence of marriage for baptized people who declare that they are non-believing and non-practicing' (*op. cit*, 504).

As a guide to the proper solution of this grave pastoral question we have the following admonitions from 1981 of the Supreme Shepherd and Legislator of the Catholic Church:

> Precisely because in the celebration of the sacrament very special attention must be devoted to the moral and spiritual dispositions of those being married, in particular to their faith, we must here deal with a not infrequent

> difficulty in which the pastors of the Church can find themselves in the context of our secularized society.
>
> In fact, the faith of the person asking the Church for marriage can exist in different degrees, and it is the primary duty of pastors to bring about a rediscovery of this faith and to nourish it and bring it to maturity. But pastors must also understand the reasons that lead the Church also to admit to the celebration of marriage those who are imperfectly disposed.

And the voice of the Vicar of Christ in this world continues, teaching:

> The sacrament of Matrimony has this specific element that distinguishes it from all the other sacraments; it is the sacrament of something that was part of the very economy of creation; it is the very conjugal covenant instituted by the Creator 'in the beginning.' Therefore the decision of a man and a woman to marry in accordance with this divine plan, that is to say, the decision to commit by their irrevocable conjugal consent their whole lives in indissoluble love and unconditional fidelity, really involves, even if not in a fully conscious way, an attitude of profound obedience to the will of God, an attitude which cannot exist without God's grace. They have thus already begun what is in a true and proper sense a journey towards salvation, a journey which the celebration of the sacrament and the immediate preparation for it can complement and bring to completion, given the uprightness of their intention.
>
> On the other hand it is true that in some places engaged couples ask to be married in church for motives which are social rather than genuinely religious. This is not surprising. Marriage, in fact, is not an event that concerns only the persons actually getting married. By its very nature it is also a social matter, committing the couple being married in the eyes of society. And its celebration has always been an occasion of rejoicing that brings together families and friends. It therefore goes without

> saying that social as well as personal motives enter into the request to be married in church.

And the Supreme Pontiff takes care to add:

> Nevertheless, it must not be forgotten that these engaged couples, by virtue of their Baptism, are already really sharers in Christ's marriage Covenant with the Church, and that, by their right intention, they have accepted God's plan regarding marriage and therefore at least implicitly consent to what the Church intends to do when she celebrates marriage. Thus, the fact that motives of a social nature also enter into the request is not enough to justify refusal on the part of pastors. Moreover, as the Second Vatican Council teaches, the sacraments by words and ritual elements nourish and strengthen faith (see Vatican II's Constitution on the Sacred Liturgy, 59): that faith towards which the married couple are already journeying by reason of the uprightness of their intention, which Christ's grace certainly does not fail to favor and support.

Regarding certain dangers the Pope urges us to beware:

> As for wishing to lay down further criteria for admission to ecclesial celebration of marriage, criteria that would concern the level of faith of those to be married, this would above all involve grave risks. In the first place, the risk of making unfounded and discriminatory judgments; secondly, the risk of causing doubts about the validity of marriages already celebrated, with grave harm to Christian communities, and new and unjustified anxieties to the consciences of married couples; one would also fall into the danger of calling into question the sacramental nature of many marriages of brethren separated from full communion with the Catholic Church, thus contradicting ecclesial tradition.

Our Supreme Pontiff, John Paul II concludes:

> However, when in spite of all efforts, engaged couples show that they reject explicitly and formally what the

Church intends to do when the marriage of baptized persons is celebrated, the pastor of souls cannot admit them to the celebration of marriage. In spite of his reluctance to do so, he has the duty to take note of the situation and to make it clear to those concerned that, in these circumstances, it is not the Church that is placing an obstacle in the way of the celebration that they are asking for, but themselves (Apostolic Exhortation, *Familiaris consortio* [LEV, 1981] 121-124, n. 68).

B. *Coram* Giannecchini, 18 December 1996 *ME* (1998) 569-573, nn. 7-8:

The simulating will must directly reach its objective totally or partially, and then the objective willed, which cannot be apprehended if unknown, or tolerated, desired, or excluded must also be revealed and proved. A will that wants, and at the same time, does not want marriage or that excludes and equally accepts any of the *bona* cannot, indeed, be conceived neither in a contracting party of sound mind nor in the nature of things in so far as the act posited cannot be, in similar situations, either conscious or deliberate.

The contracting party may be ignorant of the juridical effect of his action but certainly not of the object of his will. Resolutions that are general and common, as well as various, fluctuating, and dubious are of little use at least for the purpose of proof. All these things must be kept in mind in the alleged simulator who knows nothing about religion and the sacrament. Confusion between the sacred in general and the sacrament strictly speaking hinders the apprehending of the sacramental dignity as the object of the will, mainly because the question, although certain but subtle, is not apparent to all. And yet 'among Christians, including heretics, schismatics, and apostates, there cannot be a valid matrimonial contract without having, at the same time, the sacrament of marriage, i.e. there is no sacrament unless there is a valid marriage and, in turn, there is no marriage unless there is a valid sacrament (F. Cappello, *De Matrimonio* [Romae 1950] 25, n. 26).

Consequently, a valid marriage contract cannot exist between baptized persons without its being by the very fact a sacrament' (can. 1055, §2). However, if the party apprehends and repudiates, with mind and will, the sacramentality of marriage, the marriage is rendered invalid according to the most recent jurisprudence of our forum. The question is involved when the contracting party, although baptized and educated as a Christian and observing the Christian precepts during early youth, with the passing of time gradually abandons the early religious practices without reason, no longer thinks about the faith which he once professed, and all along lives totally without faith, not however rejecting or despising it but simply neglecting it entirely and taking no care of it. In spite of this state of mind, the party speaks here and there about matters religious, is not ashamed to go to church, takes part in ceremonies whenever convenient, and so forth. If later the person celebrates the marriage in church, his intention is certainly not turned towards the sacrament or even less towards sacredness, but the person desires only to contract marriage in accordance with local customs and using the formalities which others use to contract. He rejects nothing and despises nothing because those things that have to do with religion and faith do not matter to him. Rather than being contrary or adverse to religion, his mind and intention are absent and indifferent. 'Conforming to what others do in daily practice brings about … in the will of the marrying person a positive and specific act in which life is given to that type of society of man and woman which the canonical legislator later delineates' (O. Fumagalli Carulli, *Intelletto e votontà nel consenso matrimoniale canonico* [Milano 1974] 192-193).

Therefore, if nothing is intended against the substance of marriage and still a religious marriage is celebrated, it is to be presumed that marriage is contracted validly, in the same way that others usually contract validly, because, in that case, there is no proof of either a rejection of the faith and even less of a defect of sufficient consent. This is confirmed by the practice of the Curia which usually grants *radical sanations* to those who are married only by civil ceremony (can. 1161-1163; cf. *coram* the undersigned *Ponens*, Theatina, 10 April 1992, *RRD* 84:184-185, n. 3).

In addition, and unless otherwise proven, in those persons born and educated in the faith who have later lost it and have adhered to systematic atheism because of social and economic reasons, their error will hardly determine the will so radically as to desire to contract a different type of marriage. More often they desire a 'true' marriage, as they say, perhaps to be celebrated freely before the religious or the civil authority. Having equally neglected the demands of the faith and of atheism, they hold on to the reason and to the effects of the sacrament 'not totally aware of it' (John Paul II, *Familiaris consortio*, n. 68) because, in addition to the defect of a lost faith, error about the sacramental dignity of marriage, if it exists, does not in itself vitiate consent, and because knowledge or opinion of the nullity of marriage does not necessarily exclude consent (cf cann. 1099, 1100). Evidently a different conclusion is to be reached when the ideology of atheism so possesses the mind of the contracting party that the will intends those [matrimonial] tenets of atheism under the species of true and good.

IV. Types of Proofs Required

From the 1996 decision *coram* Ragni cited above:

> Consequently, keeping in mind the theology of the Church as handed down to us, the exclusion of sacramental dignity, carried out at the altar of God by a spouse through a positive act of the will, is an automatic rejection, that is to say, an exclusion of both the marriage and the sacrament, because that act renders matrimonial consent null and renders the entire act of marrying null in the same way in which an exclusion of the goods of fidelity, children and indissolubility destroys the entire marriage.
>
> Therefore proof of a positive exclusion of the sacramentality of marriage is obtained by the same means as the proof of an exclusion of the above-mentioned goods: namely, through a judicial and extra judicial confession of the simulator, confirmed by circumstances that are antecedent to, concomitant with and subsequent to the celebration, confirmed by testimonies that are credible and given at a non-suspect time, and based on a proportionate cause for simulating.
>
> If, therefore, these cornerstones are lacking, other motives or reasons or suppositions of a different kind are in no way able to supply for them.

V. Related Issues

See Cormac Burke, "The Sacramentality of Marriage: Canonical Reflections," *ME* (1994) 545-565.

Chapter XVI

Sources For Canon 1102

CONDITIONED CONSENT

Lynda Robitaille, JCD

I. Pertinent Canons

A. See canons 1102, §1; 1102, §2; and 1102, §3.

B. See the following allied canons: 1055, §1; 1056; 1057, §1; 1057, §2; and 826 *CCEO*.

II. Conciliar and/or Papal Teachings

No specific teachings relative to this canon. See other sections of "Sources" for general teachings concerning marriage.

III. Rotal Jurisprudence

Rotal jurisprudence considers first a) what is conditioned consent; b) future conditions; and c) the issue of future conditions or promise made in the future and d) finally past and present conditions.

A. Conditioned consent

1. *Coram* Boccafola, 27 May 1987, *Forum* 3 [1992] 87-105, at p. 90, n. 4:

   What is conditioned consent? A condition is a circumstance that is attached to a lawful act, and upon which the consent depends, i.e., the value of the lawful act is suspended or rescinded. Strictly speaking, a condition has as its characteristic note the concept of 'suspension', that is the value of a lawful act depends on a future and uncertain event. But in a wide sense, a condition is considered to be any circumstance attached to a lawful act, which either suspends its value in relation to a future and uncertain event, or depending on this event, resolves it.

2. *Coram* Boccafola, 27 May 1987, *Forum* 3 [1992] 87-105, at p. 91, n. 5:

[Conditioned consent historically] Although in the new Code the Church limits the appropriateness of a licitly attached condition, yet from ancient times, it has always admitted the possibility of conditional marriage consent because, though marriage is a sacrament, it is based on a natural contract. For it sometimes happens that a special quality in the other person or a particular circumstance is so highly evaluated by a contracting party that it prevails over the marriage. In such a case, the contracting party is not simply choosing marriage, but rather a marriage with the person endowed with this quality only or only if this circumstance is verified. Hence, a relation is established between the marriage and a quality or circumstance, which in the opinion of the contracting party precedes over marriage. In such a case, the person who is marrying would be attaching a true *sine qua non*, which truly involves or affects the very essence of the actual act of consent.

B. Future Conditions

1. *Coram* de Lanversin, 17 July 1996, *Forum* 9 [1998] 227-251, at p. 234, n. 10:

Future conditions are conditions understood in the strict sense, namely, they refer to uncertain circumstances that will be verified in the future. The determination of their fulfillment is attached to a future event. The consent of the person is subordinated to the fulfillment of the condition.

Since we are talking about condition, we mean a circumstance which is not yet verified or whose existence is not yet known, which, however, in the intention of the contracting party enters into the substance of the contract; it is 'an event, on which the will of the person who is doing something or who wishes to do something, depends' (cfr. 37, D, 12, 1). The reason is that 'there exists a condition in the strict sense when a party explicitly bound with an act of the will his consent to the existence of some quality, in such a way that if the quality is lacking, the consent too, which has been subordinated to the quality, must be lacking' (in the well known sentence of Versailles, of the 2 September 1918; *AAS* 10 [1918] 387). [Private translation]

2. For marriages that took place under the 1983 code it is sufficient to prove that a future condition was placed in order for the marriage to be declared invalid. For marriages that took place under the 1917 code, it would be necessary to prove not only that the future condition had been placed, but that it had not been fulfilled for the marriage to be declared invalid.

Coram Boccafola, 27 May 1987, *Forum* 3 [1992] 87-105, at pp. 89-90, n. 3:

> When one compares these dispositions with those of canon 1092 in the 1917 *Code of Canon Law*, a great innovation is observed in the new Code, because it simply considers as invalid every condition related to the future. [...] the provision of the 1917 Code [...] canon 1092:
>
> > "A condition once placed and not revoked:
> > 1° If it concerns the future and is necessary or impos-sible or immoral, but not contrary to the substance of marriage, it is to be considered as not having been made;
> > 2° If it concerns the future and is contrary to the substance of marriage, it renders the marriage invalid;
> > 3° If it concerns the future and is licit, it suspends the validity of the marriage;
> > 4° If it concerns the past or the present, the marriage will be valid or not, according as the matter concerning which the condition is made, exists or not."

C. Future conditions or promises made in the future

1. One distinction that is made in jurisprudence is between a future condition and a promise made in the present of something to be fulfilled in the future. It is important to recall the distinction between a future potestative condition (one that could go on for the duration of the marriage) and a future contingent condition (one that has a determined end). In the case of future potestative conditions (those which have no determined end) in theory (under the 1917 code), the marriage would never come into being because at any point one person could choose not to fulfill the condition and the other would leave. Jurisprudence tends to view such conditions as promises made

in the present, rather than permitting the validity of the marriage to be undecided for the entire lives of the parties. Conditions that might take the entire life of the parties to fulfill would suspend the validity of the marriage indefinitely. It would never be known until the marriage were over or one of the parties died if the condition had been fulfilled or not. Thus, such conditions are generally considered as promises in the present and judged as though they were present conditions.

Coram Boccafola, 27 May 1987, in *Forum* 3 [1992] 87-105, at pp. 97-99, n. 10:

> For the jurisprudence of Our Tribunal, after an accurate examination of the presumptions, which in all probability direct the will of the spouse in such circumstances, concluded that a condition concerning the future is generally equivalent to one concerning the present. For [...] a condition concerning the potential future does suspend the marriage consent. However, 'nobody, unless one is instructed in juridical subtleties, would remotely suspect about the suspension in the act of celebrating the sacrament; in the common belief of the faithful, one sacrament is similar to the others. Those approaching the altar generally intend to do what everyone else does' [...] (*coram* Canestri, 28 July 1955, *RRDec.,*. 47:668).
>
> Hence [....] arbitrary conditions, that is, those whose fulfillment depends on the will of the other party, allow a double interpretation; that is, inasmuch as they objectively concern a future fact, they assume the likeness of a true condition and hence in themselves lead to a suspension of the contract; and inasmuch as this fact, however, has been drawn into the explicit promise of the party, the condition is seen to exist or to be fulfilled in the act of the sincere promise of this party. And indeed, the lack of fulfillment is somehow drawn back in time, if the contracting party, on whose will the fulfillment of the condition depends, was, already at the time, so disposed as not to want to carry out what was being promised and hence was only feigning the promise.
>
> In the case of marriage, however, the latter interpretation seems to be more true to fact and more just, inasmuch as it fits better the nature of the sacrament; indeed, it would be odd to hold

that a contracting party actually and seriously intended to suspend the validity of a contract for an undetermined or a very long time and therefore as long as it pleased the other party' (*coram* Jullien, 26 October 1944, *RRDec.,* 57:642; cf. December 1942, *RRDec.*, 78:818, n. 2).

For those about to marry, therefore, the true object of an arbitrary condition is generally a promise concerning the present, elicited from the other party with regard to an obligation to be fulfilled in the future, or in other words, a true and sincere acceptance of an obligation. If the partner makes a sincere promise, the condition is verified at that very moment; the marriage consent (which is truly conditioned by a *sine qua non* condition affecting the consent, which condition is also verified, although unknown to the party attaching it) is elicited and, unless it is revoked, virtually endures up to the day of the celebration of the marriage; and indeed the marriage will be valid. If the partner makes a false promise, at the very moment the matrimonial consent subject to the condition is rendered null by the non-verification or non-fulfillment of the condition, whose object was the sincere acceptance of an obligation to be fulfilled in the future. Indeed, a marriage lacking 'consent [...] which cannot be supplied by any human power ...' (1081), will necessarily be null and void. (Cf. *coram* Canestri, *RRDec.*, 29:550; *coram* Di Felice, 7 July 1973, *RRDec.*, 65:555.)

2. Is this distinction still valid for the 1983 Code, which states that future conditions render a marriage null? Probably not:

Coram Stankiewicz, 30 January 1992, *RRDec.,* 84:11-22:

[...] since the prescript of law treats a future condition only in a general way (1102, §2), making no distinction between different kinds of future conditions, one can legitimately hold that the formula of law embraces even a potestative condition (i.e. one that is within the power of and depends on the will of the other party, e.g. I marry you provided you live in my house) and regards it, therefore, as invalidating a marriage." (the *in iure* section translated into English in L. Wrenn, *LS*, [Washington: CLSA, 1994] 72-81, at p. 75.)

D. Past and Present conditions

1. Past and present conditions are conditions understood in a broad sense, namely, they refer to uncertain past or present circumstances. Although the determination of their fulfillment might take place in the future, in actual fact the condition is fulfilled or not at the time that consent takes place.

2. Nevertheless, in the previous code (can. 1092, especially n. 4) and in the code which is now in force (can. 1102, §2), a marriage which has been contracted, under a condition concerning the past or the present, is considered with practically the same words and with the same reasoning.

3. The rule is the same and attention is paid to the same considerations, that is:

   a) the positive will of the contracting party, subjecting the validity of the contract to the existence or the recognition of some circumstance.

   b) the existence or verification or otherwise of the condition of a determined object at the moment of the contract. (*coram* de Lanversin, 17 July 1996, *Forum* 9 [1998] 227-251, at pp. 232-233, n. 8.)

   c) *Coram* Stankiewicz, 30 January 1992, *RRDec.*, 84:11-22: [...] Besides the prevalence over marriage, the event itself ought to be objectively uncertain, as occurs in a future condition, or at least subjectively uncertain, that is to say, in the mind of the agent, if the condition refers to the present or past. For in a past or present condition, before the person knows whether the event exists or not, a positive act of the will is made which, because of the uncertitude of the subjective doubt at the time of the contract, subordinates the validity of the marriage to the desired event. In this sense, therefore, even a past or present condition presupposes uncertitude on the part of the agent, and the uncertitude or doubt reveals the condition on the agent's part, because unless there is a doubt there is no condition. (the *in iure* section translated into English in Wrenn, *LS*, 72-81, at p. 77.)

IV. Types of Proofs Required

A. Proof of a condition is indirectly corroborated first by the importance that the party before marriage attached to the event or quality, and secondly by the way in which the party acted after marriage when it was first discovered that the attached condition was not verified. The more importance one attached to the stated condition before marriage, and the more quickly the person interrupted conjugal life after marriage, once the nonfulfillment of the condition was known, the easier it is to admit the placing of a condition.

B. Proof of conditioned consent can be difficult because the condition has to be distinguished from presuppositions, modes, causes and demonstrations. In the final analysis, the judge must look 'to the connection between the desired circumstances and the consent itself'. The main question that needs to be addressed is whether the Petitioner truly intended to marry or to place a condition. (*coram* Stankiewicz, 30 January 1992, *RRDec.,* 84:11-22; or *ME* 93:195-203; the *in iure* section translated into English in Wrenn, *LS*, 72-81, at p. 79.)

C. Conditions and not demonstrations, modes, circumstances, etc.

1. There are indeed many circumstances which can exhibit a kind or type of condition without, however, putting on its true nature.

2. There are moreover many circumstances that can cause, determine, favor [...] the contract of marriage. For this reason, doctrine and jurisprudence recall several juridical types, such as mode, cause, demonstration, day and limit, etc., which, since they have some similarity with a condition in the strict sense of the word, can be easily confused with it (*coram* Giannecchini, decision of the 24 January 1992, n. 2). (*coram* de Lanversin, 17 July 1996, in *Forum* 9 [1998] 227-251, at p. 233, n. 8.)

3. Condition is defined as a circumstance that is attached to an act and whose value it suspends for a future and uncertain time. A true condition must not be confused:

   with a mode or burden, with which we want to oblige the contracting party after the fulfillment of the act; with a cause, which denotes the 'motive for contracting'; with a demonstration or quality by which the person with whom one is contracting is determined or described; with a postulate, which affects the intention to contract, but not the consent itself; with a prerequisite, on which one's will to marry depends; with a supposition, by which a determined quality is required in the partner. (*coram* de Lanversin, 17 July 1996, *Forum* 9 [1998] 227-251, at pp. 233-234, n. 9.)

4. Quite often, those qualities, which a person desires in one's partner, are improperly called conditions; when a contracting party carries on with the courtship and then contracts marriage because he or she thought that the desired qualities are present, (for) otherwise he/she would have dismissed the partner, or because if he/she had known that they were lacking, he/she would not have contracted, it is evident that in that case we are not dealing with a condition, but rather with a prerequisite, mode, cause, an interpretative intention or error, which even though they gave rise to the contract, they do not suspend the consent, which is given rather absolutely. (*coram* de Lanversin, 17 July 1996, *Forum* 9 [1998] 227-251, at pp. 235-236, n. 12.)

5. If in the case under review the hypothesis that the object of the consent was present in the spouse only as a prerequisite or mode in relation to the celebration of the marriage, then it is a matter only of some condition which is merely interpretative. Such a condition "was never posited, but it would have been posited if the contracting party had known certain facts or had been placed in certain circumstances and which indicates nothing else but a certain disposition of the mind of the contracting party: however, a disposition absolutely has no effect on the marriage consent, which is a positive act of the will (*coram* Felici, decision of the 26 July 1951, *RRDec.,* 43:596)." (*coram* de Lanversin, 17 July 1996, *Forum* 9 [1998] 227-251, at p. 237, n. 13.)

6. Both canonical doctrine and the jurisprudence of Our Tribunal distinguish the following similar states of mind, which are often analogous to the condition act of consent, from a true condition affecting a matrimonial consent.

   a. *cause*, or reason or motive inducing a person to marry. Indeed, the contracting person would not have married without a cause, but the cause itself (I marry you because you are a virgin) is something preceding and leading to the marriage but which at the moment of the contract has no value, and does not affect the will of the contracting party.

b. *presupposition*, or something which is greatly desired by the contracting party, but which is, however, so presupposed to exist (I marry you, a virgin), that the contracting party does not in any way think of verifying its existence. The imperturbable will of the contracting party is, therefore, simply directed towards the aim of the matter, i.e., marrying; the act of consent is in no way placed under or with a condition.

c. *prerequisite* or *postulate*, or something (a quality in the other party or circumstance) so much desired by the person previous to the act of contracting marriage (I shall marry you, who are a virgin), that the decision whether to marry or not depends on its existence; hence the will of the contracting party, which is also calm after the decision of entering the marriage has been taken, is directed to the act of contracting marriage and is not affected by the object of the postulate.

d. *mode* is an obligation attached to a licit act, to which one contracting party binds the other out of justice, after the performance of the licit act. The mode, by which marriage is contracted, follows the contract that is already constituted in its essence so that the mode does not infringe on its substance. (I marry you who afterwards you will be faithful.)

e. a *promise* is something demanded by a spouse before the marriage. In itself, if a promise concerns something which has to be performed before the marriage, at most it constitutes a cause; if it concerns something which is to be performed after the marriage, it constitutes a mode. (*coram* Boccafola, 27 May 1987, *Forum* 3 [1992] 87-105, at pp. 95-96, n. 8.)

D. Presumption that what has been placed is a mode, demonstration, etc. and not a condition

1. All these elements must be deduced not from a superficial analysis of the words but from the genuine disposition of the

contracting party as the facts and circumstances demonstrate to all, especially from the proportionate and apt cause, with all the circumstances for contracting properly, and which were related during the trial by trustworthy witnesses. (*coram* Giannecchini, 25 April 1986, *RRDec.,* 78:309.)

2. If from the circumstance, from the declarations of the parties concerned, from the depositions of the witnesses, a judgment cannot be delivered with moral certainty and there remains an unsolved doubt as a result of this principle, one must stand by a mode rather than for a condition (*coram* Palestro, decision of the 17 December 1986, n. 4, 78 [1986], 729). (*coram* de Lanversin, 17 July 1996, *Forum* 9 [1998] 227-251, at p. 236, n. 12.)

E. How to evaluate the circumstances surrounding the condition:

1. With regard to the proof of a true condition *sine qua non* in the external forum, we read in a decision, Lafayetten, *coram* Egan, 18 March 1975, *RRDec.,* 67:167:

> The facts which best demonstrate that marriage has been entered under a condition may be said to be of two kinds, namely, those that show how much the contracting party valued the circumstance to which it is said he bound his consent when he married conditionally; and those that concern the behavior of the contracting party after finding out that the allegedly attached condition has not been verified. [...] Hence if someone, on coming to know about the in existence of the object of the condition which was attached to the marriage consent, immediately deserts or sends away one's partner, because one considers the obligation of the marriage consent is not binding for any reason, this may perhaps be an argument in favor of a true and proper condition attached to the consent, and this is by no means weakened by mere ignorance of the legal inferences of this condition. [...] It is also necessary that the contracting party confesses the fact of having married conditionally. However, it is not necessary that this confession, be it judicial or extrajudicial, be couched in juridical terms. [...] If such a confession exists and more so if it was made out of court, and it is afterwards referred to in court by reliable witnesses, this would constitute a solid

basis for the demonstration of the imposition of this condition. (*coram* Boccafola, 27 May 1987, *Forum* 3 [1992] 87-105, at pp. 96-97, n. 9.)

F. Positive act of the will can be either explicit or implicit:

1. The imposition of the condition must not be conceived as a big formality. Indeed the condition may be attached by an explicit agreement or by the open manifestation of one's will to the other party; but there may also be a tacit or implicit condition, provided this condition can be recognized by the contracting parties and by third persons. For a condition affects consent, which alone constitutes the marriage. This holds good, independently of whether the condition is explicit or only implicit, i.e., from the surrounding circumstances it results that the consent was truly conditional (*coram* Boccafola, 27 May 1987, *Forum* 3 [1992] 87-105, at pp. 93-94, n. 7).

2. In proving conditions it is not sufficient that the parties or the witnesses speak of "conditions" to the marriage because they may not be using the term in the juridic sense. It is more important to discover what they mean by the use of such words. In the same way, they might describe a true condition, without ever using the term. The judge must investigate the will of the person entering marriage, what the person truly wanted and what happened.

3. We read in a decision *coram* Parisella, Romana, 24 April 1974, *RRDec.,* 67:360:

   […] in order to have a true condition, it is not required that the contracting person have in sight the possible nullity of the consent which is given […] For there may be and there very often exists, a true condition together with an ignorance of the effects, rights and even duties emanating from an invalidating condition [...] it is necessary and sufficient that the will of the contracting parties is prevalently directed not so much onto the marriage which is to be contracted *sic et simpliciter*, as much as onto the marriage with the person, endowed with such a quality [...] One may be led to do such a thing, even without using the word 'condition.' The contracting party simply does not feel bound by the contract (*coram*

Boccafola, 27 May 1987, *Forum* 3 [1992] 87-105, at p. 94, n. 7.)

G. The will to place the condition must be actual or at least virtual:

1. An actual condition is placed explicitly during the marriage ceremony; a virtual condition is placed before and it perdures virtually until the ceremony. It is considered still to exist if it has not already been revoked.

2. […] it must be proved that the condition was added and never revoked and thus, at least, virtually it remains in the act of the consent which was emitted (*coram* de Lanversin, 17 July 1996, *Forum* 9 [1998] 227-251, at p. 236, n. 13).

H. The condition cannot have been revoked:

1. If the condition is revoked before the wedding, it does not affect the consent. However, it is usually presumed that if a condition is proven to have been placed, it is presumed to continue until it has been fulfilled, unless it can be proven to have been revoked. A condition can be proven to have been revoked either through words or deeds. In earlier understandings of conditioned consent, the fact that the couple had begun their intimate sexual life was considered to be a sign that the condition had been revoked. Sexual intimacy is no longer considered a sign of the revocation of a condition; rather it is a fact in itself, not one proving intent.

2. In the same way, a condition is not proven to have been revoked if, after placing the condition, the person is erroneously certain that it has been fulfilled. Such a condition remains in the person's virtual will. The presumption is that a condition is presumed to continue unless it is proven to have been revoked.

I. Element of doubt

1. At least an initial doubt needs to be proven. This is a controverted area of proof regarding conditioned consent. Most authors and judges agree that at least an initial doubt had to have existed in order for the condition to be formulated. If the person was never in doubt, how could that person have formulated a positive act of the will conditioning consent on a specific quality or action?

2. *Coram* Stankiewicz, 30 January 1992, *RRDec.,* 84:11-22. Stankiewicz makes a distinction between 'the initial doubt and the final or terminal doubt':

> […] the final doubt can cease without destroying the condition, because the subsequent certitude acquired from a false statement of another party regarding the fulfillment of the condition 'in no way destroys a condition previously placed, because the consent remains subordinated to the condition, notwithstanding the subsequent certitude that can coexist with a virtually conditioned will'. […] But the initial uncertitude is always required for the placing of a condition because initial uncertitude or initial doubt gives rise to the condition itself.
>
> […] One cannot therefore safely admit the opinion that holds that an initial doubt is not so necessary that without it a condition cannot be conceived (as Sabattani says in his decision of 17 May, 1957, *SRRD* 62:422, n. 6); even less can one hold the position that states that conditioned consent can arise without any doubt whatsoever (see the decision of 15 February, 1968, *coram* Canals, *SRRD* 60:109, n. 2).
>
> For those who hold that not even an initial doubt is required, justify their position by saying that a condition can be precipitated by some 'kind of obsession regarding a dreaded evil that is altogether opposed to conjugal life' [...] or 'by an obsessive idea' on account of which something is demanded in the other party [...] but in those cases the initial doubt, which was supposedly set aside, seems nevertheless to return in order to give rise to the condition, even though it is under the form of a pathological doubt [...].
>
> But initial uncertitude is always required for the placing of a condition because initial uncertitude or initial doubt gives rise to the condition itself. When the matter is seen from a psychological point of view 'no one is prompted to place a condition unless he or she is troubled by some doubt, whether it be objective or subjective, even though it be a pathological doubt.' [...] One cannot therefore safely

admit the opinion that holds that an initial doubt is not so necessary that without it a condition cannot be conceived [...]; even less can one hold the position that states that conditioned consent can arise without any doubt whatsoever [...] (Wrenn, *LS*, 71-81, at pp. 77-78).

3. If not logically, but at least psychologically, it is required that the imposition of a true condition originates from some doubt or uncertainty in the mind of the person placing the condition. We read in a decision *coram* Stankiewicz, 15 February 1980, *RRDec.,* 72:94:

   In both parts, it is a disputed question whether, in the attachment of a condition, a state of doubt or uncertainty is required with regards to the existence of the circumstance posited in the condition.

J. We find in the previously quoted decision *coram* Stankiewicz:

   The key to the judicial investigation in cases regarding a conditioned marriage, therefore, consists in discovering the true intention of the contractant, but it looks especially 'to the connection between the desired circumstances and the consent itself [...]'.

   In a trial, however, proof of an alleged condition, especially a past or present condition, involves three things: a) that the condition itself had been placed; b) that it was not revoked; and that it was not purified, that is to say, fulfilled.

   As regards the placing of a condition, this is directly proved through the words of the contractant who is said to have attached the condition words that are confirmed juridically by credible, firsthand witnesses, or at least by witnesses who heard from others at a nonsuspect time that the condition had been placed.

   [...] The more importance one attached to the stated condition before marriage, and the more quickly the person interrupted conjugal life after marriage, once the nonfulfillment of the condition was known, the easier it is to admit the placing of a condition [...] (*coram* Stankiewicz, 30 January 1992, *RRDec.,* 84:11-22; the *in iure* section translated into English in Wrenn, *LS*, 71-81, at p. 80).

K. One final element that must be proven in these cases is that the condition was not fulfilled. If the condition is fulfilled the marriage is valid.

One must also diligently weigh how important did the contracting party consider the object of the condition and how he manifested that to his partner. Moreover one must examine his manner of behaving when he first got to know that the condition had not been fulfilled, and so on (*coram* de Lanversin, 17 July 1996, *Forum* 9 [1998] 227-251, at pp. 236-237, n. 13).

V. Related Issues

A. When to use canon 1102 of the 1983 code and when to use canon 1092 of the 1917 code

1. Before addressing the canon itself, it is important to recall that the 1983 code changed the legislation on conditioned consent, at least regarding future conditions. Thus, for marriages that involved future conditions (1102, §1) that took place before the first Sunday of Advent 1983, it will be necessary to apply canon 1092, 3° of the 1917 code. For marriages concerning past or present condition, the legislation has not changed, thus canon 1101, §2 can be applied.

   In line with competent teaching of approved Authors and the constant application of the established jurisprudence of Our Tribunal, the principle "Time directs the act" ought to be understood in our field in such a way that the force of the marriage is to be judged according to the law which was in force at the time of its celebration, also according to the common and doctrinal jurisprudential interpretation of the same law. (*coram* de Lanversin, 17 July 1996, *Forum* 9 [1998] 227-251, at pp. 230-231, n. 7.)

B. According to canon 826 of the *CCEO*, all conditions, including past and present conditions that are truly placed, invalidate consent under the Oriental law. Thus, the requirements for verifying future conditions of the Latin Code, canon 1102, §1 would be applied to future, present, and past conditions for the Oriental law.

Chapter XVII

Sources For Canon 1103

Force And Fear

Francis G. Morrisey, OMI, JCD

I. Pertinent Canons

A. See canon 1103.

B. See the following allied canons: 125, §1; 219; 1055, §1; 1056; 1057, §1; and 1057, §2.

C. Official response of the Council for Interpretation of Legislative Texts (Promulgated August 6, 1987)

1. The Council for Interpretation recognizes the extension of canon 1103 to those who are not subject to the prescriptions of merely ecclesiastical law (see canon 11).

2. Q. – "Whether the defect of consent referred to in c. 1103 is able to be applied to marriages of non-Catholics?"

3. R. – "Affirmative."

II. Conciliar and/or Papal Teachings

A. Vatican Council II, *GS* 48:

> It is only in freedom that man can turn himself towards what is good. The people of our time prize freedom very highly and strive eagerly for it. In this they are right. [... Parents and teachers] should beware of exercising any undue influence, directly or indirectly, to force [... young people] into marriage or compel them in their choice of partners (nn. 17, 52). (Flannery, *Vatican Council II*, 1.917 and 956.)

B. Pope John Paul II, ap. exhort., *FC*, 22 November 1981, states:

The only 'place' in which this self-giving in its whole truth is made possible is marriage, the covenant of conjugal love *freely* and *consciously* chosen, whereby man and woman accept the intimate community of life and love willed by God himself (n. 11). (Emphasis added) (Flannery, *Vatican Council II*, 2:822.)

C. Pope John Paul II, allocution to the Rota, 28 January 1991, states that there must be freedom of choice when entering into marriage:

The recognition of the equal dignity of man and woman is further accompanied moreover by the ever-greater recognition of the right to freedom of choice of one's state of life and marriage partner. [...] Marriage is still, to a large degree, the result of agreements between families which do not take into account the free will of the young people. (English trans. from Woestman, *Papal Allocutions*, 216-217.)

D. Pope John Paul II, allocution to the Rota, 21 January 1999, states that the parties are to be free in entering into marriage:

This consent is nothing other than the conscious, responsible assumption of a commitment through a juridical act by which, in reciprocal self-giving, the spouses promise total and definitive love to each other. They are free to celebrate marriage after having chosen each other with equal freedom, but as soon as they perform this act they establish a personal state in which love becomes something that is owed, entailing effects of a juridical nature as well. (English trans. from Woestman, *Papal Allocutions*, 251.)

E. Pope John Paul II, allocution to the Rota, 21 January 2000, states that the human act of consenting to marriage must be a free one:

Thus the marriage bond has been established by God himself in such a way that a marriage concluded and consummated between baptized persons can never be dissolved. This bond, which results from the free human act of the spouses and their consummation of the marriage, is a reality, henceforth irrevocable, and gives rise to a covenant guaranteed by God's fidelity. (*Catechism of the Catholic Church*, nn. 1640.) (English trans. from Woestman, *Papal Allocutions*, 258.)

II. Rotal Jurisprudence

A. *Coram* Funghini, 16 January 1991, *Forum* 3 (1992) 93-129:

Funghini states in measuring the gravity of the fear that invalidates marriage:

1. It is sufficient here to recall that fear is considered to be grave if the harm is grave at least with regard to the person who is enduring it and it is prudently feared that the evil will be shortly inflicted and it is morally inevitable. Gravity is measured in view of the objective nature of the evil which is being threatened, the natural disposition both of the one who is inflicting it and of the one who is enduring it, that latter's sex, age, education, etc. [...]

2. Aversion, which is necessary in any compulsion, is to be considered not as regards the person one has to marry, but as regards the marriage one has to celebrate with that person. [...]

3. Fear that invalidates marriage is never presumed, but the one who alleges it must abundantly prove it. By law it is admissible to have proof by means of witnesses, documents, presumptions and indications which taken together can bring about moral certainty. Generic assertions, however, about compulsion having been used, but without adducing the circumstances and determining the specific qualities of the fear, do not prove coercion.

B. *Coram* Faltin, 6 July 1994, *ME* 120 (1995) 207-222.

Faltin provides criteria for determining the existence of reverential fear:

1. No one ignores that the Church, through canon 1103, protects the freedom of the future spouses, not only against common fear, but also against reverential fear. Indeed, in accordance with the principles of law, of doctrine and of jurisprudence, reverential fear, because of its juridical structure and configuration, has a special place. [...]

2. Indeed, reverential fear, as distinct from common fear, has two distinct elements: a) a *legal* qualification, from which arises a special subjection to the person legitimately

constituted in authority, and b) an *affective* qualification, from which arises, as from a cause, a bond of reverence towards those under whose power a person is placed. [...]

3. The abuse of power, especially in our times, often occurs through: a) a type of instrumental force over the person who is subject, and b) by the manipulation of affection to obtain due reverence from the subject [...]

C. *Coram* Turnaturi, 15 November 1994, *ME* 120 (1995) 232-248.

Turnaturi addresses the question whether the prescriptions of canon 1103 derive from the natural law:

1. There is considerable discussion both in doctrine and in jurisprudence as to whether the norm relating to the fear that invalidates marriage is to be considered as arising from positive law or, rather, from the natural law itself. [...]

2. The final reason why fear has an invalidating effect – as noted in a decision *coram* Stankiewicz, 24 June 1982 – according to the more probable, if indeed not certain opinion, that this derives from the natural law – is because by divine institution marriage is a community of life and love between the spouses. Where there is not love but aversion, a fundamental element of this communion of life and love is lacking. Freedom from grave coercion to institute this communion of life and love is required by the very nature of matrimony.

D. *Coram* Lopez-Gallo, 23 May 1995 (Vancouver Regional Tribunal) *ME* 121 (1996) 93-107.

In a decision of the Vancouver Regional Tribunal, the types of aversion to be considered are discussed:

1. The fear or violence must be *grave*, i.e., one that reasonably cannot be morally resisted; but grave is a *subjective* term; therefore, the fear is not only *objective* (threatened to death, to be disowned, to lose one's job in retaliation, to be expatriated, etc.) but also is relative to the person on whom fear is imposed. [...] The gravity is measured by the reluctance or

aversion a person could be affected with and which has a threefold aspect:

a) *Aversio contra matrimonium*: "I do not want *to marry;*"

b) *Aversio contra personam*: "I do want to marry, *but not you;*"

c) *Aversio contra statutum tempus*: "I want to marry and I want to marry you, *but not now.*"

IV. Types of Proofs Required

A. The nature of canon 1103

1. Presently, in line with the Turnaturi decision noted above, the majority of canonists who are writing on the subject consider that canon 1103 is an expression of the natural law, and not simply a provision of ecclesiastical law. This position was strengthened by the 1987 response of the then Pontifical Commission for the Authentic Interpretation of the Code of Canon Law. This takes on importance when determining whether the canon can be applied to the marriages of non-Catholics, or to marriages which took place before 27 November 1983 (the same unclear situation applies to canon 1098 on fraud).

2. However, some are not in total agreement with this position. For instance, Urban Navarrete, SJ, (*Per* 73 [1988] 497-510), distinguishes a number of points. He notes that it is not up to a Commission to resolve disputed doctrinal points. He does not wish to maintain that the doctrine is certain since, in his opinion, the Council did not treat the matter directly. But, he asks, even if fear did invalidate marriage by the law of nature, what are the limits within which fear can exercise the invalidating influence? Are there elements of natural law in canon 1103, as well as elements of positive ecclesiastical law? In answer, he distinguishes three issues: the injustice of the fear, its extrinsic characteristic, and the lack of freedom of choice, concluding that the response of the Commission for Interpretation did not seem to have the doctrinal authority sufficient to close definitively the question as to whether fear invalidates the marriage by the natural law itself, independently of any human law.

3. On the other hand, other authors consider that the Second Vatican Council did indeed settle the doctrinal controversy. Given the nature of marriage as taught by the Council, we could say, "one could be forced into sex, but not into love" (see L. Wrenn, *Jur* 51 [1991] 119-137, at p. 132). Wrenn holds that the Council endorsed the opinion that force and fear is not just *founded* in but is actually *present* in the natural law. He sums up his position in the following statement (which we endorse):

   > Any marriage which is entered into out of fear that is both grave and causative is invalid, and indeed by the natural law. It makes no difference whether the fear is caused justly or unjustly, directly or indirectly; the marriage is still null, by the natural law. Indeed it does not even make any difference whether the fear had an extrinsic or an intrinsic source; the marriage is null in either case; by the natural law. In the former case, however, the proper canonical ground is force and fear, whereas in the latter case, it is the lack of discretion. (Wrenn *Jur* 51:137.)

B. This matter is also addressed in detail by P. Lagges, "Force or Fear," in *CLSA Proceedings* 58 (1996) 261-282, at pp. 278-280.

C. The elements of canon 1103

1. Aversion: The first element which is considered in cases of force and fear is the *aversion* which the party feels for the other person. If the other person is the proposed partner, then practically speaking, aversion is identified with a lack of love.

   However, because the new Code has added the words "even when inflicted unintentionally," this could mean that there is aversion towards someone with whom a person is living (e.g., an incestuous father), and even though the disliked person does not want the marriage to take place (because, for instance, he would then lose the daughter), the force arising from the aversion could be such that the person cannot escape it except through entering into marriage.

2. Threat of an evil: The second element to be considered is the *threat of an evil* if the marriage does not take place. This evil is to be considered not objectively, but subjectively, as it is perceived

by the person in question. Therefore, it is immaterial to the case whether the agent links it or not to the future marriage.

3. Conditions for grave fear:

   a) *Certainty of the threat*: because of the authority of the person who is threatening, or the probability that the threats will be fulfilled.

      Reverential fear, which arises from the authority of the person who is threatening, is an internal subjective force; but it requires a connection with some outside situation or incident (see D. Smilanic, "Reverential Fear," in *CLSA Proceedings* 58 [1996] 283-291, at pp. 288-289).

      Among the sources of reverential fear, we could mention blood relationships, affection, gratitude, veneration, and subjection because of office or employment.

   b) *Gravity of the evil*: the evil must be either grave in itself or perceived as such. The party must be in a position not to resist easily, because of timidity, absence of help, exceedingly great shame, etc.

   c) *An extrinsic and free cause*: if the fear is caused only from within, then we are dealing more with a lack of internal freedom (lack of due discretion) rather than with the ground of force and fear. The fear could be the threat of blackmail or the threat of some other evil (e.g., I will commit suicide unless you marry me; I'll destroy your reputation, etc.). The Commission for the Revision of the Code decided to retain this characteristic of "extrinsic" for fear of opening the door to many abuses (see *Communicationes* 9 [1977] 376).

   d) *Unjust*: the 1917 Code specifically mentioned an unjust fear, but the Commission decided that it was unnecessary to keep this word in the revised canon because any fear inducing marriage under threats is unjust (see *Communicationes* 15 [1983] 234). Threats would not be unjust if they consisted in a criminal suit in civil court, provided that this offers a reasonable option such as: a deserved punishment, or marriage. It could be noted, though, that canon 125, §2 when speaking of fear, retains the word "unjust" since this canon applies to a number of situations, and not just to marriage.

Many years ago, the Rota decided that fear was not considered to be unjust if it is induced by local customs (cf. *RRDec.*, 47:1027). In practice, the threats are deemed to be unjust whenever marriage is *imposed* without any love on the part of the party involved.

e) *Fatality of the marriage*: if the only way to escape the fear is to contract marriage (either in reality or in the mind of the person), then the last condition prescribed by the law is met.

4. Proof of fear

a) It must be shown that the person was truly afraid of *the person* causing the fear, because of the office and authority that one has over the other. Examples of such are: domineering parents, ambitious mothers; a fiancée who threatens her fiancé, and vice versa, especially after having had illicit relations.

b) As one author notes: "As a general norm, what needs to be kept in mind in regard to the admission or evaluation of distinct kinds of proofs in nullity cases due to fear, in view of the difficulty inherent in these cases, based on the hidden character whereby the coercion is generally revealed, jurisprudence establishes a less rigorous criterion than in other causes, leading to a greater facility in admitting proofs and a certain mitigation of juridic rigor in assigning weight to these proofs" (R. González, *La nulidad del matrimonio por miedo*, Vitoria, Editorial ESET, pp. 117-118, as adapted from Lagges, pp. 280-281).

c) It must also be shown that there is indeed *evidence* of fear. A rotal decision of March 22, 1957, *coram* Staffa stated that the strongest sign of fear is the fact that a party has overcome an aversion for the other one in order to escape from the impending evil.

5. Proof of force and fear

a) There are two types of proofs used in cases introduced on the ground of force and fear:

   (1) direct proofs, arising from the force which produces the fear;

   (2) indirect proofs, arising from the aversion of the party who is being forced into marriage.

b) In the case of direct proofs, it has to be demonstrated why a given person could be said to be causing fear in the spouse, and why the spouse reacted in such a way to that person.

c) In the case of indirect proofs, the focus is placed on the person who acts out of fear. As noted above, the aversion can focus either on the marriage itself, or on the proposed spouse, or on the time of the wedding. There must be a link, though, between the aversion and the fear, and this is to be demonstrated from the acts of the case.

d) The rotal decision *coram* Funghini, noted above, speaks of indications that can be used to bring about moral certitude of nullity. P. Lagges, in his study on "Force or Fear" lists a number of these possible "indicators" (p. 282):

   (1) absence of normal exchanges of affection;
   (2) emotional or physical outbursts, refusal to discuss marriage;
   (3) postponing the wedding; celebrating it without pomp or solemnity;
   (4) signs of unwillingness during the wedding ceremony;
   (5) immoral actions in order to make that person repugnant to the other;
   (6) sexual relations with a third party during the engagement period;
   (7) uncertainty or hesitation in pronouncing the wedding vows;
   (8) refusal to consummate the union after the wedding;
   (9) refusal to take up common life; refusal to have children;

(10) refusal to convalidate the marriage when informed of possible nullity;
(11) letters expressing an aversion to the marriage.

V. Related Issues

A. The proofs must also indicate an indivisible link between the cause (force, fear) and the effect (the wedding). (See P. Pellegrino, "*La vis et metus* [can. 1103] *nel Codex iuris canonici*," *IC* 37 [1997] 529-558.) However, this does not necessarily entail that the consequences will most certainly occur. A sense of guilt, of fear, or sorrow in the person who is subject to the fear, leading to what the canonists have traditionally called "*metum patiens*," and which can find its basis in an external provocation, suffices.

B. The proofs for these elements consist in demonstrating the gravity or seriousness of the fear, whether of the person imposing the fear or of the violence that would occur. It is not necessary that the fear be considered by all persons to be absolutely grave; it suffices that it be relatively grave in regard to the person who is subject to it. Cultural factors can certainly exert an influence in this regard.

C. Likewise, the proofs should demonstrate that the consequences are, at least in the mind of the victim, inevitable. There is no way to escape the fear, except through marriage.

D. Fear, which has no relation to consent, does not invalidate marriage. Thus, for instance, a fear of elevators, or of planes, or of animals, etc., has no relation in itself to the fear that canon 1103 envisages when considering marriage.

E. It is the Judge's role to establish the proofs in the light of the above canonical and doctrinal criteria, and in accordance with the accepted practice of the Church's courts.

Chapter XVIII

Sources For Canons 1157-1160

Defective Simple Convalidation

Gerald T. Jorgensen, PhD, JCL with
Ronny E. Jenkins, JCD

I. Pertinent Canons

A. See canons 1157; 1158, §1; 1158, §2; 1159, §1; 1159, §2; 1159, §3; and 1160.

B. See the following allied canons: 1057, §1; 1057, §2; 1058; 1059; 1060; 1156, §1; and 1156, §2.

II. Conciliar and/or Papal Teaching

A. Pius XII, allocution to the Rota, 3 October 1941, *AAS* 33:421-426:

> In case validation of the marriage is impossible because of a diriment impediment from which the Church cannot or does not dispense, or because the parties refuse to give or to renew their consent, a judgment of nullity cannot be refused to a party who seeks it justly and legitimately according to canon law, provided the alleged invalidity be established with that certainty which in human affairs is called moral certainty, that is, certainty which excludes all prudent doubt, being based on positive reasons. (English trans. from Woestman, *Papal Allocutions*, 13-14.)

B. John Paul II, *FC,* 22 November 1981, n. 82:

> There are increasing cases of Catholics who, for ideological or practical reasons, prefer to contract a civil marriage, and who reject or at least defer religious marriage. Their situation cannot of course be likened to that of people simply living together without any bond at all, because in the present case there is at least a certain commitment to a properly defined and probably stable state of life, even though the possibility of a future divorce is often present in the minds of those entering a civil marriage. By

seeking public recognition of their bond on the part of the State, such couples show that they are ready to accept not only its advantages but also its obligations. Nevertheless, not even this situation is acceptable to the Church (Flannery, *Vatican Council II*, 2:887).

C. John Paul II, allocution to the Rota, 28 January 2002:

> [...] First of all, one must overcome the view of indissolubility as a restriction of the freedom of contracting parties, and so as a burden that at times can become unbearable. Indissolubility, in this conception, is seen as a law that is extrinsic to marriage, as an "imposition" of a norm against the "legitimate" expectations of the further fulfillment of the person. Add to this the widespread notion that indissoluble marriage is only for believers, who cannot try to "impose" it on the rest of society.
>
> 3. To give a valid and complete response to this problem one must begin with the *word of God.* I am thinking concretely of the passage of the Gospel of Matthew that recounts Jesus' conversation about divorce with some Pharisees and then with his disciples (Mt 19, 3-12). [...]
>
> According to the teaching of Jesus, it is God who has joined man and woman together in the marital bond. Certainly this takes place with the free consent of both parties, but this human consent concerns *a plan that is divine.* In other words, it is the natural dimension of the union and, more concretely, the nature of man created by God himself that provides the indispensable key for interpreting the essential properties of marriage. The further reinforcement that the properties obtain in Christian marriage by virtue of the sacrament (cf. can. 1056) *is based on a foundation of natural law* that, if removed, would make incomprehensible the very work of salvation and elevation of the conjugal reality that Christ effected once and for all. (English trans. from Woestman, *Papal Allocutions*, 267-268.)

III. Rotal Jurisprudence

A. *Coram* Boccafola, 12 March 1998, *SC* 34 (2000) *passim* 521-524 (translation by Augustine Mendonça, revised and approved by the *ponens*):

The notion of defect of form in the proper sense, and not however as generally used in the English-speaking world, traditionally refers to a situation in which true defect of form is verified, that is, the canonical form properly celebrated but defective, and never to the complete absence of form. Thus, a celebration which had a defective form, for example, a marriage celebrated by a priest who lacked the faculty to assist at the marriage, and other similar cases – in fact produces at least some species and figure of a true marriage.

On the other hand, should a Catholic party attempt marriage before civil authority or before a minister of some other religion [i.e., without a dispensation from the canonical form], such a celebration obviously lacks all element of canonical form and is rightly described as an "inexistent marriage," since it does not have any species or figure of a true marriage.

10. In regard to the definition of the very concept of "convalidation," proven authors explain: "Simple convalidation of marriage is an act by which an invalid marriage is rendered valid with the renewal of consent" (P. Gasparri, *De matrimonio,* II, 1932, p. 253, no. 1189); "Convalidation of marriage is an act by which that *which had only an appearance of a true marriage*, becomes such, when that which it lacked before is supplied" (T. M. Vlaming, *Praelectiones iuris canonici*, II, p. 349, no. 760).

Therefore, convalidation of marriage itself, in the first place, is a juridical notion and a *juridical act*: "Convalidation of marriage is a *juridic act* through which an apparent and invalid marriage is changed into a true and valid marriage" (L. Bender, art. "Convalidation du mariage," in *Dictionnaire de droit canonique*, IV, Paris, 1949, col. 541).

For this reason, like every juridic term, convalidation, although some use the same word in an improper and broad sense, has a precise meaning whose application is governed by definite prescriptions of law and common canonical doctrine.

A long canonical tradition, as it is attested to in the writings of many authors truly expert in canonical matters, holds that, in a strict sense, the expression and the institute of "convalidation" cannot be applied to marriage of a Catholic party celebrated merely civilly and without the observance of canonical form. For the fundamental requirement and the *terminus a quo* to which the convalidation is to be applied is always an invalid marriage. However, we have seen above that the marriage of a Catholic party celebrated merely civilly, without dispensation from the canonical form, does not meet the definition of an invalid marriage because such a civil marriage does not have any semblance or figure of a true marriage.

"The convalidation of marriage is an act by which that which had only an appearance of a true marriage, becomes such, when that which it lacked before is supplied" (T. M. Vlaming, *Praelectiones iuris canonici*, II, p. 349, no. 760). And so: "Simple convalidation is an act by which an invalid marriage is rendered valid with the renewal of consent" (P. Gasparri, *De matrimonio*, II, 1932, p. 253, no. 1189).

Here is what Conte a Coronata has to say: "Convalidation of marriage is an act *by which a marriage celebrated before according to the prescribed form, but invalid due to some defect of the form itself or of consent, or due to a diriment impediment, is sanated and becomes valid.* Therefore, there is no properly called convalidation unless there is at least the semblance of a true marriage. Likewise, nor can there be discussion of convalidation if it is a question of a valid marriage but only illicitly celebrated" (cf. *Institutiones iuris canonici, De Sacramentis*, III, p. 933, no. 673).

In a similar vein, Wernz-Vidal writes: "Convalidation of a marriage is an act by which marriage celebrated before *according to legitimate semblance and form*, but invalidly, is so restored that it attains its validity" (*Ius canonicum*, Tomus V, *Ius matrimoniale*, III editio, [1946] 852, no. 652).

In the present Code also, a "marriage" of a Catholic party celebrated only civilly or before a minister of some other religion, is not considered to have the figure and species of a true marriage, since such a ceremony is not even regarded as a putative marriage. Thus, inquiry or investigation of such a prior marriage does not require the use of actual judicial procedure for declaring its nullity. In such cases, it is only required that the parish priest or the delegate of the Ordinary, through some administrative investigation in accord with cc. 1066-1067, be morally certain about the effective state of freedom of the person marrying before he/she is permitted a canonical celebration of marriage (cf. Response of the Pontifical Commission for the Authentic Interpretation of the Code, 26 June 1984, no. II).

11. Perhaps someone may object saying that this definition is very restrictive of the concept of "convalidation" and in fact smacks of olden times so that it does not correspond with the actual ecclesial reality of our present times. Nevertheless, in no way does it seem legitimate or useful to unilaterally devise a new and broader definition and then use it to refer to an already consolidated canonical institute – that is, convalidation – with no proper consideration of the historic and traditional meaning of the term. Certainly reasons are given in a sentence *c.* Funghini of 30 June 1988 (*SRRDec*, 80 [1988] 443), explaining why a merely civil marriage of a Catholic party may be considered more kindly in our times.

However, the proper term to be used in the case of rectifying the nullity of a ceremony of a Catholic party celebrated without the legitimate canonical form, should be "canonical celebration" or "proper celebration" (cf. Hervada, Commentary on cc. 1156 – 1165, in E. Caparros, M. Thériault, J. Thorn [eds.], *Code of Canon Law Annotated*, [Montréal, 1993] 727: "A third method is added to these two ones, though it is not strictly speaking a validation, is the *new celebration of the marriage*").

For in order to remedy the inefficacy of a merely civil ceremony, those same requisites as in the first celebration of any marriage of a Catholic party must be met, that is, actual *consent de praesenti* of the parties, properly manifested through the legitimate canonical form and absence of any diriment impediment. It matters little if we call this consent *first, new or renewed*, provided that it is clear to all that there was an actual, effective matrimonial consent, present at the moment of the canonical celebration of the marriage. [...]

13. A few excerpts from some cases already judged at the Roman Rota under this ground of "invalid convalidation" clearly demonstrate that the real fundamental question concerns total

simulation of marriage, since the sentences in these cases generally concluded in favour of the invalidity of the marriage on the basis of proven total simulation. [...]

Also in a well-known case judged *c.* Rogers of 21 January 1969 (*SRRDec*, 61 [1969] 63), where the *ponens* greatly emphasized the concept of "renewal of consent" – and in our opinion, not sufficiently taking into account the above-cited opinion of Wynen, concerning the naturally innate awareness of the inefficacy of the prior ceremony when the parties are required to express anew their consent before the parish priest – the fundamental ground of nullity of the accused marriage concerns either a consent that was refused or one that was totally simulated: "One who is not only ignorant of the invalidity of the previous marriage, but really fights for its validity, is certainly impeded from giving a new consent: *should the person pronounce anew the words expressing consent, he/she can intend nothing other than either to simulate consent totally or to confirm the inefficacious consent*; in neither instance is a true consent produced in the case."

And finally, in a sentence *c.* Funghini of 30 June 1988 (*SRRDec*, 80 [1988] 444), we read, first of all, the citation from the sentence by Rogers: "*The defect of the new consent in case of convalidation of marriage must be considered as equivalent to total simulation of consent.* For the essence of total simulation consists in the fact that the object of will is not the marriage itself but something else, that is, the subject's particular purpose [*finis operantis*]," and then Funghini continues: "For this reason, it is not necessary to deal separately with total simulation [...] *For, if the absence of consent is acknowledged, by that very fact total simulation is admitted as the cause of non-convalidation of marriage.* If, on the other hand, the accused absence of consent is not admitted, by that very fact one must affirm that there was convalidation of marriage, which, as we said above, does not come about except through a formal and positive act of will to marriage which is to be contracted in a proper form." Therefore, in this case the doubt was formulated at the Rota by a more accurate and precise formula, namely: "Whether there is proof of nullity of marriage in the case *due to lack of matrimonial consent in one or the other party at the moment of the ecclesiastical 'convalidation' of the civil marriage* of the parties (cc. 1160;

1157), that is, due to invalid 'convalidation' of the marriage contracted on 8 March 1967."

B. *Coram* Wynen of 1 June 1940 *RRDec.*, 32 (1940) 432:

The *ponens* indicated that when the spouses celebrate the canonical form after a civil ceremony, "*it follows from the nature of the thing* that those newly contracting [marriage] before the parish priest and witnesses *know that their previous marriage was null, and that both parties elicit a new consent.*" For this reason, it does not seem necessary to inquire about the knowledge of the spouses concerning the nullity of the previous ceremony or concerning their new or renewed act of matrimonial consent, because from the very nature of the thing, that is, from the repeated ceremony, they know the inefficacy of the previous ceremony and in this repeated ceremony they express anew their matrimonial consent (*coram* Boccafola, ibid. 524).

IV. Types of Proofs Required

A. 'For the validity of a juridical act, it is required that it be performed by a person who is legally capable, and it must contain those elements which constitute the essence of the act, as well as the formalities and requirements which the law prescribes for the validity of the act (c. 124).' The canonical invaliditiy of a particular juridical act, including marriage, therefore, can be seen to arise from natural law or from positive law, i.e., either the elements which constitute the essence of the act itself are lacking, or those formalities prescribed by the positive law under the pain of invalidity are lacking (*coram* Boccafola, ibid. 520).

B. Indeed, whenever there is a new celebration in canonical form of a marriage void due to lack of legitimate form, there is necessarily present, from the very words used in the canonical form of celebration, a new expression, that is, an external manifestation, of consent. For this reason, it is the Petitioner's responsibility to demonstrate that the consent given in the canonical ceremony (and therefore, *de facto*, the new act of consent itself) was not a true, actual act of matrimonial *consent de praesenti*. Consent *de praesenti* is, in fact, the will to give and accept at this moment and from this moment for perpetuity all the essential rights-duties of marriage.

Therefore, *the real question in these cases is precisely whether or not there is total simulation*. For, the nullity in this case is claimed either because it is maintained that the party had truly not given or accepted the true matrimonial consent at the canonical celebration, since he simply acquiesced in the consent already given during the civil ceremony, or because it is maintained that the party had consciously simulated, refusing to give consent at that moment and unwilling to recognize any efficacy and validity of the canonical ceremony (*coram* Boccafola, ibid. 523).

C. There is a presumption in law that a well-informed Catholic will know that he or she ought to have been married in a church. Such a presumption may be rebutted only by strong evidence that the Catholic party did not know the requirement of canonical form (*Summ.* I, p. 774) [*coram* Boccafola, ibid. 527].

D. 20. The phenomenon of an interpretative will is known to all. By such a will, one who ardently desires the declaration of nullity of his/her marriage, convinces him/herself about the presence at the moment of celebration of the marriage, i.e., at a prior moment of time, of some defect in his/her intention or in the act of will, whose actuality and significance he/she has come to know only recently, i.e., at the time of introducing the cause. Probably this is the way the subjective conviction of the Petitioner about the absence of true matrimonial consent *de praesenti* at the time of the celebration of his canonical marriage must be interpreted (*coram* Boccafola, ibid. 527).

E. In view of the Church's concern to reduce obstacles to marrying validly and the favor of the law which marriage enjoys, one cannot ignore the reductive definition of awareness of nullity called for by canon 1157's addition of *aut opinatur* to *scit.* This is an amendment of 1917 canon 1137, and it was added to settle a controversy among the authors (Bogdan, art. cit., 513). [...] Hence, in order to hold for the nullity of a validation one must invincibly prove a *pertinacious* rejection of validation tantamount to a determining error about the sacramentality of marriage or total simulation, which results in *entirely* empty words expressing consent, *mere* confirmation of the original consent, or renewal of the vows as a pure formality. Otherwise, one must hold for the validity of the validation according to canon 1060 (C. Hettinger, "The Law of Invalid Validation in U.S. Tribunals," *ME* 124 [1999] 568).

V. Related Issues

A. Ecclesiastical laws do not apply to the marriages between: the non-baptized, a non-baptized person and a doubtfully baptized person, baptized non-Catholics, and a baptized non-Catholic and a non-baptized person. As Bogdan explains:

> All that would be required for a convalidation between persons in the above categories would be the perduring naturally sufficient consent of both parties and the cessation of the cause(s) of nullity. For example, once a diriment impediment binding such persons in the above mentioned categories ceases (e.g., cessation of *ligamen* by the death of a previous spouse), and the previously given naturally sufficient consent perdures, marriage is convalidated by natural law without any further formalities on the part of the couple, provided no obstacles of natural law stand in the way. Furthermore, it would follow that neither party would have had to know or suspect the marriage in question was previously invalid (ibid. 517) [L. Bogdan, "Simple Convalidation of Marriage in the 1983 Code of Canon Law," *Jur* 46 (1986) 511-531; as found in Patrick S. Morris, ed., *Law Section for the Adjudication of Marriage Cases*. Catholic Marriage Tribunal: London, Ontario (2000) 196-197].

B. Clarence J. Hettinger, "The Law of Invalid Validation in U.S. Tribunals," *ME* 124 (1999) 554-568.

C. Some distinguish between a *null* and a *void* (inefficacious) marriage: they say that a void marriage is one whose effect is impeded by some diriment impediment, even though it was celebrated with due form; however, they call a marriage null *which has neither a form or a figure of a true marriage* (cf. *Institutiones iuris canonici, De Sacramentis,* III, p. 33, no. 30 as cited in *coram* Boccafola, ibid. 521).

D. "An invalid marriage is said to be putative if it has been celebrated in good faith by at least one party. It ceases to be such when both parties become aware of its nullity (c. 1061, §3)." The marriage of the one who, being conscious of the nullity of the act, celebrates the marriage in bad faith is called *attempted marriage* (*coram* Boccafola, ibid. 521).

E. *An inexistent marriage* is an empty and ineffective celebration which, according to canon law, creates neither the semblance nor the form nor the appearance of a true marriage. "Generally, a merely civil marriage for those who are bound by the form prescribed by the Code, is not considered to have the semblance and form of marriage (A. De Smet, *De sponsalibus et matrimonio,* p. 158)." A merely civil marriage of a Catholic party cannot be considered even a putative marriage (Decision of the Commission for the Interpretation of the Code, 26 January 1949, *AAS* 41 [1949] 158).

Appendix I

Canons on Matrimonial Consent Cited in this Text

Can. 1095 — The following are incapable of contracting marriage:

1° those who lack the sufficient use of reason;

2° those who suffer from a grave defect of discretion of judgment concerning the essential matrimonial rights and duties mutually to be handed over and accepted;

3° those who are not able to assume the essential obligations of marriage for causes of a psychic nature.

Can. 1096 — §1. For matrimonial consent to exist, the contracting parties must be at least not ignorant that marriage is a permanent partnership between a man and a woman ordered to the procreation of offspring by means of some sexual cooperation.

§2. This ignorance is not presumed after puberty.

Can. 1097 — §1. Error concerning the person renders a marriage invalid.

§2. Error concerning a quality of the person does not render a marriage invalid even if it is the cause for the contract, unless this quality is directly and principally intended.

Can. 1098 — A person contracts invalidly who enters into a marriage deceived by malice, perpetrated to obtain consent, concerning some quality of the other partner which by its very nature can gravely disturb the partnership of conjugal life.

Can. 1099 — Error concerning the unity or indissolubility or sacramental dignity of marriage does not vitiate matrimonial consent provided that it does not determine the will.

Can. 1100 — The knowledge or opinion of the nullity of a marriage does not necessarily exclude matrimonial consent.

Can. 1101 — §1. The internal consent of the mind is presumed to conform to the words and signs used in celebrating the marriage.

§2. If, however, either or both of the parties by a positive act of the will exclude marriage itself, some essential element of marriage, or some essential property of marriage, the party contracts invalidly.

Can. 1102 — §1. A marriage subject to a condition about the future cannot be contracted validly.

§2. A marriage entered into subject to a condition about the past or the present is valid or not insofar as that which is subject to the condition exists or not.

§3. The condition mentioned in §2, however, cannot be placed licitly without the written permission of the local ordinary.

Can. 1103 — A marriage is invalid if entered into because of force or grave fear from without, even if unintentionally inflicted, so that a person is compelled to choose marriage in order to be free from it.

Can. 1156 — §1. To convalidate a marriage which is invalid because of a diriment impediment, it is required that the impediment ceases or is dispensed and that at least the party conscious of the impediment renews consent.

§2. Ecclesiastical law requires this renewal for the validity of the convalidation even if each party gave consent at the beginning and did not revoke it afterwards.

Can. 1157 — The renewal of consent must be a new act of the will concerning a marriage which the renewing party knows or thinks was null from the beginning.

Can. 1158 — §1. If the impediment is public, both parties must renew the consent in canonical form, without prejudice to the prescript of can. 1127, §2.

§2. If the impediment cannot be proven, it is sufficient that the party conscious of the impediment renews the consent privately and in secret, provided that the other perseveres in the consent offered; if the impediment is known to both parties, both are to renew the consent.

Can. 1159 — §1. A marriage which is invalid because of a defect of consent is convalidated if the party who did not consent now consents, provided that the consent given by the other party perseveres.

§2. If the defect of consent cannot be proven, it is sufficient that the party who did not consent gives consent privately and in secret.

§3. If the defect of consent can be proven, the consent must be given in canonical form.

Can. 1160 — A marriage which is null because of defect of form must be contracted anew in canonical form in order to become valid, without prejudice to the prescript of can. 1127, §2.

CONTRIBUTORS

Carlotta Bartone, SHCJ, has been a tribunal judge and Defender of the Bond since 1990. She earned a BA and MA in French and her JCL from The Catholic University of America. Currently she serves as a judge in First and Second Instance for the Metropolitan Tribunal of the Archdiocese of Philadelphia.

Marianne Burkhard, OSB, is Associate Judge and Judge Instructor for the Tribunal in the Diocese of Peoria, Illinois. She earned her PhD in German and French Literature from the University of Zurich/Switzerland and her JCL from St. Paul University, Ottawa, Canada. She is a member of the Benedictine Sisters of Rock Island.

Michael J. Cariglio, a priest of the Diocese of Youngstown, Ohio, has been serving the diocesan tribunal in various roles since 1978. He served as Adjutant Judicial Vicar since 1988 and was named Judicial Vicar in 2003. He also has served as parochial vicar, has taught in the diocesan high schools and has been a pastor since 1986. He holds master's degrees in Philosophy and Education, an STL in Theology. He received his JCL from The Catholic University of America in 1980. In 1997 he was named a Chaplain of His Holiness.

John P. Donovan is a priest of the Diocese of Syracuse, New York. He earned a JCL from The Catholic University of America. He has served in parishes and campus ministry as well as a Judge in the Tribunal of the Diocese of Syracuse. He currently serves in the Office for Vocation Promotion and as Adjutant Judicial Vicar for the Diocese of Syracuse.

Ronald W. Gainer is Bishop of the Diocese of Lexington, Kentucky. He earned his JCL from the Gregorian University in Rome. From 1994 through 1999, he was adjunct professor of canon law at St. Charles Borromeo Seminary, Philadelphia. Prior to his appointment as diocesan bishop and episcopal ordination, he served as the Judicial Vicar for the Diocese of Allentown, Pennsylvania.

Margaret Gillett has worked for the Tribunal of the Diocese of Dallas, Texas, since 1981 and in 1983 she was appointed Secretary to the Tribunal. In 2003 she was appointed an Assessor as well as an Auditor for the diocesan tribunal.

Clarence Hettinger was a priest of the Diocese of Peoria, Illinois for more than 60 years, having been ordained in 1942. After nine years as a parochial vicar and two years of graduate canon law studies, he was appointed *Officialis* of the Tribunal in 1954. He served in that capacity for many years. He also served as pastor at St. Clement Parish, then at St. Jude Parish in Dunlap, Illinois. Most recently, until his death in November 2003, he served at the Tribunal of the Diocese of Peoria as associate judge and resident Latinist. He published articles in various scholarly journals in canon law.

Ronny E. Jenkins is a priest of the Diocese of Austin, Texas. He has an STL in Patristic Studies from the Pontifical Gregorian University and a JCL and JCD from The Catholic University of America. He currently is assistant professor of canon law at The Catholic University of America. Prior to coming to Catholic University, he served as Judicial Vicar of the Diocese of Austin, Texas, and as lecturer in canon law at Oblate School of Theology. He has published articles in various scholarly journals and presented papers at regional and national conventions of canon lawyers.

Gerald T. Jorgensen, a deacon of the Archdiocese of Dubuque, Iowa, is a judge in the Metropolitan Tribunal and a consulting psychologist for the Archdiocese. He earned his JCL from The Catholic University of America and his PhD in Psychology from Colorado State University. He is a licensed psychologist in the State of Iowa and certified as a Health Service Provider in Psychology by the State of Iowa and the National Register of Health Service Providers in Psychology. Prior to being appointed to the Metropolitan Tribunal, he was an Associate Professor in Psychology and Education, as well as Vice President for Student Development, at the diocesan college. He has published articles in various scholarly journals in psychology and canon law and presented papers at regional and national meetings of psychologists and of canonists.

Francis G. Morrisey, OMI, is a priest of the Oblates of Mary Immaculate. He has earned several advanced degrees from the University of Ottawa and Saint Paul University, including a PhD and JCD. He was Dean of the Faculty of Canon Law, Saint Paul University, 1972-1984, and presently is a titular professor. He has served as consultor for the Pontifical Council for the Interpretation of Legislative Texts and the Congregation for Institutes of Consecrated Life and Societies of Apostolic Life. He is the author of some 200 titles in the area of canon law, church history, etc. and has presented at numerous regional and national meetings of canonists and Church leaders addressing various issues in canon law.

Margaret Anne (Peggy) Ramsden, SFCC, is a Judge for the Tribunal in the Diocese of Orange, California. She earned her JCL from St. Paul University, Ottawa, Canada. She has served at both First and Second Instance levels during her career as a canon lawyer and has been involved in tribunal ministry in one form or another since January 1978. She has been a member of the CLSA since 1979. She is a member of the Sisters for Christian Community.

J. Brian Rejsek is a priest of the Diocese of Peoria, Illinois and in 2003 he was named a Chaplain of His Holiness. He holds advanced degrees from Kenrick Seminary, St. Louis, and from the Pontifical University of St. Thomas Aquinas (Angelicum), Rome. He is Episcopal Vicar for Hispanic Ministry for the Diocese of Peoria and also currently serves as Defender of the Bond and Promoter of Justice for the diocesan tribunal. In June 2003 he was appointed Rector of the Cathedral of St. Mary of the Immaculate Conception in Peoria.

Lynda Robitaille earned her JCD from the Gregorian in 1990. Her doctoral dissertation was on conditioned consent, which is the topic of her contribution for this resource. She is an assistant professor of canon law at Saint Paul University, Ottawa, Ontario, Canada. Currently she serves in a consulting capacity to several Canadian and US tribunals. Also she has published articles in various scholarly journals in canon law and presented papers at regional and national meetings of canonists.

Melissa L. Schools currently serves as a judge in the Metropolitan Tribunal, Archdiocese of Philadelphia, Pennsylvania, although working on only a part time basis. She earned her JCL from the Katholieke Universiteit Leuven, Belgium. She did her undergraduate work at Thomas More College of Liberal Arts in New Hampshire.

Girard (Jerry) Sherba, a presbyter of the Diocese of Raleigh, North Carolina, has been Vice Chancellor of the diocese since 1988 and Vicar Judicial since 2000. He earned his JCL from the Angelicum, Rome, Italy and his JCD from St. Paul University, Ottawa, Canada and his PhD from the University of Ottawa. He has served as parochial vicar and pastor in his diocese. He has served as an Adjunct Professor of Canon Law, The Catholic University of America, in its Canon Law Para-Professional

Program, and summer JCL program. Presently, he also serves as Rector of Sacred Heart Cathedral in Raleigh.

Richard Soseman is a priest of the Diocese of Peoria, Illinois. He has received graduate degrees from Marquette University, Milwaukee, Wisconsin, and Mt. St. Mary's Seminary, Emmitsburg, Maryland. He earned a JCL from the Pontifical Lateran University. Since 1996 he has served as Judicial Vicar of the Diocese of Peoria. He also currently serves as Pastor of St. Mary of the Woods Parish in Princeville, Illinois. He has published articles in various scholarly journals in canon law and presented papers at regional and national meetings of canonists. Most recently he was appointed a judge in the beatification cause of Archbishop Fulton Sheen.

Lawrence G. Wrenn is a priest of the Archdiocese of Hartford, Connecticut where he is currently a judge on the Metropolitan Tribunal. He received his JCD from the Lateran University in Rome and is the author of several articles published in various scholarly journals as well as the author of several books. He has presented at numerous regional and national meetings of canonists.

The Canon Law Society of America

Membership in the Canon Law Society of America is open to degreed canonists and to interested persons who wish to collaborate in the promotion of the pastoral ministry of the Church within the context of its legal/canonical structures.

The Society's constitution identifies four (4) kinds of membership: Active, Associate, Student, and Honorary. Active membership is open to those who have earned at least a licentiate degree in canon law; active membership is also open to other practitioners in canon law who demonstrate a broadly based competence in canonical issues and who have fulfilled the stipulated requirements established by the Board of Governors of the Society as enumerated in the By-Laws. Associate members are any others who wish to associate themselves with the purpose of the Society. Student membership is open to those enrolled in any school of canon law engaged in studies to obtain a licentiate degree in canon law. Student members enjoy the same prerogatives as associate members in the Society. Honorary members are (a) *ex officio* all the Most Reverend Bishops of the United States and Canada, and (b) those persons, who by reason of outstanding contributions in the field of canon law or in support of the Society, are proposed for this distinction of honorary membership by the Board of Governors and accepted by a majority vote of the active members at the General Meeting.

Membership information and applications are available from the Society's Administrative Office and through our website at clsa.org. Payment of the initial dues is required after approval of the application.

For questions and further information, please contact:

Administrative Office
Canon Law Society of America
415 Michigan Ave., NE, Suite 101
Washington, D.C. 20017
Tel: (202) 832-2350
Fax: (202) 832-2331
executivecoordinator@clsa.org

[Updated 2022]